My Baby's Father

My Baby's Father

Unmarried

Parents

and

Paternal

Responsibility

Maureen R. Waller

CORNELL UNIVERSITY PRESS

Ithaca & London

Parts of chapter 2 appeared as "Meanings and Motives in New Family Stories" in *The Cultural Territories of Race*, ed. M. Lamont, © 1999 by the University of Chicago and Russell Sage Foundation. All rights reserved.

First published 2002 by Cornell University Press
First printing, Cornell Paperbacks, 2002

Printed in the United States of America

Library of Congress Cataloging-in-Publication Data

Waller, Maureen Rosamond, 1967–
   My baby's father : unmarried parents and paternal responsibility/
Maureen R. Waller.
      p. cm.
Includes bibliographical references and index.
   ISBN 0-8014-3988-4 (cloth : alk. paper)—ISBN 0-8014-8806-0 (pbk. :
alk. paper)
   1. Unmarried fathers—United States. 2. Fatherhood. I. Title.
   HV700.7 .W35 2002
   306.874'2—dc21
                                    2002002432

Cornell University Press strives to use environmentally responsible suppliers and materials to the fullest extent possible in the publishing of its books. Such materials include vegetable-based, low-VOC inks and acid-free papers that are recycled, totally chlorine-free, or partly composed of nonwood fibers. For further information, visit our website at www.cornellpress.cornell.edu.

Cloth printing   10 9 8 7 6 5 4 3 2 1
Paperback printing   10 9 8 7 6 5 4 3 2 1

For my parents,

Anne and Paul Waller

Contents

Acknowledgments

This project has reminded me that support comes in many forms and that some of the least obvious expressions of support are the most critical. The greatest contributions to this book are from the men and women who shared their lives with me and entrusted me with their stories. For many, participating in this study was a risk, and I am deeply appreciative that participants decided to take this risk with me. I am also thankful that several parents I met during the course of this fieldwork invited me to visit their children and relatives, to come to church, to attend birthday parties and family meals, and to otherwise hang out. I benefited more from this kindness and generosity than they probably realize. Although I promised to keep participants' names confidential, and cannot mention them here, they should know that my thanks go out to all of them. With a sigh of relief, I can finally tell them, "Yes, the book is finished." At the same time, their words and perspectives have enriched my life, and I'll carry them with me. This might not be exactly the kind of book they expected, but I hope they see value in it.

A critical type of support comes in the form of guidance. This project began at Princeton, where I was privileged to work with two scholars and mentors who showed me—each in her own extraordinary way—how to be a sociologist. My sincere thanks go to Michèle Lamont for her early and sustained interest in my intellectual development and her faith in this project. In addition to providing a superb model of theoretically informed qualitative scholarship, Michèle advised me on the nuts and bolts of interviewing and generously read all of my preliminary drafts and proposals. Many thanks also to Sara McLanahan whose remarkable body of research inspired me to study low-income families. Sara's sharp logic and deep policy interest pushed me toward greater clarity and relevance in this research. Over the years, I have been extremely fortunate to reap the benefits of her knowledge and support.

Others who read drafts of the manuscript at various stages of completion have also guided me on this journey. I am indebted to Kristin Luker for, among other things, encouraging me to interview "absent" fathers. She also showed me that scholarship could be rigorous while also being compassionate and socially relevant. I thank Kathy Edin whose early discussions with me about fieldwork in inner-city communities motivated me in this work. I also benefited from Frank Fustenberg's ever-wise and innovative insights into family relationships and from his recommendations for improving the manuscript. Special thanks are reserved for Bob Plotnick and Peter Richardson, who I worked with at later stages of this project. Bob helped me to refine the policy discussion in this study and allowed me to draw on our collaborative work in the latter chapters of the book. Peter read and responded to each part of the manuscript, and the final product bears the mark of his exceptional intellectual and editorial counsel. With good humor and grace, Peter also nudged me to keep going each time I wavered. I cannot thank him enough for this.

I am grateful to Cornell University Press, and to Fran Benson in particular, for their first-rate production of the book. I appreciate Fran's enthusiasm, concern, and the easy but attentive manner in which she moved the book through the publication process. Thanks to Ange Romeo-Hall, my manuscript editor, and Kathy Gohl, my copyeditor, for improving both the presentation and quality of the text. I am also thankful to the anonymous reviewers who offered valuable suggestions for revising the manuscript. Although I have received excellent advice on the book, I am responsible for any error that should exist.

Still others have contributed to this research in important ways. In particular, James Moore helped me design and implement an effective strategy for sampling fathers. Sunday Parker and the WIC staff in Mercer and Middlesex County graciously allowed me access to their programs. Michelle Coyne expertly transcribed the interviews. Earl Johnson introduced me to social service providers who work with low-income fathers in Trenton. Paul King, Terry Dean, and Ron Heckart at U.C. Berkeley provided invaluable library support; Wendy Nardi, a historian and curator at the Trenton Public Library, also deserves my thanks. At various points, Sterling Bland, Jennifer Borkowski, Casey Crawford, Jean Knab, Diep Le, Julie Leavitt, Hugh Louch, Tara Mead, and Jonathon Simpson provided help in bringing this book to fruition. For all of these contributions, I am grateful.

Financial support was also critical to the success of this project. I would like to acknowledge the generous funding I received from the National Science Foundation, the Woodrow Wilson Foundation, the Eastern Sociological Society's Orlandella/Whyte Urban Research Fellowship, and Princeton University's Center for Domestic and Comparative Policy Studies. Many thanks to David Lyon, Michael Teitz, Joyce Peterson, and Debbie Reed at the Public Policy Institute of California who granted me the time and resources I needed to revise the book, and to all of my colleagues at PPIC who created a pleasant environment in which to do so. I also appreciate the in-kind assistance of Sara McLanahan and Irv Garfinkel who allowed me to use data from the Fragile Families and Child Wellbeing Study before its public release.

Research for the Fragile Families and Child Wellbeing Study was supported by the following grants: 5R01-HD-35301 and P30-HD-32030 from the National Institute of Child Health and Human Development through the Office of Population Research, Princeton University. Funding was also provided by the California HealthCare Foundation, the Commonwealth Fund, the Ford Foundation, the Foundation for Child Development, the Fund for New Jersey, the Healthcare Foundation of New Jersey, the William and Flora Hewlett Foundation, the Hogg Foundation, the Kronkosky Charitable Foundation, the John D. and Catherine T. MacArthur Foundation, the A. L. Mailman Family Foundation, the Charles Stewart Mott Foundation, the National Science Foundation, the David and Lucile Packard Foundation, the Department of Health and Human Services (ACF and ASPE), the Public Policy Institute of California, the Robert Wood Johnson Foundation, St. David's Foundation, St. Vincent Hospital and Health Services, and the William T. Grant Foundation.

In the end, the tremendous emotional support I received along the way made all the difference. For their encouragement over meals, drinks, long nights in the office, and long-distance phone calls, my deep affection and appreciation go out to Tim Baldwin, Sean Bayliss, Carolyn Weisz-Djornsen, Toby Eckert, Monica Groth Farrar, Steve Forte, Amy Halpin, Tammie Harkey, Tyrone Harvey, Steve Hudner, Steve Kantrowitz, Erin Kelly, Aaron Meskin, Susan Turner Meiklejohn, Michael Moody, Christine Morton, John Randolph, Belinda Reyes, Kim Rueben, Shira Stone, Christine Sullivan, Jeff Troiano, and Jon Wentz. I am especially thankful for the friendship of Fran Hirsch who has been there through it all. Writing is an unusually solitary task, and I am grateful to my friends for understanding those times I had to slip away to do this. Aaron Russel came as a blessing to me as I finished the project. As my best friend and staunchest supporter, he helped me through some of the most trying stages of the book, giving me the confidence to see it through to completion and, eventually, to let it go. I thank him not only for keeping me sane during this time but for making me happy.

As one of eight siblings, I couldn't help but become interested in family relationships. Mary Eleanor, Paul, Joe, Michael, Kathleen, Anne Marie, and Margaret—you and your families have been with me through this process even though I've never been within easy driving distance. At last, I thank my parents, Anne and Paul Waller, and my late grandmother Winifred Hartman.

My Baby's Father

Introduction

Alarmed by the high proportion of single-parent families in contemporary America, a relatively small but vocal group of commentators and academics has identified "fatherlessness" as one of the most important issues of our time.[1] A much larger group of academics and policymakers has expressed concern about the consequences of inadequate paternal involvement and support. Two consecutive administrations—one Democratic and the other Republican—have funded programs to promote "responsible fatherhood" among low-income men with child support obligations. Federal agencies have also been asked to include fathers in programs and research studies that have traditionally focused on mothers and children.[2]

Among the most popular images of the irresponsible parent is the deadbeat dad who casually fathers children outside of marriage to prove his manhood and then stands by indifferently as his children fall into poverty.[3] Social commentary, political discussions, and scholarly studies often endorse the view that low-income, unmarried fathers fail to support their children because they lack a sense of paternal responsibility. Although these discussions vary in their sophistication and rigor, they point to serious problems of paternal absence and nonsupport and the negative consequences for children. They also respond to a growing uncertainty about the meaning of fatherhood in contemporary culture. What these discussions lack, this book seeks to provide: a useful account of which beliefs about fatherhood prevail in low-income communities, how parents express their beliefs through informal practices, and how these beliefs and practices interact with public policy and conflict with the assumptions and regulations of the child support system.

Drawing on in-depth interviews with unmarried mothers and fathers whose children receive welfare, I pose in this book a series of basic, related, and vital questions and find some unexpected but surprisingly consistent answers. How do low-income mothers and fathers make sense of their experiences as unmarried parents? How do they define unmarried fathers' obligation to their children and explain "irresponsible" behavior among fathers? How do they use informal practices to acknowledge and care for their children? And how do these informal practices interact with mandatory welfare and child support regulations?

Among other things, the interviews show that low-income, unmarried parents believe that fathers have an unconditional responsibility to their biological children. Parents articulated coherent standards of paternal responsibility that blended new ideas about involved fatherhood with more conventional ideas about guidance, role modeling, and breadwinning. These standards, which were consistently invoked to evaluate unmarried fathers in their communities, did not center on economic provision—the foundation of the child support system. Equally consistent, although often incommensurable, were the accounts mothers and fathers offered when discussing failures to meet these standards of paternal responsibility.

The interviews also indicate how parents' ideas about paternal obligation, their informal systems of paternal recognition and support, and their sometimes dire economic circumstances conflicted with the assumptions of child support policy. Parents caught at the intersection of child support and welfare regulations often believed that the child support system detracted from their children's well-being, increased antagonism between parents, and punished poor fathers. Faced with a mismatch between public policy and their own beliefs, practices, and circumstances, many parents preferred informal support arrangements to participation in the child support system. Some also circumvented child support regulations that they perceived to be unfair, counterproductive, or punitive. Even parents who wanted to follow these regulations faced a variety of challenges that made it difficult for them to do so. Although many of these parents may have overestimated the long-term viability of informal arrangements, their preferences and constraints help explain why the system is not more effective for unmarried parents and their children.

Why Study Unmarried Parents?

Approximately 33 percent of all births in the United States now occur to unmarried parents, a figure that has risen from 4 percent in 1940 and 11 percent in 1970. Recent studies show that about half of these parents are living together at the time of their child's birth (McLanahan et al. 2001). However, paternal contact drops sharply as children grow older and the parents' relationship breaks apart (Sorensen, Mincy, and Halpern 2000). There is evidence, too, that children who grow up in families headed by a single parent have worse socioeconomic outcomes than do those raised by married, biological parents (McLanahan and Sandefur 1994). Because never-married parents and their children are also among the poorest demographic groups in the United States and make up the majority of families receiving welfare, the prevalence of nonmartial childbearing presents significant public policy challenges.

In response to these challenges, many policymakers have called for states to increase the numbers of paternities established for children born outside marriage and to promote tougher enforcement of child support orders. As a strategy closely aligned with welfare policy, child support policy is intended to privatize welfare costs, encourage self-sufficiency, and promote paternal responsibility. Privatization is accomplished in two ways: first, by helping poor mothers avoid entering the welfare system and, second, by reimbursing the costs of aid for those mothers already in the system. Mothers who receive welfare are required to identify their child's father and assign to the state their rights to the child support payments made by the father. Despite the state's intensive efforts to crack down on "deadbeat dads," however, child support enforcement has been relatively ineffective for families headed by unmarried mothers. In 1997, less than half of all never-married mothers had a child support award, and only about one in five received child support payments.[4]

Even as policymakers have expressed a strong interest in paternal obligation and provision, they have had little information about the ability of low-income, unmarried, nonresident fathers to pay child support. For a variety of reasons, these fathers are often missing from national surveys, which makes accurate assessments of their economic characteristics difficult (Garfinkel et al. 1998).[5] Emerging research indicates that approximately one-quarter of all unmarried fathers are poor by official definitions, and approximately half have incomes near the poverty line (McLanahan et al. 2001). New evidence also shows that nonresident fathers who do not pay child support have many of the same barriers to employment as do the mothers of their children (Sorensen and Zibman 2000b).

In addition to the effort to gather more information about fathers' economic circumstances, social responses can be improved by knowing more about the way unmarried parents perceive their own situations and the policy regulations that affect their families, and how they act on the basis of these perceptions. By gathering, analyzing, and placing the findings from the interviews in a social and regulatory context, this book will help academics, policymakers, and community leaders better understand the lives of unmarried parents and encourage them to reconsider programs that affect these parents and their children.

Approach

This study relies on intensive, qualitative interviews with unmarried, African American and white parents who were living in New Jersey and whose children received welfare. These interviews show how such parents—who were directly affected by changes in family formation, ideas about fatherhood, and welfare and child support policy—interpreted these changes at the ground level. By engaging parents in a dialogue about these issues, I was able to identify collective beliefs and informal practices not easily discernible through survey methods and to explore these issues in significant depth.[6] At the same time, this study incorporates and builds on survey results, especially the Fragile Families and Child Wellbeing (FFCW) study, a recent nationwide survey of unmarried parents and their children.[7] The FFCW study was designed to provide information about unmarried parents (particularly fathers) that has been unavailable from other national surveys.

In this analysis I investigate the language parents use to define collective standards, make sense of their situations, and explain their actions. Because people's explanations mediate and integrate action, this approach regards language and action as inseparable (Mills 1940, 907–908).[8] The analysis also considers the cultural repertoires or tool kits used by unmarried parents to organize and coordinate their beliefs and actions over time (Swidler 1986, 2001).[9] It is further informed by the view that the cultural resources unmarried parents have access to, as well as the structural conditions in which they live, push them toward particular ideas and practices (Lamont 2000, 7). In this study, I am especially concerned with the way unmarried mothers and fathers use available ideas and practices to define, evaluate, justify, and express paternal responsibility within a specific socioeconomic context defined by poverty, nonmarital childbearing, and welfare and child support regulations.

Discussions of reproduction, marriage, and paternal responsibility have historically been cast in moral terms—particularly when the discussion pertains to parents who receive public assistance. This tendency is likely to persist well into the future. My aim in this research is not to offer a moral evaluation of the cultural system I am studying. Rather, my goal is to describe this cultural system and to explain its internal logic. For this reason, I sought to identify the collective ideas and formulations that gave rise to the consistent (indeed, predictable) discursive and behavioral patterns I observed.[10]

This book builds on an important body of qualitative research about low-income fathers. Clark's *Dark Ghetto* (1965), Liebow's *Tally's Corner* (1967), and Rainwater's *Behind Ghetto Walls* (1970), among others, offered rich insights into the lives of low-income fathers and made important contributions to our understanding of poverty and the family. Because these studies appeared when they did—at the onset of de-industrialization, when the breadwinner model was culturally dominant, before the federal Office of Child Support Enforcement was created in 1975, and before the steep increase in single-parent families—they could not address the demographic, cultural, and policy changes that have occurred since 1970. However, Anderson (1989) and Sullivan (1989) reopened the discussion of low-income men and their families in provocative essays.[11] Their contrasting observations of poor fathers' relationships with their children raised questions that motivated the work presented here.

Despite the important contributions of these studies, most research on low-income families has addressed the perceptions and experiences of single mothers. This book gives voice to the "absent" fathers, who often have been excluded from academic and policy discussions, even as it pays careful attention to unmarried mothers and their beliefs. It also documents the experiences of African American and white parents simultaneously.[12] In so doing, the book illustrates the extent to which beliefs and practices are likely to cross racial or gender lines. It also shifts the focus from teenagers to adults, who constitute the largest group of unmarried parents but who have received less attention in the scholarly literature on nonmarital childbearing.

Overview

The book begins by presenting the context for my interviews with low-income, unmarried parents in New Jersey. After describing the demographic and socioeconomic characteristics of the parents, as well as how they were selected for the study, I discuss some of the study's methodological challenges, including the problem of gaining access to unmarried fathers. I then turn my focus to how mothers and fathers made sense of their experience of having a child and remaining unmarried. This investigation considers how unmarried parents regarded reproduction and marriage both in their own lives and more generally.

I next examine the ways that unmarried parents framed their expectations for and experiences with paternal involvement and support. After outlining important models of fatherhood in American culture, the book investigates how unmarried parents interpreted the responsibilities of fatherhood. In particular, it asks: How do parents explain why unmarried fathers are obligated to their children? In what ways are fathers expected to support their children? What is the significance of different types of support? From here, I examine how mothers and fathers described variations in paternal behavior and how they accounted for their partner's or their own disengagement from their children.

The analysis then looks at how unmarried fathers accept and express responsibility for their children. After examining how these fathers acknowledged their biological and social paternity, the study goes on to investigate the ways in which the ideas and practices of unmarried parents played out under welfare and child support requirements. In particular, it identifies points at which parents said the child support system broke down for their families. It also documents why many of these parents were reluctant to participate in the child support system and how they reconciled their views and practices with welfare and child support requirements.

These interviews indicate that the child support system has been slow to respond to changes in family formation and contemporary views of fatherhood. After examining these changes as they apply to low-income families with unmarried parents, I suggest how policymakers can shape more effective child support policies and increase the long-term stability of relationships between unmarried parents and their children. The book concludes with specific recommendations for social policies that are suited to unmarried parents' socioeconomic situations and are responsive to the collective ideas about and practices of responsible fatherhood in low-income families.

CHAPTER ONE

Studying Unmarried Parents

Trenton just can't grow. Like at one time, you know that sign—Trenton Makes, the World Takes—that was actually true. Now-a-days there ain't nothing you can take from Trenton. . . . Trenton's not productive. [There used to be] a whole lot of factories here. Raw materials. You know, stuff like that. Yeah. They all moved from Trenton. (Andre)

[Trenton is] depressing. Basically, that's it. It's depressing. . . . There's nothing to do here. There's not really any opportunity. Even those people that go to school and get degrees still have a hard time in this area. . . . If I had a chance for my children not to grow up here, I wouldn't have them grow up here. . . . Kids are getting into a whole lot more stuff now than they were when I was younger. Like now they in all these gangs and jumping people and stealing cars. And drugs is all around. Everything is right at their doorstep. (Joe)

I want to move, I don't like it around here. . . . Drugs and the violence, it's terrible around here. Now it's quiet 'cause it's early in the day. But honey you try coming through here at night. Psss it's terrible. I can't stand it. I hate it with a passion. . . . I don't even let my son go outside and play. When he comes home from school, he's secluded in this house unless I take them over to their grandma's house and they play over there. That's where their dad at. . . . But, it's just terrible. I'm telling you, I don't like it. I hate it with a passion. . . . My goals [are to have] a nice house, a nice car, put [money in a] savings account, and move the hell away from here as far as I could possibly go. I don't care where. It could be in the suburbs some-where. . . . I'll move around a bunch a dog-gone white people. I don't care.

At least I could send my kids out in my yard, like go outside and play and not be worried about running to the door every five minutes. (Shakeema)

The research for this study was conducted in central New Jersey, primarily in the city of Trenton and the nearby suburbs of Mercer and Middlesex counties, during 1994 and 1995.[1] Trenton is a medium-sized urban area (the 1995 population was 86,165) with characteristics similar to other de-industrialized cities in the Northeast and Midwest, such as middle-class flight, concentrated poverty, and a high incidence of welfare receipt (Wilson 1996, 1987). In 1989, approximately 27 percent of the children in Trenton lived below the poverty level—about two and one-half times the state rate of 11 percent.[2] The percentage of households in Trenton receiving public assistance was twice as high as that of the state (12 and 6 percent, respectively). Furthermore, 43 percent of children lived in a family headed by a single mother, and 45 percent of these children were living below the poverty level (U.S. Census Bureau 1990).

Trenton, the capital of New Jersey, emerged as an important industrial city during the nineteenth century and remained a relatively strong manufacturing center until the 1960s when de-industrialization began to change the economic structure of many Northeastern cities (see Cumbler 1989).[3] A bridge that crosses the Delaware River between Trenton and Morrisville, Pennsylvania, supports a large sign that reads "Trenton Makes, the World Takes" and stands as a poignant testimony to the blue-collar factory jobs that have disappeared from the area. Between 1976 and 1994, manufacturing jobs in the state of New Jersey declined by approximately one-third, from 756,000 to 510,000. Mercer County, where Trenton is located, was particularly hard hit by the loss of manufacturing jobs with such companies as General Motors and Roebling Steel. In early 1995 alone, the county lost about 5,400 jobs as the result of factory pullouts by Lockheed, Mobil Oil, and Hill Refrigeration.[4] During this time, another 1,200 state jobs were cut, hundreds of which were located in Mercer County (Goodnough 1995).

Statistics reveal some of the economic problems that Trenton experienced at the time of this study. In 1995, when a "new economy" based on information technology was taking hold in much of the country, Trenton had an average unemployment rate of 11.4 percent, compared with that of 5.4 percent in Mercer County, 5.5 percent in Middlesex County, and 6.4 percent throughout the state as a whole. After the period of economic recovery between 1998 and 1999, the unemployment rate in Trenton dropped to 8.7 percent (U.S. Bureau of Labor and Statistics 2001). Although the cost of living in the Northeast Corridor between New York and Philadelphia is high, in 1990 the per capita income in Trenton was about $11,000—more than 40 percent below the average for the state (U.S. Census Bureau 1990).

"Trenton Makes, The World Takes": A slogan from the city's more productive times. Photo courtesy of the Trentoniana: Local History and Genealogy Collection, Trenton Public Library.

The 1990 Census shows that approximately 48 percent of Trenton residents were black and 38 percent were white, in contrast to the racial composition of Mercer County as a whole (which was about 73 percent white and 18 percent black) and Middlesex County (about 77 percent white and 7 percent black) (U.S. Census Bureau 1990).[5] By 2000, the total population of Trenton was close to what it had been in 1990, although now 52 percent of the residents were black and 33 percent were white, indicating a further depopulation of whites (U.S. Census Bureau 2001a).[6]

Trenton covers a small area of approximately 7.5 square miles and is divided administratively into four geographical areas (North, South, East, and West Trenton). These four sections, or wards, create a basis for neighborhood identification among its residents. Trenton's white residents are typically segregated from African American residents and live in higher-income neighborhoods. One Italian working-class area of the city is symbolically divided from poorer African American neighborhoods adjacent to it by a major street running through the city. Both white and African American residents expressed their anxiety about crossing over into the "wrong" neighborhood. Some white residents noted their fear of being victims of violent crime in the poor, drug-ridden neighborhoods that surround them, at times citing a highly publicized incident in which a white woman was murdered while driving through an African American neighborhood. Similarly, some African American residents said they avoid entering certain white neighborhoods for fear of a racially motivated attack.

Low-income neighborhoods are represented within each of the four sections of Trenton and contain housing projects, Section 8 (federally subsidized) housing, and private housing. Many of the Trenton public housing units are low-rise brick buildings. The most obvious indicators of other impoverished areas are the many abandoned, "bombed out," and boarded-up buildings. Although low-income neighborhoods in Trenton have a number of storefront and larger churches, check-cashing facilities, bars, and liquor stores, there is only a scattering of restaurants, stores, or other businesses on many blocks. In fact, about 18 percent of the land in Trenton is vacant (Kaufman and Bailkey 2001).[7] With the exception of the outdoor mall built around a complex of state buildings, many residents of Trenton had little access to shopping or entertainment. The African American parents I spoke with often attributed the tendency for young people to use drugs or to hang out on the street to the lack of diversions, such as a movie theater, available in Trenton. Taking a bus to movie theaters, malls, and restaurants about fifteen minutes from Trenton was an option, but the effort, cost, and stories the parents heard about incidents of racial discrimination and harassment by police deterred many.

This study was conducted during 1994 and 1995—the last two years in which the Aid to Families with Dependent Children (AFDC) system was in place. At that time, the typical single mother with two children in Trenton could receive a maximum of $424 a month in AFDC benefits and $276 in food stamps.[8] The New Jersey legislature had passed a "family cap" in 1992 that denied additional cash benefits to women who gave birth to a child while receiving welfare. The state had also begun to rely more heavily on the penal system in the effort to crack down on fathers for nonsupport. Paternity establishment emerged as an important issue in the 1993 governor's race between Christine Todd Whitman and Jim Florio. Whitman condemned a Florio-backed bill that would have denied welfare benefits to women who refused to identify the fathers of their children. After she was elected, however, Governor Whitman reversed her position and created a controversy when she suggested that young black men played a game called Jewels in the Crown to impregnate as many women as possible (Sullivan 1995). It was in this context of rising nonmarital birth rates, increasing crackdowns on deadbeat dads, and limitations onpublic assistance leading up to the passage of the Personal Responsibility and Work Opportunity Reconciliation Act (PRWORA) that I investigated how unmarried parents with children receiving welfare interpreted paternal responsibility and interacted with the child support and welfare systems.

Research Design

The sample for this study consisted of 40 African American parents (20 mothers and 20 fathers) and 25 white parents (16 mothers and 9 fathers) whose children received welfare.[9] All of the African American parents and 75 percent of the white parents in this study lived within the Trenton metropolitan area.[10] However, many more African American parents (85 percent) than white parents (25 percent) lived in the city itself. The remaining 25 percent of white parents lived in Middlesex County, which is adjacent to Mercer County.[11]

An important objective of this study was to interview unmarried fathers as well as mothers. Because unmarried fathers are underrepresented in national surveys, much of the data available about low-income, unmarried fathers come from interviews with women. Some of these fathers are missing from surveys because they are difficult to sample, and some who are included in surveys do not acknowledge that they have children (Garfinkel et al. 1998). I used qualitative sampling and interviewing methods to gain better access to and information about unmarried fathers. Compared with surveys, open-ended, qualitative interviews provide richer data for interpreting the meaning of parents' responses.

My sample included only parents who had a child outside of marriage and who were unmarried at the time of the interview. All of the African American parents and approximately 75 percent of the white parents I contacted had never been married. This pattern is consistent with those in other studies of nonmarital childbearing, which show that white women who have a nonmarital birth are more likely than African American women to have been previously married (Driscoll et al. 1999). I also selected mothers whose children lived with them, and I selected fathers who did not have sole custody of their children. (Most of these men were also nonresident fathers.) Although this study does not capture the experiences of single fathers or many fathers currently cohabiting with their children, it represents the typical living arrangements of families headed by unmarried parents.[12] These nonresidential arrangements are likely to affect parents' feelings about fathers' engagement with children and account for their involvement with the child support system.

I sampled parents who were eighteen years or older because adults make up the majority of parents who have children outside of marriage.[13] Most of these men and women had young children, allowing me to compare mothers and fathers in similar parenting situations. Because fathers with children receiving welfare incur a child support obligation to the state, I made a sampling decision to interview parents with a child who had received welfare. However, three children of white parents had received Medicaid only and not AFDC.[14]

Most parents in this sample were in their twenties, with low levels of education and limited employment; mothers were about twenty-five years old and fathers about twenty-seven (see Appendix B, tables 1 and 2). Approximately 42 percent of mothers did not have a high school diploma, 8 percent had a high school diploma or General Equivalency Degree (GED), and 50 percent had some education or training beyond high school. This sample includes a relatively high proportion of mothers with post–high school education because many of these mothers had participated in training programs through welfare. Approximately 31 percent of fathers did not have a high school degree, 31 percent had a high school diploma or GED, and 38 percent had some education or training beyond high school.[15] About 17 percent of mothers were employed at the time of the interview and did not receive AFDC, whereas about 62 percent of fathers I spoke with were employed. The white fathers in this sample were older than the other parents (their average age was thirty), and they had lower employment rates than did the African American fathers, in contrast with the general employment patterns of African American and white males.[16]

The Fragile Families and Child Wellbeing (FFCW) study helps put the characteristics of this sample in a broader context. As a representative survey, the FFCW study does not select parents on the basis of criteria such as race or welfare receipt.[17] Therefore, the two samples are not directly comparable. However, the characteristics of parents I interviewed are not unlike those of unmarried parents in the FFCW sample. In the FFCW study, the average age of the mothers was twenty-four and the average age of fathers was twenty-seven. About 38 percent of mothers did not have a high school diploma, 32 percent had a high school diploma or GED, and 30 percent had education or training beyond high school. About 34 percent of fathers did not have a high school diploma, 39 percent had a high school diploma or GED, and 27 percent had some education or training beyond high school. Only about 73 percent of fathers were working at the time of the interview, despite a strong labor market in the late 1990s.[18] Unlike my sample, more white fathers were employed (84 percent) than black fathers (64 percent).

Understanding the composition of unmarried parents' families and the characteristics of relationships between unmarried mothers and fathers is also important for interpreting their responses. The typical parent I interviewed had two children, and the average age of the focal child was three.[19] Although about two-thirds of parents were involved in committed relationships with their child's other parent at the time of the birth, only one-third reported to be involved in any kind of romantic relationship with the other parent at the time of the interview. More than half of parents said they had lived with the other parent for some period of time, but only 15 percent were cohabiting when we spoke. In the FFCW study, parents also had two children on average. About 83 percent of unmarried parents were involved in romantic relationships at the time of their child's birth, with over half of unmarried parents living together.[20] Early evidence suggests that parents who were cohabiting at the time of the birth had relatively stable relationships in the first year of their child's life, but parents who were living apart were more likely to end their relationships than to stay together, indicating the fragility of these relationships (Waller 2001).

Out in the Field: Sampling Strategies

I contacted more than half of the mothers in the study through the Women, Infants, and Children (WIC) program from locations in Trenton and in Mercer and Middlesex Counties.[21] The rest were contacted primarily through referrals from other parents participating in the study.[22] I talked with women informally at the clinics and provided informational fliers about the study to schedule interviews (see Appendix A for a longer discussion of the research experience). Following the example of other researchers who have successfully interviewed low-income parents, I obtained personal referrals or met each parent before the interviews rather than sample through the state welfare and child support offices. Although drawing from an administrative list of welfare clients might have given me a targeted sample, I did not think it would allow me to gain the trust of prospective participants. The issue of trust was particularly important given the sensitivity of some of the issues raised in the interviews and the fact that my class, and, in many cases, race and gender, differed from those of the respondents.

Sampling from WIC clinics involved visiting their sites, which are located in churches, community centers, and recreational facilities. Because of the location of the WIC sites, I was not seen as part of their staff. I typically sat in the waiting area, struck up conversations with individual mothers, and told them about the project.[23] Some women had already heard from the WIC staff or from other social service providers that I was writing a book. If a woman told me that she was unmarried and that she was interested in participating, we would exchange names and home telephone numbers and set up an appointment. I always called to finalize the time and place of our meeting, to tell her more about the project, and to answer any questions she had. When respondents did not have telephones, I tried to schedule the appointment for the following day and answer questions before the interview. The majority of interviews with mothers took place in their homes, but approximately one-third of white mothers asked to be interviewed in fast food restaurants or coffee shops.[24] The length of the interviews with mothers and fathers ranged from about ninety minutes to more than four hours.[25]

Replicating other qualitative approaches (e.g., Edin and Lein 1997), I also "snowballed" off of these contacts to generate the remainder of my sample. At the end of each interview, I asked women for a maximum of four referrals to other unmarried parents to ensure I would reach diverse networks, and I included a subgroup of those parents who fit my sampling criteria.[26] Some participants would call their friends or introduce me to their neighbors immediately after the interview. Others would ask their friend's permission to be contacted and call me with their numbers. A few women who seemed particularly excited about the interview had arranged for friends to come over before I even asked for referrals, perhaps wanting to give their friends a chance to earn $20 or to participate in this experience. In these situations, we also had group conversations about men, child support, living in New Jersey, and other issues that were raised in the interview.[27] Almost all of the women who said they had friends who were unmarried mothers offered to introduce them.

As a general rule, I did not ask for referrals from mothers to the father of their child. Although I have three couples in my sample, early conversations with parents suggested that I would be much more likely to reach both parents if they were on good terms or still involved in a romantic relationship. Because I typically interviewed parents three years after their child was born, many of their relationships had dissolved. A number of mothers also indicated that the father was inaccessible because he lived in a different area, was in jail, or (in one case) was no longer alive. Although the strategy of sampling men and women independently prevented me from comparing the consistency of couples' accounts, it allowed me to interview many parents who were raising their children in separate households and who were likely to have experience with the child support system.

While interviewing mothers, I received some referrals to men but had difficulty finding institutions in Trenton that served a large number of low-income fathers. I considered conventional qualitative methods of sampling through community organizations, through a random selection of residences, and through personal networks. These plans were complicated by the fact that noncustodial fathers do not interact with social service agencies to the same extent that women do. Men also have not been as involved in community institutions, such as churches, as women are (Lincoln and Mamiya 1990). In addition, low-income fathers are more loosely attached to households, thereby making this group difficult for researchers to sample. Given that African American men were a visible presence in the neighborhoods in which I interviewed women but "invisible" in formal organizations, I decided to go directly onto the street to find my sample.

Because Trenton neighborhoods are racially segregated and groups on the street were typically segregated by gender, I stood out as a white woman in African American neighborhoods, and it might have appeared strange if I had sought interviews by myself. James Moore, an African American research assistant at Princeton who grew up in Trenton, helped me develop a plan to sample from areas in which young men in Trenton hang out: in front of housing projects, on street corners, in front of stores and houses, and in barber shops. Typically, James would approach groups of five to six men, introduce me, and briefly describe the study. I provided additional information and answered any questions the men had.

We encountered most men outside of housing projects or on neighborhood streets lined with abandoned row houses. Often we approached groups of men who were sitting on front porches. On sunny days, we saw families having cookouts, men shooting dice, children doing flips off old mattresses piled in back of housing projects, and men getting their hair cut by friends on their lawns. We also saw some men wandering around drinking from bottles in paper bags, selling drugs, and hanging out in gangs. Our approach to "street sampling" was greeted with varying levels of curiosity, enthusiasm, and suspicion. Typically, about half of the men in each group would give me their names and telephone numbers. Some of the remaining men were not unmarried fathers and others, presumably, were not interested in participating.[28]

I returned from these outings with a list of names, telephone numbers, and times at which men could be reached. Several men who gave me their names, however, told me that they did not have a telephone and asked me to call them at a neighbor's or relative's residence. When I began to call these numbers I realized how transitory many men's living situations were. Although three-quarters of the African American fathers in this sample said they lived with their mother or with their mother and other family members, quite a few of the men seemed to reside somewhere else (such as their girlfriend's home) for part of the week. I usually made a few attempts at each residence and asked fathers to call me collect at home. Some men's telephone numbers were disconnected by the time I called. Other men could not return toll calls from telephones they had access to or did not return calls when they saw an unfamiliar number on their caller I.D. or on their pagers. Because I was not always near my telephone, collect calls were also difficult to receive. Some men probably never received my messages, whereas others did not return my call for other reasons. Given the selectivity of men who gave me their names and returned my calls, I assume that my sample of fathers probably over-represented men who were involved with their children and wanted to talk about their experiences as fathers.

Despite these problems, I managed to speak to about two-thirds of the men I met on the street, and all but one of these men agreed to be interviewed. A set of logistical obstacles followed, however. I decided to interview most fathers in public places, primarily in fast food restaurants. Because there were so few restaurants in black neighborhoods in Trenton, men sometimes had a long walk, bike ride, or bus ride to meet me. In a few cases, I would arrange to meet men on the street for an interview if no other reasonable alternative existed. In several situations, I gave the men a ride home after the interview.[29] Fortunately, almost all of the men I spoke with offered to refer me to other participants or to help with the project in some other way.[30] In the end, about half of the African American fathers in the study were sampled from the street and the rest were sampled through personal referrals or fliers.[31]

Given the complications involved in interviewing low-income African American fathers, it is ironic that white fathers—a group more integrated into the mainstream economy and housing market—were the most difficult group to reach. Like unmarried white mothers, white fathers of children on welfare usually reside in mixed-income, suburban communities in New Jersey. In these neighborhoods, men rarely hang out on the street, in part because the majority of white men hold jobs. Other locations where men socialize (for example, bars) also reflect the mixed income distribution of the community. As noncustodial parents, these fathers were absent from organizations or social service agencies that assist low-income children. Therefore, they were contacted through referrals from other interviewees and through a program for noncustodial fathers in Trenton.[32] Overall, my sample is probably less characteristic of unmarried white fathers than of unmarried white mothers and African American parents.

A Note on Racial Comparisons

As a group, African Americans have faced more severe socioeconomic problems than whites have, given their historical experience of slavery and their exposure to racial discrimination, persistent poverty, and unemployment. The literature on African American families suggests that a father's ability to be involved with his children has been associated with this particular set of economic, social, and historical experiences (see McAdoo 1988). Therefore, many researchers interested in low-income fathers have rightfully turned their attention to African American families. By focusing on low-income fathers within a single racial category, however, researchers risk conflating race and class characteristics, sometimes with the unintended effect of reinforcing negative stereotypes about black family life and overlooking nonmarital childbearing in low-income, white families.[33] Today, most unmarried mothers are white (40 percent), despite the greater proportion of births to unmarried black mothers (69 percent) than to white mothers (22 percent) (Ventura and Bachrach 2000).[34] I interviewed African American and white parents to represent the experiences of both groups.

At the same time, the research design used in this study lends itself to looking at unmarried parents as a group and to comparing the responses of mothers and fathers, rather than examining differences between African American and white parents. Although I note some differences in responses by race, this study is primarily concerned with analyzing pooled information about unmarried parents—now an important demographic subgroup that challenges conventional thinking about how to design policies for low-income families. I was particularly interested in studying those unmarried parents whose children receive public assistance and who are at the intersection of child support and welfare regulations.

Furthermore, I found that the data pointed to more similarities than differences between African American and white respondents. Because these parents were sampled according to the same criteria, such things as their marital status and use of public assistance were "controlled." Almost three times the proportion of births to African American women occur outside of marriage compared with those to white women, and I would have likely seen more differences in a sample that had included married parents (most of whom have higher incomes than unmarried parents).

Compared with white respondents, African American respondents in this study had more in common with each other as a group. Therefore, I elaborate on the responses of African American parents at various points in the text. Whereas low-income white families in this sample had varied residential and class backgrounds, African American respondents had grown up in more similar socio-economic situations, attended many of the same schools, and shared local experiences as residents of Trenton. As noted earlier, for example, 85 percent of African American respondents lived in the city of Trenton compared with 25 percent of white respondents. This pattern reflects the fact that in this area, low-income whites tend not to live in pockets of concentrated poverty. The African American parents also had had more exposure to parenting outside of marriage than the white parents and probably had had more experience with poverty as a result of growing up in households headed by unmarried parents (two out of five African American parents in this sample said their own parents had never been married to each other while all white parents said their biological parents had been married, at least for some time). Given these issues of sample size and composition, the data allow me to speak with the most confidence about commonalities in the sample as a whole and within the subgroup of the African American parents.

In the next chapter I turn to the information I received from the unmarried mothers and fathers who participated in this study. These responses, gleaned from more than two hundred hours of discussion, show how low-income unmarried parents are responding to the changing cultural, economic, and policy context. I begin by looking at how mothers and fathers make sense of their experience as unmarried parents.

CHAPTER TWO

The Separation of Reproduction and Marriage

[Having a] kid never crossed my mind before I was twenty-two. Nope. Never. Never even thought I had to worry about it. When I found out I was pregnant, you know, here I am in a relationship for a couple years and I thought it was everything it was supposed to be . . . and I was confused. And I kept it to myself because he took off on me, and then I was left in this little insecure ball. And I didn't tell anyone for months. I was about five months pregnant before I let my friends know. Which, at that time, you know, to look back from the outside was a mistake. I should have talked to people because I was very unprepared for everything. I really didn't know what was available, and I didn't even see a doctor until I was twenty-three weeks. You know, things like that. I just didn't know what to do because I was scared.

Julie, a mother of one who had recently left welfare, told me the story I've quoted above over diet sodas one evening after returning home from her new job. Her small one-bedroom apartment was on the top floor of a row house in an Italian working-class section of Trenton. Her three-year-old daughter hid in a cardboard box, which she used as a playhouse, occasionally coming in and out of the room to inspect the stranger sitting on her couch. Julie recounted what she had seen as her options during pregnancy:

I didn't consider abortion. You know, I'm not against it. I'm not out there rallying, but for me it wasn't a choice. And I really considered having her adopted. I spent, up until, like, eight months I said, "I'm not ready for this." I knew at twenty-two I was still immature, and I wasn't prepared to be a mother. I didn't think I was. And, almost last minute, I said no. I didn't go to any agency or anything, but I said, no, this is my responsibility and I'm going to regret it . . . so I just winged it.

It was morning when I knocked on the door of Crystal's apartment in one of Trenton's low-rise housing projects. Crystal, a mother of three, greeted me warmly and asked me to sit down. She instructed her two older children to play in their bedroom, while her one-year-old baby slept on the couch. Almost immediately she launched into a story about her last pregnancy, which had occurred while she was involved in an "on-and-off" relationship. Like Julie, Crystal had reservations about having a baby but cited a moral motivation in responding to her pregnancy:

I was surprised about being pregnant with him . . . it's not like you plan to have a baby. It just happens. But at that point it was my fault because I know, if you're not using no protection, there's a 100 percent chance that you can get pregnant again. And it happened again. It happened again. Mm hmm. But you know, I'm dealing with it. . . . I never had an abortion. Never. I'd be kinda skeptical about doing that. I was kinda skeptical about [having] him because I wasn't with his father when we made him. We wasn't into a deep relationship. We were just seeing each other. And I was, like, why should I have this baby? I'm not with him. But I had to think about it. My baby is always going to be here. You have to think about the child first, before you think about the man. You got to think about: this child did not ask to be born. I did lay down and make it.

Julie and Crystal struggled with their decisions to become mothers but dismissed the idea that marrying the father would have resolved their situations, or that it was even a viable option. Although both women said they wanted to marry eventually, neither believed that pregnancy was a good enough reason to do so. Describing her unhappy experience living with parents who fought constantly, Julie attributed many of her current economic and emotional problems to her volatile childhood. Her mother, she said, had a "horrible experience" with marriage. She explained, "Both my mother and stepmother were married when they were twenty and had their first kid at twenty. They were both, like, pregnant, like, at their wedding." Julie believed that having a child in the context of a troubled marriage was worse for the parents and child than having a child as a single person. Her advice to other young couples dealing with an unexpected pregnancy was that

If they stay together, more power to them. But don't get married, because it's harder to undo than to do. There's time. Five, six years down the road when they're stable, do it. There's no stopping you from getting married. The hard part is putting the child through a horrible marriage and getting out of it.

Similarly, Crystal rejected the idea of a shotgun wedding:

A couple shouldn't get married because of a baby. A couple shouldn't get married because the woman's pregnant. That's not for the right reason, you know what I'm saying? You just getting married because you're pregnant from this man. No. I really think he should try to get a job to help her out. He should really get a job to try to take care of the baby. And if he can't, then she could get on some type of program and get some type of assistance.

In contrast to Crystal and Julie, more than half of the parents I interviewed described themselves as having been open to the pregnancy when it occurred or as planning the pregnancy, typically within the context of a committed relationship. However, these parents mentioned similar considerations about marriage. Both groups emphasized the importance of finding the right person and being ready to make a commitment.

I talked to Simone, a first-time mother, in a crowded, two-story house where she lived with her mother, grandparents, siblings, and cousins. Simone said she was happy about her pregnancy and felt good about being a mother:

I always wanted to have a baby. . . . I had got pregnant before [and] I miscarried. And it seemed like it took me forever to get pregnant again. And when I did, the thought in my mind of having an abortion was not even there. I wanted my baby.

Although Simone was living with her son's father when she became pregnant, they were forced to move out of their apartment because of plumbing problems. She said that the father saw their son almost every day and bought him "whatever he needs." She also had the support of her extended family. However, Simone hoped that she and her son would live with the father again as a family:

I want me and his father to be able to stay together, 'cause I want [our son] to have his mother and his father together. Not his mom here with somebody else and his dad is somewhere else, married to somebody else. I would want them to be together.

Simone's immediate plans were to move into a new apartment, find a job, and leave welfare. She also expected to marry but did not plan to do so in the near future. Simone explained, "He wants to marry me, and I'm not sure yet. . . . I think we'll wait a little while longer." She planned to follow her mother's advice: "Not to get married just for the name or nothing. Just make sure I really love him. And that's what I want to do."

I interviewed Jeff at a fast-food restaurant on the outskirts of Trenton. Although he and his child's mother were no longer romantically involved, Jeff described living with her in a "marriage-like" relationship for five years. They were not trying to become parents but were open to having a child when the pregnancy occurred:

> I kind of knew all along that it would happen. I think that she did, too. She claimed at the time that she was on the pill. And I think at some point in time she'd stopped taking them. . . . I guess I was being irresponsible myself. But in a sense I didn't care, because I loved her and I felt that if we had a child together it would bring us closer. So, I could go either one way or the other. It didn't bother me.

In principle, Jeff believed it was a good idea to be married when you had children. But like other parents, he and his partner did not consider marriage a necessary response to the pregnancy. Jeff explained that they had talked about marriage, but he "figured what the hell—we're already in it together. You know, I consider us husband and wife. So, I didn't see a point in making it official like that. And at the time, she didn't either." Jeff attributed their later breakup to the frequency of arguments in the relationship and felt that marrying the mother would have been "all for nothing," given the likelihood of divorce. He said he would advise other people thinking about marriage to look for the "telltale" signs in relationships:

> Can you see yourself with this person? Maybe this person is a good lover. Maybe this person is a good companion. But is he gonna be a good husband? You have to make that decision. There are basic telltale signs of whether he's fit for that or not. Is he the impulsive type? Is he the type to run out when the going gets tough? So, it's a personal decision. And I don't think it will always be a good idea to just do it, just for the sake of doing it.

All of these parents or their partners made a series of decisions—to continue a nonmarital pregnancy, to keep their child, and to remain unmarried—within particular economic and social constraints. In this chapter I discuss how parents drew on ideas and explanations from their cultural repertoires to make sense of these decisions and their options for marriage (Mills 1940; Burke 1989).[1] After briefly describing reasons why the separation of reproduction and marriage has become so prevalent, I examine how unmarried parents talk about reproduction, romantic relationships, and marriage in their own lives and more generally. Despite the fact that parents interpret and perhaps revise their own stories in interviews, their retrospective accounts and general beliefs provide insight into how men and women in similar situations regard marriage after they have become parents.

Declines in Marriage

Julie, Crystal, Simone, and Jeff were part of one of the fastest-growing types of American families in the 1990s—those that consist of unmarried parents and their children. Although nonmarital childbearing rates have leveled off in recent years, approximately one-third of births now occur outside of marriage in the United States. Scholars observe that the separation of reproduction from marriage has occurred across social groups and in other industrialized countries.[2] However, this separation has not affected all groups equally. A majority of the births to unmarried parents are to low-income, white, adult women, but a disproportionate number are to African American women.[3]

Social scientists point to a complex set of economic and cultural factors that have led to the steep increase in rates of nonmarital childbearing in the latter half of the twentieth century. Research suggests that much of this increase results from changes in marital behavior that have heightened the risk of having a nonmarital birth.[4] Recent cohorts of adults have postponed marriage or chosen not to marry, and men and women are more likely to divorce and less likely to remarry (Ventura et al. 1995).[5] Instead, more couples are choosing to live together, and most of the increase in nonmarital childbearing since the early 1980s has occurred to cohabiting parents (Bumpass and Lu 2000).[6] Finally, fewer men and women today are deciding to marry in response to a nonmarital pregnancy (Ventura et al. 1995).

Economic factors explain some of the change in marital behavior. Over the last three decades, a narrowing of the gender gap in earnings has altered the conventional gender bargain in marriage in which men act as the primary or sole provider.[7] For men at lower skill and educational levels, absolute declines in male earnings have made the provider role much less attainable. Between 1979 and 1997, for example, the real hourly wages of men who had not completed high school dropped by about 30 percent. Of those with a high school diploma, wages decreased by about 17 percent (Mishel, Bernstein, and Schmitt 1999, 157).[8]

In poor, urban, African American neighborhoods, economic trends affecting the employment and earnings prospects of low-skilled workers have been even more pronounced (Danziger 2000). Wilson (1996, 1987) argues that joblessness—along with incarceration and high mortality rates—has rendered fewer African American men "marriageable" and has led to in-creases in nonmarital childbearing in poor neighborhoods.[9] In sum, scholars suggest that the diminishing ability of men to support a family because of decreased earnings and joblessness makes men less attractive marriage part-ners to women.

At the same time, economic factors explain only part of this increasing trend of delayed marriage or nonmarriage (Mare and Winship 1991; Lichter 1995; Moore 1995). The past decades have brought an increasing cultural ac-ceptance of divorce, cohabitation, and sexuality outside of marriage. Survey data indicate that nonmarital sexuality and cohabitation are much more ac-cepted among younger cohorts, while marriage is viewed as less central to their lives (Thornton 1995). Young men and women now perceive fewer ad-vantages to marriage than in the past (Thornton and Freedman 1982) and seem to have higher expectations for realizing cultural ideals, such as equal-ity and emotional gratification, in their relationships (Furstenberg and Cher-lin 1991; Luker 1996). Also, women may be less willing to tolerate abusive or extremely hierarchical relationships (Stacey 1991; Luker 1996). Other re-search suggests that a male revolt against commitment to family preceded women's resistance to inequality in marriage (Ehrenreich 1984). Finally, an increasing emphasis on individualism in American culture may have con-tributed to the reluctance of men and women to marry (Lichter 1995). These new cultural beliefs and gender expectations may have influenced changes in marriage and family structure that occurred earlier in low-income families than in the rest of the population.[10]

Although researchers offer different interpretations of changes in family structure, they consistently express concern about the high incidence of poverty among families headed by single mothers. Compared with children who grow up with both biological parents in intact families, those who grow up in single-parent families run a greater risk of dropping out of high school, having a child as a teenager, and being idle (that is, out of school and out of work) during their late teens and early twenties, in large part because their families have lower incomes (McLanahan and Sandefur 1994).[11] The poverty of families headed by never-married mothers (the majority of all unmarried mothers) is even more severe and of greater duration than that of other single-parent families.[12]

Becoming an Unmarried Parent

When I interviewed parents, I asked them to tell me how they had made the decision to have a child. More than half said they had not had reserva-tions about having a child; this group included those who characterized their last pregnancy as "planned"—about 15 percent. However, like Jeff, most of these parents described themselves as accepting the pregnancy when it occurred rather than making a conscious decision to have a child outside of marriage.[13] That is, they were open to the idea of children or were pleased when they found out about the pregnancy, but they did not try to control the exact timing or the conditions under which it occurred.[14]

Parents who easily accepted the birth tended to be involved in committed relationships or to be living with the other parent at the time of the birth. Yusef, who was living with his child's mother when she became pregnant, discusses his reaction to the pregnancy:

> It happened where she got pregnant. It wasn't planned or nothing. And as soon as it happened, I wasn't thinking about abortion or nothing like that. I wanted to have it, you know. I was excited.

In contrast, just under half of the parents said they felt significant ambivalence or apprehension about the pregnancy.[15] Some of these parents considered terminating the pregnancy, and others considered adoption. Parents who initially had reservations typically represented their decision to become parents as an ethical and emotional resolution to their pregnancies. These parents used therapeutic and religious discourses, collective stories, and popular wisdom to explain their decisions. They also discussed their choices in terms of anticipated consequences (Mills 1940).

Research shows that abortion rates among unmarried women have fallen approximately 18 percent between 1980 and 1995, and the figures are similar among black and white mothers (Ventura and Bachrach 2000, 11).[16] Responses from the parents I interviewed showed that in almost equal numbers they supported abortion unconditionally, supported abortion in particular circumstances, or opposed abortion in general. Those who supported abortion conditionally often considered the circumstances and timing of the pregnancy. In particular, they identified age as an important factor when deciding whether to carry a pregnancy to term, mainly because young teenagers typically were not thought to be emotionally and economically prepared to raise a child and because pregnancy often disrupts their education. Some mothers and fathers who said they or their partners had had abortions as teenagers decided to continue pregnancies as adults.

Several women considered abortion but decided to continue their pregnancies after experiencing a moral or emotional crisis. Women sometimes said they chose not to have abortions against the wishes of their parents or partners. Some men I interviewed also said they had wanted their partners to have an abortion but that their partners chose not to. Parents often framed their reluctance to have an abortion in moral terms, arguing that abortion destroys a human life. The majority of African American parents in this study were raised in an evangelical Protestant church, and the majority of white parents were raised Catholic and drew on these traditions.

> From my understanding, my belief, we are put here to replenish the world, not to destroy or not to stop kids from living. That's all life is about . . . in the books, in the Scriptures, it says we are put here to replenish the world not to not replenish it. So that's one of the main reasons I'm against abortion. (Andre)

Using a religious framework to denounce abortion reflects not only an individual's belief but also various sanctions that friends and family impose on each other. One father told me that he discouraged his partner from having an abortion after his mother "took him to the Bible" and talked to him about the immorality of taking a life.

Another reason given for opposing abortion concerned the value of life and the happiness derived from becoming a parent. Parents often countered arguments for abortion with expressions that children are "precious" or that "life is beautiful" and should not be destroyed. These accounts emphasized the high value placed on children and represented parenthood as a natural human desire. Kareen said, "I feel as though everybody wants a child at one point or another. Everybody wants to experience the father and the mother part. 'Cause it's beautiful."

The white parents I spoke with were more likely than African American parents to consider adoption to be an emotionally and morally appropriate option. Jean, a white mother of three, explained:

> Being a single mother's hard. 'Cause sometimes, you know, look, you got your kids. They were unplanned. You thought about what you were gonna do. Your parent's screaming adoption, your other parent's screaming abortion. Your other parent's screaming, "You made your grave, you lay in it." I thought about all my choices. And if I could not keep my kids, like, if I thought I'd be unfit, I would've put them up for adoption.

In contrast, as Janet observed, "Being the fact that we young, black women, you don't hardly hear too much about adoptions." African American parents expressed a great deal of concern over where a child would be placed in a formal adoption. Rather than characterizing adoption as a principled decision, African American parents sometimes criticized parents who had given their children up for adoption.

It's bad to have a baby and get an abortion, you know. Then it's bad to have a baby and give it up for adoption because you never know what kind of parents are gonna adopt the kid. You know, kill[ing] and the people these days getting crazy. . . . It could go to a foster home. And how could you risk knowing you got a baby out there in the world [and] you don't know if he's being taken care of? (Mariah)

Although African American families have a long history of informal adoption, their formal adoption rates have been low. Formal adoption has also decreased significantly among white parents in recent years as nonmarital childbearing has become more common.[17]

Marriage after a Nonmarital Pregnancy

By the time I interviewed these parents, approximately two out of three were no longer involved in a romantic relationship with their child's other parent. Thus the decision not to marry the other parent had already been made. However, I asked parents what they thought of the once common shotgun wedding and whether they had considered marrying in response to the birth of their child. Rather than viewing marriage as a natural resolution to an unintended pregnancy, parents typically said the decision to marry should be made independently and should be considered on its own terms.[18] Although parents pointed to advantages of marriage, especially for children, they overwhelmingly argued that "forced" or "rushed" marriages should be avoided, given their high risk of failure. When I asked them what advice they would give to young parents in an unstable economic position after an unexpected pregnancy, almost all parents I interviewed said they would advise against marriage. The only respondents who thought marriage was a viable option added that the parents should wait until after the baby was born and they felt economically and emotionally prepared to make this commitment.

These responses speak to the transformation that has occurred in family structure in recent years following complex cultural and economic changes. If an unmarried woman became pregnant unexpectedly three decades ago, a typical response was to marry the father of the child; today she more often chooses to stay single. Between 1960 and 1964, approximately 60 percent of women whose first birth was conceived when they were unmarried opted to marry before the birth of the child. Between 1990 and 1994, only about 23 percent of "premaritally" pregnant women did so (Ventura and Bachrach 2000, 10).

Perhaps most people would agree that teenagers should wait to marry, but why would unmarried adults decide not to marry or to delay marriage until after a pregnancy, particularly if they had been open to the pregnancy? Parents typically framed the decision not to marry in terms of minimizing the high likelihood of divorce. Citing numerous stories of failed marriages, the parents I interviewed suggested that exposure to divorce in their own families and in the larger society made them approach marriage more cautiously. Because parents could draw on personal anecdotes and publicly available information to identify the kind of marriages that might lead to divorce, they suggested that it was futile, and perhaps detrimental, to marry under certain conditions.

In the view of many parents I interviewed, the average marriage was at a high risk for divorce, and marriages between young couples with a marginal attachment to the labor force were even more likely to fail. Sonny warned other parents, "Don't get married just for the kids. No, you'll be divorced just as fast. That's proven." Similarly, Andre observed, "Marriage, nowadays, you can break up like a relationship. That's why, if I get married, it'll be for the right reasons. I mean, we ain't gonna be breaking up just like that." Although Larry says that he had never wanted to have a child outside of marriage, the pregnancy happened unexpectedly in the context of a casual relationship. His own parents had been married for thirty-seven years, and, he explained, "I haven't gotten married, 'cause I don't believe in divorce. And so I want to be absolutely sure when I do it. Divorces are a dime a dozen. Do your own for $5.99."

Rather than embracing a casual attitude toward marriage, parents maintained that they postponed marriage precisely because they thought marriage should last "forever":

So she got a baby by you, things happen, okay? Then you got to think about—is this the one you want to spend your life with, for the rest of your life? You know what I'm saying? Marriage is forever, so that's something you gots to deal with everyday. (G.)

Parents believed that transforming a fragile relationship into an unstable marriage was unwise not only because it was likely to dissolve but because of the emotional damage a "bad" marriage could cause for their children. Chastity explained:

I'd rather not get married and be able to give my child a happy home than be married and have a mom and dad that fight all the time. Even if they both love the child and give the child a lot of love and affection and attention. If both parents fight all the time, that's just as much abuse as if you do it against the child itself, I feel. 'Cause, you know, they love mom and they love dad. And they don't want to see either one get hurt.

Mothers and fathers also suggested that persistent economic insecurity exacerbated such emotional difficulties in relationships as distrust, communication failure, and incompatibility, which makes marriage a worrying prospect for many men and women in contemporary society. Arthur, who was living with the mother of his child and planned to marry her, described the barriers to marriage that they were facing:

> We're going [to get married], but we just don't know when. The way things have been going for us. Just been through everything. Can't get breaks for nothin'. Nobody, nobody can even let us live with them, you know, pay them rent. Can't afford really an apartment. And everything just so expensive. . . . Until I get a car, I can't move too far or I'd never be able to get to work.

African American parents in particular seemed to doubt whether they could realize the kind of economic stability necessary for a good marriage. Joe believed that declining economic opportunities and families' inability to "pull together," as they had in previous generations, undermines couples' ability to form a stable relationship that can lead to marriage. In response to my question about why people are not getting married, he also connected emotional barriers to the economic problems facing men and women:

> Times is just frustrating. Times is hard, and people aren't as happy as they used to be. So, I think basically that has a lot to do with it. I mean, if times wasn't so tough and people wasn't so aggravated and frustrated all the time, then people could be more loving.

The parents I interviewed typically believed it was better for children if their parents were married, an opinion held by approximately 64 percent of unmarried mothers and 77 percent of unmarried fathers in the Fragile Families and Child Wellbeing (FFCW) survey. Although parents in my study said they wanted to marry, they often viewed marriage as part of the American dream that was not easily attainable for lower-income men and women. Joe continued:

> As a child, you want to be with your mommy and daddy. You want them to be married in a big house and a dog and all that. So, that just one step to getting that American Dream, I guess. You know that dream you want fulfilled as a child.

Parents also identified other specific threats to relationships that are endemic to poor neighborhoods or environments. Like other parents, Carl stressed the destructive effect of drugs on relationships: "I hate them drugs. Them drugs tear up anything." He said that couples needed to have an exceptional relationship to keep a marriage together in the face of these obstacles. Like other mothers and fathers, Debra suggested that "the streets" could ruin young men and women and interfere with their ability to form stable relationships:

> The only way I see marriage is, like, you're in college and you meet a guy in college. And after you get a career and he get a career and he find he love you then. But once they get a taste of the streets out here . . . you don't want to marry nobody like that.

The prospect of marriage introduced particular concerns for mothers, who typically had the primary responsibility for raising their child. Some warnings about marriage were passed down from their female relatives and friends:

> I want to get married, but if I can't find the right person, I ain't marrying him. I don't want no man that's gonna put his hands on me either. My grandma always told me, if he hits you, leave him . . . 'cause if he hit you one time, he'll do it again. . . . Not no drug dealer [either]. Next thing you know, he locked up in jail. See, I'm stuck. I'm on my own again. . . . I'm getting a divorce. (Evette)

Among parents who were no longer together, most of the women I interviewed said they had initiated the breakup with their youngest child's father. In addition to women claiming more agency in breaking off their romantic involvement with the father, women drew on a shared vocabulary of motives to explain or legitimate the conclusion of their relationship. Women usually represented their decisions to break off the relationship not as a choice to be single but as a way to eliminate relationships they found untenable or detrimental.[19]

In addition to citing general relationship problems around such issues as responsibility, commitment, and fidelity, approximately 17 percent of mothers I spoke with cited abuse as a reason for leaving their partners. These mothers believed that in escaping abusive relationships, they were protecting their children from emotional and physical danger and from negative images of male/female relationships. Marie explained why she decided not to marry the father of her children:

> I was always brought up to, like, you get married, you have kids, and that's how it was. That's why . . . I was with their father eight-and-a-half years,

but we never got married. But we tried to make it work. I mean, because I thought that, you know, that was the way it was supposed to be. But he had a problem with his hands, so eventually I just turned around and left. 'Cause he was an alcoholic and he beat me all the time. So, I just left him. But I tried to make it work . . . 'cause I guess that's just the way I was brought up, like, you're supposed to have a little family and make it work. So, I tried, but it just did not work at all.

While portraying her situation as a deviation from a conventional family model, Marie, like other women I interviewed, was confident in explaining her motive for leaving the father: being a single mother was preferable to tolerating a partner's abuse and alcoholism.

Minimizing Risk by Choosing the Right Time

The parents I interviewed argued that to avoid untenable or destructive relationships and to manage economic uncertainties, men and women should evaluate whether the conditions are "right" and whether they and their partners are "ready" for marriage. But in what circumstances do parents feel they are prepared to make this commitment, and how does this relate to the timing of reproduction?

Most parents hoped to marry, but they argued that emotional maturity and economic stability are required to make a marriage work. Shakeema described what it means for couples to be ready for marriage:

[When] they are responsible, mature. Both parties want something out of life, and they know what they aiming at once they're married. . . . They both have good jobs, saving up money.

The responses of parents I interviewed are not atypical. In the FFCW survey, approximately 89 percent of unmarried mothers and 85 percent of unmarried fathers identified the "husband and wife being emotionally mature" as very important to a successful marriage; a similar proportion of mothers (89 percent) and slightly higher proportion of fathers (92 percent) identified the "husband having a steady job" as very important. The third highest percentage of parents indicated that the "wife having a steady job" was very important to a successful marriage, although mothers were more likely to respond this way (67 percent) than fathers (48 percent). Black parents placed more emphasis on the wife's employment than did white parents.[20]

The mothers I spoke with often associated "being ready" for marriage with finishing school or securing employment after leaving welfare. A twenty-two-year-old mother explains her decision to delay marriage:

My youngest son's father, he's talking about getting married. But I'd rather be in a better situation than I am now when I get married. I want to finish school, get certified [as a physical therapy assistant], get myself all situated, and have a lot more things than I do now. And for him too, I want him to get all his running and stuff out now before he really do that.

As this example suggests, both mothers and fathers regarded young men as generally less mature and less able than young women to make an emotional commitment. In addition to achieving economic stability, more fathers felt the need to be emotionally ready before settling down.[21] Looking back on the relationship with his child's mother, Jason explained that he proposed after she unexpectedly became pregnant, but he still wanted to "run around":

We were talking about getting married. We were engaged. She had a ring and everything. It got thrown back at me. Never happened. She wanted to get married, that was the whole thing. But, I was a procrastinator. Commitment and all that. I was young . . . I wanted to go out and do things, you know. I loved her and everything, but I didn't want to get married.

To explore how unmarried parents think about the relationship between being ready for marriage and for reproduction, I asked what advice they would give to other young couples about the appropriate timing of these events. Most parents said these two events should be timed to coincide. Although parents typically associated the ideal timing of these events with a certain level of personal development or stability, they generally said that the transition to marriage and parenting should not occur until after finishing high school or securing stable employment (usually during their early to mid-twenties).

At the same time, the majority of parents did not report planning the exact timing of their own pregnancies. Emphasizing that parents have an unconditional obligation to their child, whether or not they feel emotionally ready for its arrival, Carl explained,

Sometime it just happen, and when that time come, when you become a parent, you just got to rise to the occasion. Just take care of your responsibility. . . . No time's a good time to be a parent.

In fact, the idea that there is "good time" economically to become a parent may stem from the opportunities men and women have available to them. Although young adults who hope to achieve economic mobility through higher education and employment may believe it is beneficial to delay parenthood, poor parents may not believe their economic situation will improve significantly in the future.[22]

A minority of parents set the appropriate age of reproduction earlier than that of marriage. Although parents did not always notice that they timed these events differently until I asked them to explain their responses, these accounts illustrate how parents come to decisions about reproduction and marriage through separate processes. Both white and African American parents sometimes distinguished the timing of these events, but African American parents more clearly articulated the rationale behind their decisions.

Some parents argued that mothers and fathers who are "too old" would have difficulty understanding and relating to their children. According to this view, older parents would have more trouble interacting with their children and passing on cultural capital. At the same time, these parents also drew a lower limit (for example, younger than age eighteen) below which they believe a person is too young to become a parent. Given this fairly narrow age range in which it is desirable to become a parent, they either opened themselves up to the possibility of becoming parents during certain years or consciously planned to have children at this time. Again, this decision was typically made within the context of a committed relationship, but not necessarily one leading to marriage:

> When I was going to school, me and all my girlfriends always said we ain't never gonna have kids till we finish high school. 'Cause we don't never want to be a mother in school. Like some mothers go to school pregnant. We didn't want that when we was young . . . we always used to have fun. We never wanted kids. That was out. So I decided at twenty-two I wanted to have a baby before I turned twenty-five. I said if I was over twenty-five, I didn't want no kids. (Diamond)

According to Diamond, twenty-two was a "nice age" because she had been working for four years after high school and had saved up some money to buy things for her baby. She continued to live at home and, with the help of her family, planned to return to work next year.[23] Although the father of her child and his parents also helped with child care, she explained that his immaturity and unwillingness to assume more economic responsibility made him a bad candidate for marriage. After watching her sisters' marriages end in divorce, she says she would prefer to wait.

I'll say by thirty I won't mind getting married. . . . I don't want to get married and next year I'm divorced. I'm not like that. I don't never want to rush into anything. Not me, never.

Despite parents' confidence in their ability to take care of their children regardless of their marital status, research shows that the social and economic circumstances that unmarried parents experience often make parenting more difficult and may disadvantage their children. For example, children growing up in poverty are more likely to experience health problems and to live in neighborhoods with high crime, less adult supervision, and less access to playgrounds, child care and health care facilities, parks, and after-school programs.[24] Certain parenting and family strategies can help buffer these risks of living in poor neighborhoods and produce more positive outcomes, but these risks remain (Jarrett 1997, 276). Mothers and fathers recognized these risks but felt they could be good parents even in these circumstances.

Although parents typically were confident about their parenting abilities, they expressed more doubt about their chances of marital success. This apparent inconsistency reveals how parents perceived the options available to them. When parents described their reproductive decisions, they said that they felt competent to care for a child or made a moral or emotional decision to accept their responsibility as parents following an unintended pregnancy. Women, in particular, said they felt capable of loving and providing for a child, although most expected help from the child's father, regardless of the status of their relationship.

Given the nature of the study, parents talked about their fertility decisions retrospectively but usually talked about their marital decisions prospectively. Many parents who said they had felt apprehensive about pregnancy thought it was morally questionable to characterize their child as a "mistake." Rather, they described their child as "wanted" and considered parenthood a positive experience.[25] Unlike their decisions about reproduction, which could not be reversed, decisions about marriage were still ahead of them, and they wanted to approach these decisions with caution. Although a minority of parents were still involved with their child's other parent and anticipated marrying him or her, most were no longer involved and expected to marry someone else. Evidence from the FFCW survey shows that at the time of their child's birth, approximately 58 percent of unmarried mothers and 74 percent of unmarried fathers thought there was a good or almost certain chance they would marry the other parent.[26] In this study, many parents whose relationships had ended, like those who were still involved, had expected to stay together and even marry. However, their relationships had not worked out, and they were now trying to make sense of why their relationships had ended and to imagine how future relationships could succeed.

Minimizing Risk by Choosing the Right Person

Both mothers and fathers viewed romantic relationships, and love more generally, as something that could not be "forced." Because these relationships were based on voluntary commitments, they emphasized the importance of selecting the right partner to make their relationships more predictable. Parents realized they could not fully control the feelings or behavior of their partner or the outcomes of their relationships. As one mother observed, "You can't make someone who doesn't want to marry you." Precarious economic circumstances, abuse, drug addiction, infidelity, and the unpredictability of romantic love could all undermine relationships and make marriage unfeasible.

Parents' views of marriage seem to invoke both "realist" and "idealist" ideas about relationships, which Illouz (1997) has identified as the two dominant models of love in contemporary American culture.[27] The idealist model represents love as an "all-consuming force," whereas the therapeutic and economic discourses underlying the realist model suggest that love must develop over time after a process of information gathering and "work" on the relationship. The realist model also emphasizes the importance of choice to bring love under rational control and to ensure the compatibility of couples. Because irreconcilable ideas about love are available simultaneously in the general culture, people are often frustrated in their attempts to unite the ideas in a single model (Illouz 1997, 77). In the context of low-income communities, Furstenberg (2001, 240) observes that "by holding a set of inconsistent, if not contradictory, views [about marriage], inner-city youths are prepared for all eventualities."

Ideas about love that follow the realist model encourage unmarried parents to evaluate their partner's potential for marriage. Many parents I interviewed thought that couples should get to know each other well and perhaps live together before marriage. One father stopped living with his child's mother after she became addicted to crack; he advised, "You need about three to five years under your belt before you even think about marriage." Long-term relationships, including those that involve living together, provide an opportunity for couples to assess the other partner and their compatibility as a couple. Mothers also look at a man's behavior as a father, or her new partner's acceptance of her children from a previous relationship, to evaluate his potential as a marriage partner.

Furstenberg (2001) suggests that this process of gathering information is part of a "culture of gender distrust" in poor communities, a phenomenon Hannerz (1969) observed more than three decades ago. According to Furstenberg (2001, 232), women "enter relationships expecting them to fail, and their sensitivity to the failings of men leads many to monitor relationships closely, looking for early warning signals of distress." Aware that they are being watched closely for signs of failure, the men lack confidence in their own abilities and also have low expectations for success in their relationships. My conversations with parents suggest that mothers were particularly cautious and might be more likely than fathers to end harmful relationships. At the same time, the men I interviewed also emphasized the importance of selecting the right partner to avoid negative outcomes. In this highly charged situation, expectations for failure may become self-fulfilling.

Both idealism and realism also influence parents' expectations of what it means to be a good spouse. Mothers and fathers emphasized the importance of compatibility, equality, and companionship in a marriage. Furthermore, they hoped to experience strong emotional connection to their partners. When asked what kind of spouse they were seeking, mothers talked about the capacity to be supportive, caring, responsible, accepting, hardworking, trustworthy, financially secure, and a good father figure. Although fathers mentioned similar qualities for a prospective spouse, they usually valued self-sufficiency and the ability to share financial burdens more than they did reliability.

Parents also mentioned qualities that would make partners less attractive as spouses. Mothers and fathers both mentioned their employment status—an important measure of "marriageability"—as a factor in their decisions about relationships and marriage (Wilson 1987, 1996). Men expressed reluctance about assuming financial responsibility for partners who did not have jobs or who were not "trying to do anything for themselves." Women's accounts also indicated that men may be "unmarriageable" if they are abusive, "into the streets," involved in selling drugs, or "haven't got the running out of their system." It is likely that women on welfare were afraid that marrying an equally poor man would threaten the economic stability they were trying to achieve. Poor men may also have been unable or unwilling to take on the economic burdens of a mother and her children, particularly when these children were from a previous relationship. African American and white parents held similar ideas about the qualities of a desirable spouse, but African American parents described more clearly how their social and economic environments influenced the kind of partners available to them.

In the following exchange, Crystal described her options for marriage in Trenton and the kind of husband she would choose.

C: I say out of a hundred, it's like 10 percent good dads because you can't find too many good fathers to be there. Most of the dads are in jail. Most of the dads are on drugs. Most of the dads are just not there period. There's not too much good dads. And then people wonder why would you want to have a baby from a guy like that. Why would you want to be involved with someone like that? Because at that point of time, that person was not like that. You don't really know a person 'till you get to know them. And then there's a big difference when you get pregnant with them. And then they start to actin' stupid. Can't take the trials and tribulations and things like that. You never know who Mr. Right is until he put that ring on your finger and say I want to marry you. That's what I'm waiting for.

M: What kind of man would you want to marry?

C: I don't know. I guess I'd have a storybook wedding. Sweep me off my feet. A good provider. Someone to love me the way I love him. I want us to be equal. I want us to be able to do things together, go places and experience things. A good father figure to my children. I want him to have a good job, a education. I want him to have money but . . . sometime you can't always get what you want. But that's what I would like.

Using an idealist model of romantic love, Crystal wants to be swept off her feet by her prospective husband. But given the "trials and tribulations" many low-income parents face, Crystal also invokes a realist model by acknowledging that she could only determine if someone was right after observing his willingness to be there through difficult times.[28] In fact, Crystal could not be sure she had found the right person until he had already demonstrated his commitment to marriage.

Unmarried parents' decisions about marriage also take place in a larger cultural context in which expectations for marriage have increased even while marriage is viewed as less important to people's lives. Beyond the minimal requirements for a "marriageable" partner, parents hold other ideals for marriage—ideals valued by men and women of their generation—such as equality and emotional fulfillment.

*   *   *

These accounts show that unmarried parents did not necessarily view marriage as an appropriate resolution to a pregnancy. In fact, parents whose pregnancies were unintentional often represented the decision to have their child as a moral response to the situation. Rejecting the feasibility of a shotgun wedding, parents argued that forced or rushed marriages were likely to fail. Parents living in impoverished neighborhoods and women concerned with protecting their children from harm also viewed marriage as untenable, detrimental, or futile in many circumstances. In general, they regarded marriage as a risk and typically framed their decisions not to marry in terms of minimizing the high likelihood of divorce. To decrease the risk of divorce, parents argued, men and women should evaluate whether the conditions and their partner were "right" for marriage and whether they and their partners were "ready" to take this step. Although most parents expected to marry at some point, and a minority still hoped to marry their child's mother or father, they wanted to approach the decision cautiously. Despite this hesitancy about their relationships, mothers and fathers were confident that they could love and care for their children in the absence of a marital relationship. As we shall see in later chapters, the fact that these unmarried parents did not feel an obligation to marry their child's other parent does not imply a minimal paternal obligation. At the same time, previous research shows that fathers often lose a connection with their children when their relationship with the mother ends. After reviewing available models of fatherhood, the next chapters explore how low-income unmarried parents view a father's obligations to and engagement with his children.

CHAPTER THREE

Models of Fatherhood

Although there has been a good deal of continuity in ideas about fatherhood and paternal responsibility in American society, these ideas have changed in response to shifting social and economic conditions. Researchers have identified at least four models of fatherhood that became prominent during different historical periods (e.g., Lamb 1987; Pleck 1987).[1] In contemporary culture, these models are not mutually exclusive but rather provide a cultural repertoire or tool kit of symbols, stories, and practices that shape men's and women's understanding of fatherhood.[2]

In pre-industrial America, the most prevalent model of fatherhood emphasized the father's role as teacher and moral leader. During the colonial period, fathers assumed a broad range of responsibilities while taking the lead in the moral and religious education of their children (Demos 1986, 44–46; Pleck 1987, 84–86). Because children were regarded as inherently sinful and unrestrained, fathers were encouraged to impose moral standards and to promote children's rational development. Women, who were presumed to be less rational than men and more susceptible to emotional impulses, were assigned the duty of caring for young children (Demos 1986, 49–50; Pleck 1987, 84–85). As property owners and primary parents, fathers made childrearing decisions and assumed custody of their children in cases of marital separation. Many scholars have observed, however, that this pattern exhausted neither the experiences of men nor the representations of them (Demos 1986, 48; Gerson 1993, 18). For example, this model fits uneasily with the experience of African American families, both during slavery and after emancipation.[3]

When economic activity moved outside the home during industrialization, a second model of fathers as breadwinners emerged (Demos 1986, 51–52; Pleck 1987, 86–90). Changes in childrearing practices, family law, and the state's role in family life led to a decline in direct paternal authority over children (Griswold 1993, 10–33). Early nineteenth-century advice books cast mothers as the primary and essential parent, especially during a child's infancy (Demos 1986, 49). Courts increasingly awarded custody of children to mothers, maintaining that maternal custody was in the best interest of the child (Demos 1986, 57–58; Pleck 1987, 86–87). As masculine gender roles consolidated around breadwinning, feminine roles focused on domesticity in a privatized, nuclear family. In particular, a "cult of domesticity" glorified motherhood and supported the division of men's and women's spheres. Women's purity made them the appropriate parent for nurturing children and guiding their moral development, whereas men were suited to participate in economic and political life (Pleck 1987, 86–87; Gerson 1993, 20). Because men were expected to be the sole economic support of their families, the basis of paternal authority also changed. Men's status as breadwinners, rather than as moral leaders and teachers, justified their privileged position in the home (Demos 1986, 52; Gerson 1993, 19–20). However, many African American fathers and lower-income white fathers were unable to earn a "family wage"—an amount that would allow them to be the sole family breadwinner. Their wives and children also worked to help support the family (Gerson 1993, 19; Griswold 1993; 34–67).[4]

Psychologists in the early and mid-twentieth century helped produce a third model of fatherhood one that revolved around sex roles.[5] Concerns about the formation of sex-role identity appeared in popular discussions during World War II, when more fathers were absent from their families. These concerns exacerbated anxiety about the consequences of mothers' disproportionate influence on children (Griswold 1993, 172). Even as this model developed, however, the economic prosperity after the war reinforced the association between fatherhood and breadwinning and the gender-based division of labor in the family.[6] Fathers were expected to provide for their children financially while promoting their psychosocial development (Griswold 1993, 174–175).[7] The childrearing practices of white middle-class fathers were thought to promote such traits as emotional stability, heterosexuality, and tolerance more effectively than did the practices of working-class fathers (Griswold 1993, 206–211). In popular culture, too, the absence of a strong father figure was associated with homosexuality and juvenile delinquency (Pleck 1987, 90–93).

Writers and commentators later argued that the absence of fathers and the prominent role of women in African American families caused a host of problems, including unemployment, poverty, and crime. The most controversial public statement about the "black matriarchy" was Daniel P. Moynihan's *The Negro Family: The Case for National Action* (1965). Moynihan restated many of the findings of a 1939 study of black families by E. Franklin Frazier, who argued that slavery, Jim Crow laws, urban migration, unemployment, and poverty had undermined the black family structure. In particular, Moynihan traced the roots of female "dominance," the marginal status of fathers, and their defeated sense of masculinity to the effects of racism, unstable employment, and the compensatory effort of women to provide income through work or welfare receipt. Moynihan also argued that black "broken homes" were linked to low educational achievement, juvenile delinquency, and crime among young males (see Griswold 1993, 213–217). During the 1960s and early 1970s, however, the civil rights and black power movements portrayed black men as strong forces in their families and communities. These representations contrasted with the "black matriarchy" image (Wallace 1979).

At least four important economic and social trends worked together to change the shape of fatherhood in the latter part of the century. First, the real wages of many men began falling in the 1970s, and families had more difficulty surviving on a single income. Second, a greater number of women entered the paid labor force. Third, divorce and nonmarital childbearing rates rose significantly, thus changing the structure of families. Finally, a feminist movement during the 1970s initiated a cultural rethinking of the gender division of labor and differential power of men and women within families.[8]

During this time, the breadwinning model of fatherhood lost cultural resonance, and a fourth model of involved fathers has emerged. Fathers now are expected not only to make an emotional connection with their children, as in previous periods, but also to share with women the work of caring for children (Lamb 1987; Griswold 1993). As Pleck maintains, "This new father differs from older images of involved fatherhood in several key respects: he is present at the birth; he is involved with his children as infants, not just when they are older; he participates in the actual day-to-day work of child care, and not just play; he is involved with his daughters as much as his sons" (1987, 93).[9] These revised expectations for fathers followed feminist critiques of men's reluctance to share household responsibilities. Concerns that the breadwinner ideal placed unreasonable expectations on men and prevented them from nurturing their children also supported this new idea about fatherhood. Furthermore, a therapeutic culture drew attention to the personal growth and satisfaction men might realize through fathering and the emotional loss they experienced when absent from their children's lives (Griswold 1993, 245–250).

The current state of fatherhood in the United States is characterized both by fathers' increased involvement and by their increased disengagement

(Furstenberg 1988; Gerson 1993; Griswold 1993).[10] As a result, an image counter to that of the involved father—the deadbeat dad, who abdicates paternal responsibility—has also become familiar.[11] Gerson (1993, 9) observes the paradox of a pattern of involved fatherhood emerging alongside a retreat from family commitment. Furstenberg (1988, 193–194) argues that the ideal and the counterimage are "two sides of the same cultural complex" that results from the declining division of labor in the family.

Disengagement is even more possible for the large number of divorced and unmarried fathers who now live apart from their children. Research on nonresident fathers shows wide variations in their relationships with their children. Among unmarried fathers, some evidence indicates that at least half of unmarried fathers live near their children, visit them often, and make child support payments, whereas the other half do not. Unmarried fathers' contacts with their children also decline considerably over time, with only two-thirds of these fathers maintaining contact by the time their children reach age six or seven (Lerman 1993, 46).

Images of both involved and uninvolved fathers have become widespread in popular culture. Representations of the active, involved, and nurturing father have appeared in popular films, television shows, and books (Lamb 1987, 6). Although these fathers are often represented as white middle-class or professional men (for example, Dustin Hoffman in *Kramer v. Kramer* and Robin Williams in *Mrs. Doubtfire*), black representations of involved or "new" fathers have also appeared. Bill Cosby's character on the "Cosby Show" and his best-selling book on fatherhood, for example, attest to the cultural significance of this model. Images of irresponsible fathers are also culturally pervasive. The middle-class version of the deadbeat dad is often represented as men "who make car payments but find it impossible to make child-support payments" (Griswold 1993, 221) or who support a new wife and child but not his first family. Lower-income deadbeat dads are more often portrayed as sexually irresponsible as well as financially unreliable. Popular music presents both positive and negative images of unmarried fathers, or "babydaddies."[12] Although some rap songs celebrate masculinity and denigrate women, others lament the absence of the rappers' own fathers and encourage men to share parental responsibility with women.[13]

As these cultural representations proliferate, a group of mostly white middle-class men have embraced more traditional notions of fatherhood in an effort to recover a lost, neglected, or fugitive sense of manhood (Griswold 1993, 265–267). Conservative social movements such as the Promise Keepers encourage men to accept family leadership and responsibility. Other traditional models of paternal responsibility have emerged in African American social movements. The Million Man March, organized by Louis Farrakhan and Benjamin Chavis, assembled a large group of African American men in

Washington, D.C., to "atone" for their transgressions against their families and communities and to reclaim leadership positions within both.[14] Prominent in the list of issues that called for atonement was nonpayment of child support. A diverse array of fatherhood and "male-involvement" programs have also appeared across the country, which often focus on strengthening low-income fathers' emotional bonds with and economic support of their children (National Center for Children in Poverty 1999; Levine and Pitt 1995). Some of these programs encourage men to act as role models for their sons and other young males in their communities.

During a period when the images and practices of fathers have become more varied and the meaning of fatherhood less certain, Gerson (1993, 22) argues that no single model of fatherhood is now dominant: "Now, as in an earlier era, 'good providers' vie with 'autonomous men' and 'involved husbands and fathers' for ideological and social support. But no clear successor has taken the place of the once-ascendant but now embattled ethos of male breadwinning." Older models of fathers as moral overseers and as sex-role models also retain cultural currency and are made available to men through the media, popular culture, therapeutic influences, and religious involvement (Pleck 1987).

Fatherhood in Low-Income Communities

During the past thirty years, sociologists and anthropologists have documented "local" interpretations of paternal obligation in a collection of qualitative accounts. The first wave of these studies was conducted at the onset of de-industrialization, when the breadwinning model of fatherhood was dominant. The second wave of studies began in the late 1980s, after the model of involved fatherhood had appeared in popular culture. Each study suggests that paternal culture in poor communities has adapted to conditions of extreme economic insecurity and, often, racial discrimination. The studies, however, offer different explanations for how this adaptation occurred and how it relates to models of fatherhood in the larger culture.

Alternative Subcultures

The culture-of-poverty perspective was introduced by anthropologist Oscar Lewis (1959) in *Five Families,* a study of poor urban families in Mexico City. In that work, Lewis argues that members of poor subcultures adopt a unique but incoherent set of values, attitudes, and behaviors that deviate from "mainstream" culture. Although the members of these cultures are aware of dominant values, they do not live by them. Furthermore, Lewis suggests that these subcultures are reproduced in succeeding generations.[15] Although researchers holding the culture-of-poverty perspective did not focus specifically on fatherhood, they drew attention to the problems facing single-parent families in poor communities and influenced how subsequent research would be framed. For example, Lewis (1959, 29–30) writes about the frequency of "illegitimacy," acceptance of children born to couples in common-law unions, and abandonment of these families by men, and among the families he studied he notes an emphasis on male dominance and masculinity. He also indicates that fathers had weak emotional ties to their children, were authoritarian, and often spent time away from the home. Lewis's work suggests that the behavior of poor fathers was distinctive in that it did not comply with the provider model present in the larger society.

Social scientists of the 1970s reevaluated cultural values and behaviors in poor communities as positive adaptations to economic and social deprivation. Ladner (1995 [1971], xxii–xxiii) introduces her study by noting that although much has been written on the "pathology" of black communities, "Few authorities on the Black community have written about the vast amount of strength and adaptability of the people." This approach presents the values, attitudes, and behaviors adopted in black communities as part of an autonomous culture shaped by African "survivals." In *All Our Kin,* a classic study of black family life in a poor community, Stack (1974) contests the representations of poor black families as deviant versions of the white middle-class nuclear household; instead, she describes survival strategies as autonomous cultural patterns with their own integrity. By viewing family relationships based on reciprocity as functional adaptations to poverty, the survival strategies approach stresses the salutary aspects of attitudes and behaviors in poor communities. Instead of casting low-income unmarried fathers as failed breadwinners, Stack (1974, 119) writes, "Mothers generally regard their children's fathers as friends of the family—people they can recruit for help—rather than as fathers failing in their parental duties. While fathers voluntarily help out their children, many fathers cannot be depended upon as a steady source of income." Stack also observes that although fathers' primary responsibility was to their own kin network, they were expected to provide what they could for their biological children. They could also offer their children the resources of their kin network.

Elijah Anderson (1989), like his precursors, describes the problems faced by young men who cannot prove their manhood as husbands and breadwinners. Anderson finds that the young men and women he studied seemed to embrace two different cultural models. Although the breadwinner model had waned in the larger society at the time the study was conducted, Anderson found that young mothers in this community dreamed of establishing a conventional family life with the father as provider. However, young fathers attached themselves to their peer groups rather than their families because they could not form a masculine identity as providers. These men preferred to have sexual relationships with multiple women, to remain in their own mother's home, and to "play daddy." In this way, they received the benefits of being a father without marrying the mother or assuming any real responsibility for their children.

Value Stretch

The value stretch approach adopts some of the assumptions of the culture-of-poverty approach but also offers a corrective to it. In particular, it questions the cultural distinctiveness of poor communities and maintains that their members were not only familiar with mainstream values but often endorsed them (Valentine 1968). According to Rodman (1963), those who are poor "stretch" mainstream values to fulfill them at a lower standard of success. Although poor men and women have a broad range of values, they have weak commitments to them.

Three important studies of fatherhood in the first wave of ethnographies of poor communities adopted the value stretch perspective (Clark 1965; Liebow 1967; Rainwater 1970). All three conclude that fathers evaluated themselves and were judged by others according to their performance as breadwinners and that paternal support was closely linked to perceptions of masculinity. Perhaps the best-known description of low-income African American fathers, Liebow's study of "streetcorner men" in Washington, D.C., suggests that poor communities embraced the mainstream breadwinner ideal while at the same time acknowledging that this role was unattainable for most poor men. To deal with their failure as providers, these men chose to separate themselves from their own children but offered limited support to the children of the women with whom they were currently involved.

Cultural Repertoires

Hannerz (1969, 185–193) presented an alternative to these approaches in which he observes that residents of poor communities have a broad cultural repertoire, or "items of culture which are somehow stored in [them]," based on their exposure to "mainstream" as well as to "ghetto-specific" beliefs and modes of behavior. These residents use elements of their repertoires that are most relevant for a particular situation, and they may be more skilled in using some parts of their repertoire than others.

Similarly, Swidler (1986, 273) approaches culture as a repertoire or tool kit of "symbols, stories, rituals, and world views" that people use to construct strategies of action. She also observes that people develop strategies of action for which they have the "cultural equipment" (275). For example, members of poor communities share the same preferences and aspirations with those from more advantaged communities, but members of each community identify lines of conduct, and organize their actions, around things they are able to do well. Therefore, practices may take on different configurations in high- and low-income communities (and, as Hannerz points out, within poor communities themselves), not because their residents adopt different values but because their cultural repertoires enable and constrain the strategies they can pursue. Swidler writes (1986, 275),

> The culture-of-poverty example suggests a misdirection of our explanatory efforts. Students of culture keep looking for cultural values that will explain what is distinctive about the behavior of groups or societies, and neglect other distinctively *cultural* phenomena which offer greater promise of explaining patterns of action. These factors are better described as culturally-shaped skills, habits, and styles than as values or preferences.

Rather than examining whether low-income unmarried parents adopt subcultural values that contrast with those in the rest of society, my analysis follows the cultural repertoires approach in assuming that these parents draw their ideas, justifications, and practices regarding fatherhood from various sources, including their families and communities, other institutions, and the general culture.[16] Unlike the value stretch perspective, my approach also assumes that people in all social positions—not just those who are poor—actively interpret and redefine ideas and expressions of paternal responsibility in ways that are appropriate to their social, economic, and personal circumstances. This investigation proposes that unmarried parents are not only in dialogue with culturally available models but also have developed new interpretations of and responses to fatherhood. Furthermore, it assumes that parents continually modify the culture of fatherhood in their own communities.

Although the following discussion highlights the diversity of unmarried parents' cultural repertoires, people's access to cultural resources as well as their socioeconomic positions push them toward some cultural resources rather than others (Lamont 2000, 7). The availability and use of resources are also shaped by parents' membership in race, gender, and generational groups. This analysis focuses on the way that unmarried parents' use available ideas and practices about paternal responsibility in response to the socioeconomic contexts, such as poverty, nonmarital childbearing, and involvement with the welfare and child support systems, that they face. This analytical approach is generally compatible with those in other recent studies of fatherhood (Sullivan 1989, 1992; Furstenberg 1992, 1995).

Families and Communities

Ethnographic research on fatherhood in low-income communities primarily examines the cultural codes people learn in their neighborhoods or immediate environments. As such, the central concern is to analyze cultural transmission through the peer group, family or extended family system, and social networks. Gadsden (1999, 223) describes the influence of family cultures, or a "repertoire of beliefs, knowledge, skills, and experiences that are as likely to strengthen as to debilitate its members, depending upon the family's access to resources and upon the family's ability to rise above the constraints, social practices, and laws that circumscribe opportunities."[17] In my interviews, for example, parents often mentioned the positive and negative influences of their biological fathers. Hannerz (1969, 191) argues that the cultural skills that residents of poor communities learn (often unintentionally) when interacting with others in the same social location often constitute the most relevant aspect of this repertoire.

Residents of communities with high rates of poverty, unemployment, and welfare receipt exhibit many common beliefs and behaviors as a result of their isolation from other communities and shared socioeconomic situations (Wilson 1987, 1996).[18] Many of the parents I interviewed were living in the same neighborhoods or communities in which they had grown up, and their social networks were comprised of neighbors and family members. At the same time, their extended families included members with diverse class and regional origins, and their communities (particularly among white parents) included higher-income residents and two-parent families (see Newman 1992). As a result, the parents I spoke with were able to learn interpretive and behavioral codes from members of their neighborhood while at the same time being exposed to demographic, class, and cultural heterogeneity within their families and neighborhoods.

Other Institutions

Not only do parents have access to ideas and practices within their neighborhoods, but they can draw on models of fatherhood through their institutional memberships and social networks, some of which extend outside their communities. About one-quarter of my interviewees participated in churches or mosques (which often provided social support services, food, and clothing), and the majority were raised in families that had some religious affiliation. Others cited involvement in drug and alcohol counseling and rehabilitation programs, community mental health centers, Planned Parenthood, domestic abuse and sexual assault counseling, parenting classes, day care centers, programs for noncustodial fathers, programs for adolescents at risk, or programs for single-parent families. Furthermore, these parents interacted with state institutions, social workers, and nurses through their participation in programs such as welfare, food stamps, Head Start, job training, WIC, prenatal care, the Department of Youth and Family Services (which deals with child neglect and abuse), and foster care. Finally, several men and a small number of women I interviewed had spent time in jail and juvenile correctional programs or institutions. All of these groups and institutions contribute to each person's interpretive and behavioral repertoires.[19]

The General Culture

As we have seen, American culture offers various models of fatherhood that come from such sources as law, religious tradition, social movements, and media and popular culture, including music, television, film, and self-help books. The diffusion and proliferation of these models contribute to the diversity of parents' cultural repertoires. Because these models are not only diverse but carry multiple meanings, low-income unmarried parents can appropriate ideas about fatherhood (for example, through popular culture) but not always "read" them in the same way as do people in other socioeconomic strata.[20] As a result, parents can actively interpret and redefine the resources available to them, as well as offer new interpretations of fatherhood. The next chapter documents how the men and women I interviewed used elements of their cultural repertoires, or tool kits, to define paternal responsibility.

CHAPTER FOUR

Interpreting Paternal Responsibility

[A father's] love's gonna carry a lot farther in respect than money will. You don't have to have money to take [your child] somewhere. You can just spend time with him in the park somewhere and talk to him about what men and boys talk about. (Michelle)

What claims do parents make about an unmarried father's obligation to his children? What language do parents use to describe the way in which a father is expected to support his children? In this chapter I am particularly concerned with these two questions, and I ask them in the course of examining whether the unmarried parents I interviewed held collective beliefs about paternal obligation and, if so, what these beliefs entailed.

To answer my two questions, I examine how unmarried parents use elements of their cultural repertoires to define standards of paternal responsibility and interpret them in specific socioeconomic and family situations. By combining and modifying culturally available ideas, these parents create a hybrid model of paternal obligation that includes elements of contemporary and traditional models.[1] These standards of paternal responsibility, in turn, provide a foundation for evaluating the behavior of individual fathers. As part of this analysis, I also explore how parents distinguish between "good" and "bad" fathers when discussing paternal responsibility.[2]

I am also concerned with the extent to which economic provision—the model of paternal obligation reflected in child support policies—corresponds to the collective beliefs of unmarried parents, who now comprise a significant segment of welfare and child support populations. Understanding the meaning of economic support relative to other forms of paternal support is also important in a context in which unmarried fathers are often as poor as unmarried mothers. Recent findings from the FFCW study show, for example, that approximately 65 percent of unmarried fathers have incomes below $20,000, with about 19 percent reporting incomes below $5,000. The average income of an unmarried father with children on welfare is even lower (McLanahan et al. 2001).

My conversations with unmarried parents indicate that they believe fathers have an unconditional obligation to support their biological children. Although parents regard economic support, along with paternal love and guidance, as a primary component of paternal responsibility, they believe that economic support alone is an insufficient expression of this responsibility, and they emphasize non-economic forms of paternal engagement.

Why Are Fathers Responsible?

If they [men] didn't want the child, they should learn to strap up. That's what I say. If you didn't want the child, why [did] you go through the whole nine months and then have the child? You should have spoke up then. If she want to keep it, then you gotta deal with it, because you knew what you was doing when you was laying down. Just like I knew what I was doing when I was laying down. It's not up to [fathers] if they want it or not. The child's here now . . . this is your child. This is part of you. You should always take care of part of you. This is like a reincarnation of you. You're gonna take care of your kid; you're gonna take care of yourself. [If you say] this is not my child, this same child gonna laugh in your face when he get older . . . They didn't ask to be here. You bring them here, take care of them . . . that child could grow up to be president or whatever and they look at you, like—well, my father didn't play a role in my life. (Andre)

The majority of parents I interviewed referred to the biological connection between fathers and their children to explain why unmarried fathers have an obligation to them. Parents typically supported these claims with popular expressions about the biological bond, such as, "That child is part of him" or "That's his flesh and blood." When I posed questions suggesting that some men might not feel obligated to support their child if the pregnancy had been unplanned, if he had not wanted to have the child, if the parents had decided to end the relationship, or if either parent had started a new relationship, almost every parent countered that unmarried fathers have a responsibility to their children regardless of the circumstances under which the children had been born. Only five parents expressed uncertainty about whether the biological father should assume full responsibility for children when he had been "trapped" into having a child by the mother or when he had opposed the pregnancy.[3]

These findings about the obligations of biological fathers are supported by those in the FFCW survey: more than 94 percent of unmarried mothers and fathers believe that fathers should be required to provide financial support to their biological child if the mother has a new partner. Similarly, more than 96 percent of these parents said that the father should be required to provide financial support to a biological child from a previous relationship if he has a baby with a new partner.

Almost all of the parents I interviewed were critical of men who do not recognize their children as their own. In fact, the denial of paternity represents one of the most common descriptions of what it means to be a "bad father." I asked one father who had participated in a responsible fatherhood program to explain why men sometimes deny paternity:

> Because, to me, they ain't no man. They ain't no man. They rather lay with them, screw them, stick them, and get a reputation. . . . Some dudes get mad 'cause I always jump in a lot of dudes' face. And they be talking about, "Yeah, man I'm about to have me another baby and what not." [I ask] "How old is your last baby? When is her birthday? Or his birthday?" [They say] "You're trying to be funny now. Me and mine don't get along." "Why is that? Who's fault [is it] that you all don't get along?" . . . "Only thing you doing is bringing a child into the world that ain't gonna know his dad cause you ain't gonna be around long enough to know them." (O'Shen)

Although O'Shen's response resembles that of other parents, his participation in a fatherhood program may have caused him to express his feelings more strongly.

According to the parents I interviewed, biological paternity also incurs an obligation of paternal involvement and support. Although parents often naturalized maternal commitment, their accounts suggest that paternal ties with children must be achieved. Therefore, parents distinguished a father's biological relationship with his child from his social one, and suggested that these relationships may or may not coincide. According to one mother I interviewed,

> Anybody can say they a daddy, but they can't say they a father. A father to me is where they would come get their kids and spend time with them. Spending time with them—that's the most important part—and giving

them love. Where a daddy, they just say they got a child except they don't do nothing for them. (Belinda)

If most unmarried parents I spoke with regard paternal obligation as unconditional, what is the basis for this social obligation? Parents advanced four general arguments framed around the needs of the child and the mother or around the interests of the father.[4] The first argument is that men are active subjects who have the ability to prevent a pregnancy from occurring. Bucky, a father who lives with one of his two children and her mother, remarked:

I say if the father's no longer here on this earth, then somebody could step in. But other than that, I believe the biological father should be the one to raise them for the simple fact they made them. . . . Like they say, you do the crime, now you got to do the time. You made the baby, you got to take care of the baby, simple as that. . . . If you didn't want the baby, [you've got] two choices, two routes: protection or abstinence; either one or the other.

Other parents argued that men also have some say in whether their partners have an abortion. However parents defined men's options, most thought they were responsible for the consequences of their sexual behavior. Some of the fathers I interviewed used metaphors about prison, military service, or car accidents to emphasize the seriousness of becoming a father and the need to "deal with" this situation, whether or not it was anticipated.

The second argument focuses on children's need for a relationship with their father. This need was defined both positively—a relationship with the biological father benefits the child—and negatively—the father's absence leaves the child feeling hurt and abandoned. Parents typically suggested that the obligation to develop this relationship was morally nonnegotiable. If fathers were angry or frustrated about this obligation, mothers often responded, "The child didn't ask to be here," "It's not the child's fault," or "It's not fair to take it out on the child." To illustrate the effect of the biological father's absence on children, parents frequently mentioned their experiences with their own fathers. In particular, men who saw their children regularly said that their relationship with their father had had an important effect on them. Some men attributed their own involvement with their child to having a good relationship with their father, whereas others said that they were involved because they knew what it meant to have an absent father. For example, a highly involved twenty-four-year-old father explained how his father's absence had affected him:

When I used to see him, he'd be like, "Nah, that's not my son." He be like, "But you all, he looks so much like you. Nah." You know, he was denying.

And from then on I just started growing a bad feeling towards him. Like, for instance, one day we was down there, and my mom told him that I wanted to speak to him. He came in the kitchen; I had nothing to say to him though. But he made me feel bad because I was fourteen and the first thing he gave me I gave it back to him. 'Cause it couldn't do me no good. And I still remember it: two dollars and forty-seven cents. That's like a smack in the face. After fourteen years you didn't give me anything, and you finally give me this. I gave it back to him. I don't get no calls, no letters, no cards for any of the holidays, my birthday, just to see how I'm doing, or for my mom, you know? We don't get nothing from him. It's like if you get gangrene and you cut off their arm and/or the leg and forget about it.

African American men told particularly poignant stories about growing up without their fathers. Daniel, an unemployed father, recounts how when he was twelve years old he was placed in foster care with a woman who eventually died of problems related to alcoholism. Daniel met his brother in jail after a corrections officer called out their last names. He was later introduced to his natural parents and the rest of his siblings.

I didn't have no father when I was growing up. And that's why I say, that's why I'm glad I'm still alive today. I know I got a father, but back then, he was nowhere around when I needed him. I would have been in school, playing ball for a college [if he had been there]. Boxing. I wouldn't had any kids. I needed somebody to really stay on my back, you know?

African American parents, compared with white parents, seem more easily able to imagine how an unmarried father can be actively involved with his child, perhaps because nonmarital childbearing is more common in African American communities. Although only three African American women I interviewed (about 15 percent of this group) expressed uncertainty about their youngest child being in contact with his or her biological father, about seven white women (almost 50 percent of this group) and two white fathers had reservations about the father's, or their own, involvement. These two fathers did not acknowledge paternity, and the mothers who resisted paternal involvement indicated that the father had been abusive to her, that the father was threatening to take custody of the child to "get back" at the mother, or that a new partner now acted as a father figure to the child. The accounts of both African American and white mothers, however, suggest that they were much more likely to encourage than to resist contact with the natural father. These statements are also consistent with those of unmarried mothers and fathers in the FFCW survey who overwhelmingly desired involvement by the biological father or who themselves wanted to be involved with their child.[5]

A third argument about paternal responsibility, which was made primarily by the women I spoke with, is that men are equally responsible for creating the child and should therefore share equally in that child's care and upbringing. Women often maintained that because men helped "make" the child, "it's theirs just as much as mine." Mothers framed this argument around their need for support from the father and the inequity women experience by having to accept most or all of the responsibility for raising children. According to the women I interviewed, mothers are expected to care for their children but fathers can avoid this responsibility. Beth, who became pregnant unintentionally, contested the idea that women more than men had a "natural" responsibility for children:

> I guess there are some fathers that would say they didn't want the babies so that it's not their responsibility. It's just unfortunate that it's only the woman that got to [take responsibility]. Maybe she didn't want it either, but she got it inside, and she's the one who's stuck. It's not like it's in him, and he's got to decide. It's just as much their responsibility. . . . I mean, it's part of you. You created this thing. How can you not want anything to do with it?

Finally, parents argued that it was in the emotional and moral interest of fathers to be involved with their children. These parents maintained that men who deny their obligations will experience a host of negative feelings and will forfeit the benefits of fatherhood. Also, many African American parents and a small number of white parents connected the recognition of paternity with masculinity, saying things such as "Any man can make a baby, but it takes a real good man to take care of his child." They also argued that fathers risk losing the recognition of their children and their respect as men. Parents said they consider the "real" man to be the one who acts not only as the biological but also the social father to the child. When I asked Robert what he would say to someone who did not accept responsibility for his children, he replied, "He's less than a man." When elaborating on this response, Robert associated manhood with other moral qualities: "Just being able to face up to reality. I mean, if you make the child, then you should have the guts to support the child—the wisdom to support him or her, you know, not just abandon them."

To explain how men can be embarrassed, hurt, or disrespected when they abdicate their paternal responsibilities, parents often cited stories of fathers who try to enter a child's life after a long absence. According to these stories, the child may refuse to recognize the father by making the statement "You ain't my dad." To add insult to injury, children may recognize another man as their social father if their biological father is not involved. Many parents suggested that it was especially painful to fathers when their children began calling another man "daddy." In fact, some men said that their anxiety about this issue motivates them to see their children. Again, Bucky explained:

> I couldn't see myself if I broke up with my daughter's mother, somebody else raising my daughter. I don't have to raise her, some other guy raising her. No. My daughter's gonna know who her father is. I could not have that. I could not see that or stomach my daughter calling somebody else "daddy." . . . You know, it's something that hits you inside. It's like almost being stripped of all your honor.

To illustrate the effects on fathers of denying responsibility, Salaam described why his brother's daughter may disavow her father if he tries to enter her life:

> I got a brother, and he got a daughter. She got to be about twelve now. And sometimes me and him could be in the neighborhood, and he would never acknowledge that she lives there. I know he's scared too. And I guess he don't want to accept the fact that all these years went by, and he hasn't done nothing for her. I think he's scared that he don't know how she gonna react if he go up to her and be like, "Hi. How are you doing?" First thing that might come out of her mouth is, "You wait all these years to find out how I'm doing?" First thing kids will say is, "You ain't my father." And their mom might have another boyfriend that taking care of her more than her original father is. That causes a lot of conflict. But see, it's nobody's fault but the original father. 'Cause if you would have been there from the door, from the start of things, you wouldn't have to go through this problem.

According to Salaam, his mother and sisters "throw this in [his brother's] face" and have lost respect for his brother. Salaam believes that his brother's guilt over his behavior has immobilized him and made it increasingly difficult to establish contact with his daughter:

> It'll make you feel real bad, especially if you got a gorgeous little kid and your kid turned out to be something. And the first thing you gonna holler, "That's my child." It wasn't your child when it was nothing, but now that it's something, it's your child. You know, then guilt would be all over.

These four arguments about the link between biological relationship and social responsibility carry with them a set of beliefs about the needs and interests of family members. I explore these beliefs by discussing how fathers are expected to satisfy their paternal responsibilities.

How Are Fathers Responsible?
Being Emotionally Involved

Parents identified emotional involvement as a primary component of paternal responsibility, referring to children's need to have their fathers present in their lives. When defining what this obligation entails, parents endorsed the involved or new father model, a model that encourages men to nurture their children, establish emotional bonds, and provide direct care for them (Griswold 1993). At the same time, they tended to emphasize the emotional component of this model more than the direct care component (see chap. 5). This finding is supported by the FFCW survey, in which the majority of unmarried mothers and fathers ranked "love and affection" as the most important paternal activity and ranked the importance of direct care lower.[6]

This new model of fatherhood emerged as the breadwinning model became less attainable and lost cultural resonance. It also evolved out of a therapeutic discourse about the personal growth and satisfaction that men can realize by being involved with their children. As we saw in the previous chapter, these ideas have been disseminated through television, film, and popular books and are now pervasive in American culture (Lamb 1987). Moreover, parents had access to therapeutic discourses through their involvement in such things as drug rehabilitation courses, parenting classes, and community programs for low-income families.

When describing a "good" father, parents said that fathers have an obligation to develop a healthy emotional relationship with their children. In particular, they identified the activities of loving, caring, listening, respecting, understanding, and supporting as essential to good fathering and good parenting more generally. Parents identified two primary ways that fathers can be emotionally involved with their children. First, parents said that fathers should "be there" or establish a reliable emotional presence in their children's lives and spend "quality time" with them.[7] Second, fathers should actively communicate with their children.

To "be there" means not only that fathers see their children regularly but also that they are easily accessible.[8] In situations in which children live apart from their fathers (as was the case for most parents I interviewed), parents claimed that it is critical for children to know that their fathers care about them and that they can depend on them. Parents also emphasized the negative effect of paternal absence on children, with several parents saying that they became aware of this need through the experience of having an absent, unreliable, or neglectful father in their own lives. Bayshawn argued that men can teach their sons the meaning of paternal responsibility through their involvement: "The baby . . . needs his father's attention and love. The baby grow up with no father, you know. I didn't do it, so he ain't gonna do it. I had a father, he gonna have a father."

O'Shen took pride in the time he spent with his children every weekend. However, he acknowledged that he learned the importance of being reliable only after his behavior hurt them:

> M: If you could say what you think a really good father would be like, what would that be?
> O: A caring father, responsible father, and a loyal father. That's number one. Got to be loyal and dedicated to your kids. You just can't promise them, "Oh, I'm coming over to come take you to the park" and, you know, never come. And then you're gonna tell them you're gonna be there. At least [be] decent enough to call or come or something. You can't come, call. That's all they want, you know, 'cause I used to always do that myself—tell my kids, "I'll be there at 5:00 and come get you." Bang, something come up. I never call them or do nothing. They wouldn't see me two or three days. And that hurts my daughters.

In addition to noting the disappointment children feel when fathers do not show up for a visit, parents insisted that a father's absence throughout their children's lives or at critical times could have lasting emotional effects.

Unmarried fathers can also "be there" for children by spending quality time with them. Although the concept of quality time originated among higher-income working parents who wanted to make the limited time they spent with their children meaningful, parents I interviewed used the term to describe diverse parenting arrangements. In fact, one twenty-four-year-old father who lived apart from his son told me that selling drugs gave him a flexible schedule, which allowed him to spend quality time with his son. This striking, although atypical, example shows the extent to which these ideas have become part of a standard cultural script for talking about fatherhood. Other parents described more conventional situations when explaining the importance of quality time:

> A father that would not just come home: "Hi, honey. Hi son, hi daughter," and then go about his business. Someone that comes in and spends time with them and sits down and reads to them. Just play with them. They love it when you play with them. They just want to be loved. If they don't have that attention then they feel like they're not being loved. (Robert)

As this example suggests, parents regularly distinguished good fathers from bad fathers on the basis of the attention and love they show their child.

A second way fathers can offer emotional support is through communication. In particular, parents argued that by actively talking and listening to children, fathers expressed their love and concern for them. For example, Mariah defined a good father as "someone that has time for the child and patience and can sit down and talk to the child." Bad fathers, in contrast, are "the ones out there trying to hang out with their friends and doing drugs, and don't have time for their child." G. felt that although he received adequate economic support from his father, he did not have sufficient opportunity to talk to him. Attributing some of his personal problems to his father's lack of involvement, G. said that he wanted to be able to communicate more with his own son.

> My pop [would] never sit down and talk. He was there as far as buying [for] me or whatever. But as far as sitting down and talking to me man to man, he was never like that. I started thinking of holding some of that against him.

Parents also interpreted the importance of communication in relation to raising children in poverty. Ray described the psychological effect on children when their fathers are absent, leaving mothers economically overwhelmed with the responsibility of raising a child alone. In these cases, neither parent spends the time creating a relationship with their children based on communication. Ray explains:

> [Spending time is] a bond, and without that bond you can't have communication. Without that communication, you just passing through. They be calling you by your first name then. 'Cause I went through that. It's real hard, 'cause you lock yourself up. You close yourself in. You be in your room pouting and stuff. It's like a miniature depression. 'Cause [you're thinking], "[I] don't know if my parents love me or not. They never spend time with me. They never take me to the park."

He said that children who feel unloved will begin to call their fathers by their first name (a sign of disrespect) and "cut up," or get into trouble. He also said he continues to feel "all bottled up" as an adult because he never had a father to express his feelings to or to talk with about his problems.

African American parents often expressed the need for communicating with children in terms of their experiences of living in an urban neighborhood in which drugs and crime are everyday problems. Marilyn voiced these concerns:

I'm sticking with the reality part about it. Nowadays I would say the most a parent could do for their child is . . . to be there, to understand, you know. 'Cause there's so many things going on out there. Children, you know, teenagers and drugs, shootings, killings, you know? And if the parent isn't there for that child, they gonna have to go. . . . They say it's rebelling; like, a lot of children would be dead today [if] their parents would not have [had an] understanding of them, you know? You know what's going on especially if you living in a drug-infested environment and you have a thirteen- or fourteen-year-old staying out until ten, eleven o'clock at night. . . . It's understanding, knowing your child needs. If you're a true parent, you know, you know your child needs; you'll be there for them, for whatever it is.

Many parents said they want to have a closer relationship with their children than they had with their own parents. They hoped that open communication and accessibility would encourage more understanding and prevent their children from rebelling against their authority.

Providing Guidance

The parents I spoke with mentioned guidance as another important component of paternal responsibility, invoking conventional discourses about the importance of paternal role models, teachers, and disciplinarians and more specific ideas about role models for young black males in urban communities.[9] This view is also consistent with the responses of unmarried parents in the FFCW survey when asked about the most important things fathers do for their children. The combined responses of "teaching children about life" and "serving as an authority figure" were ranked as the second most important paternal activities, just below "showing love and affection."[10]

Although the idea of fathers as teachers and role models derives from traditional models of fatherhood, parents modified these models to fit within an involved father framework, suggesting that fathers need to spend time and communicate with children to effectively provide guidance.

[A father should] help them with their homework and encourage them to do good things. Even if they're not doing good, encourage them anyway, 'cause I do. Encourage them and just be there. Be a role model, at least. Kids need a role model. (Debra)

While identifying good fathers as men who supervise their children in daily activities, Debra said that bad fathers are those who put their own needs before those of their children—for example, fathers who are in jail, are out "running the street," deny or abandon their children, or are addicted to drugs. Similarly, William criticized men who fail to see the importance of parental guidance:

> I don't see how you can turn your back on something that needs upbringing, that needs help. You know, has no direction in life. You have to be there to guide the child. When you abandon that responsibility, you're just leaving that child out there with no direction, and [the child] can go in any way.

Parents also described the negative effects of not having a role model and often believed children would need another father figure to turn to if their biological father was not involved. Evette worried about her own son because his father has little contact with him:

> When he get to that age where he gonna need a male to talk to, I hope he can find somebody to talk to. He don't have to go out into the street and take it out in anger. You know, he can find a male figure to talk to.

As this example suggests, African American parents' ideas about a child's need for a paternal role model often speak to the risks children face in poor neighborhoods. Kareen portrayed his mother's boyfriend as a good father, not only because he spent time teaching his daughter new things but because his interest kept her "off the streets": "He spends a lot of time with his daughter. He has a lot of things for her to do while she in the house to keep her attention from off the streets. . . . He teach her a lot of things, that's good for a father."

Parents' claims about the importance of paternal guidance were closely associated with beliefs about masculinity and respect. Both mothers and fathers argued that a "man is needed to raise a man" and that fathers gain respect as men by becoming role models for their sons. These accounts associated manhood with the ability to provide guidance for their children, especially for sons. In particular, parents distinguished maternal and paternal roles in the areas of identity formation, learning about the streets, and discipline. According to parents' accounts, the gender of parents becomes particularly important when their children reach puberty, in part because they believe adolescents feel more comfortable asking questions of a parent of the same gender. Parents also suggested that mothers and fathers could give their own gendered perspective on romantic relationships to their adolescent children.

An important part of fathers' involvement with their sons is teaching children masculine styles, knowledge, and skills, ranging from those needed to play sports to those required to manage a dangerous urban environment.

> A father is not gonna baby his son. He's not going to be holding his son like a mother. He's not going to be petting him up all the time. Every time he falls . . . the boy is going to run to the father and expect the father to pick the baby up and say, "It's going to be okay." No, I think that's the mother's job, because the man is going to teach the little boy to be a man. He want the little boy to be independent: "You's a boy, you's going to be a man. You have to take these things." So they be more harder on a boy than they do a girl. That's why I say, a boy listens to a man more. (Crystal)

In an area in which job opportunities were limited, the parents I spoke with were often faced with ethical choices different from those of higher income parents. Drug dealers represented an extremely visible, alternative model available to young men in Trenton. Fathers said that they could draw on their own experiences to help children avoid making the kinds of mistakes they made, particularly in regard to selling or using drugs. As a Muslim, Kareen argued that other fathers should teach their sons respect for themselves and for women. After describing his experiences with selling and being addicted to drugs, living on the street, imprisonment, and returning to the Nation of Islam for moral guidance, Kareen talked about how he would like to teach his son the lessons he has learned in life so that he and other men do not become role models:

> I would tell him the things that I went through at a young age and the things that I don't want him to go through now. You know, it's pretty much the opposite of my life . . . like my uncles told me how to get out here and try to manipulate the system. I won't teach him how to do that. I teach him how to work with the system, how to get jobs. You know, start doing that at an early age so then he knows there's a lot to work. See when I started working, I felt good when I started getting a check. I know I ain't got to be out there; I don't have to run from the police no more. I ain't got to run with gangs no more. You know what I'm saying? I pretty much do what I want to do now.

Parents also argued that fathers play an important role in providing discipline for children. Because parents often regarded men as "harder" and more intimidating than women, they believed that the ability to discipline children came more easily to them.[11] Therefore, fathers could raise their voice or give their child a certain kind of look, and the child would take them seriously, without relying on physical punishment:

It's important to have fathers around because sometimes they [children] get out of control and they won't listen to their mothers. So it's good to have a deeper voice around, to talk to them so they can understand more. 'Cause the deeper the voice, the more they listen because they be scared and they listen. (Daniel)

With large numbers of nonresident fathers in their communities, parents talked about the negative consequences of children growing up without paternal guidance, role modeling, and discipline. These sentiments paralleled parents' feelings about children who grow up without the emotional presence of their fathers in their lives. Nicole explained the possible consequences of her daughter's father being absent: "[The father should] spend time with her. It's not all about money. Your time and your impression on your child—that may change how she feels about men in her life." Once more, we see that parents emphasized the importance of unmarried fathers providing love and guidance in addition to offering economic support.

Providing Economic Support

Parents identified economic support as a third important component of paternal responsibility. According to parents' accounts, making an effort to provide material support is a basic responsibility of fatherhood. However, economic claims were typically "internally dialogized," or made in reference to claims about the emotional and developmental needs of children, to explain why economic support is a necessary but insufficient condition for adequate fathering.[12]

In my interviews with parents, about 9 out of 10 mothers and fathers described a good father in terms of love or guidance compared with only 4 out of 10 parents who described a good father as one who provides material support for his children.[13] These findings were consistent among mothers and fathers and among African American and white parents. The responses of unmarried parents in the FFCW survey also revealed some ambivalence about the importance of economic support. Approximately 12 percent of unmarried mothers and fathers reported that providing regular financial support is the most important paternal activity. Overall, parents ranked this activity third (out of five responses), after measures of love and guidance. At the same time, about 27 percent of mothers and 19 percent of fathers considered financial support to be the least important activity (also ranking this the third least important activity).[14]

Parents' statements about the importance of economic support were often accompanied by the argument that simply providing for a child does not make someone a good father. Reflecting the sentiments of many other parents, one mother observed, "Money comes and goes, but love will always be there." Jacqueline explained that she had more interest in what the father can provide emotionally, rather than financially, for their child, given the difficulty of the job market for many unmarried fathers:

> If you can't do it financially, at least he can be there. 'Cause it's hard nowadays, it's hard for everybody out here. 'Cause that's all your child really needs is for you to be there. Of course, they need clothes and things like that, but you can get clothes from anywhere. Like you can go to a Salvation Army or to a church or anything. There's help out there. But you can never just go to a church and find that father for your child.

Although these accounts suggest that parents were resigned to the fact that fathers often could not offer much financial support, they also demonstrate the parents' belief that emotional resources are more precious than economic resources.

When parents talked about the responsibility of providing economic support, they typically described situations in which the mother had custody of the children and they were living in poverty. In these cases, the father was expected to support the mother's efforts to ensure that the children's basic subsistence needs were being met, or that the children were not "hungry and dirty" and that they had "clothes on their backs," "food on the table," and "a decent place to live." These statements often emphasized the harm to children of inadequate economic support rather than the positive benefits of adequate support.

Fathers were minimally obligated to provide small, in-kind items such as diapers, food, clothing, and shoes. Depending on a father's financial resources, he might also be expected to pay for more expensive items such as strollers, car seats, cribs, and medical care. Cash and in-kind assistance (for example, food stamps and Medicaid) covered some of these basic needs, but the welfare grant was usually not enough to meet all of the children's expenses. Contributions from the father could help fill this gap (Edin and Lein 1997).[15]

> Like if she goes to the hospital and they got to do surgery and she comes up with this big, extravagant bill and I'm not able to pay it, then he [the father] should make sure it can get paid. That's just like an example. Because see when I take them to the doctors and they got medicine that like my insurance [Medicaid] won't pay for, I take it right to him. I take the majority of the bills to him. Like I buy them clothes and Pampers and stuff like that. But when they come up with all this doctor bill stuff. 'Cause see my son has asthma. He had to get this asthma machine that costed like one hundred and something dollars. The medicine was separate 'cause it like fifty

dollars for each medicine. I mean his father got it. I was like, I can't afford this, this is too expensive. I wasn't working then. I was only receiving a grant every month. I was like I can't afford it. And he was working and everything, so he got it. (Shakeema)

Only a minority of parents suggested that fathers should have the primary or sole responsibility for supporting their families. Parents who expressed this belief typically described situations in which the parents were living together. As William explained:

My father always told me the man should be the head of the household. That's how he was brought up, so that's how I feel. You know, the father should take care of everything. . . . He's supposed to be the man of the house as far as laying down the rules or talking if something goes wrong in the house. He should be the one to dictate what happens. Plus, financially, he should be taking care of the mother and the children.

Although William seemed to tie economic provision to a breadwinning model, he also emphasized other important aspects of fatherhood, such as guidance and direct care, in other parts of the interview. In fact, parents who believed that fathers should be the primary providers also said that they should be involved with their children in other ways.

According to parents' accounts, obligations for support varied with the relationship between the mother and father. If the parents were in a relationship, and especially if they were living together, the father was expected to help support the mother and the household as well as the child. (A father might also do this if he were in a relationship with the mother but not living with her.) If the parents were not in a relationship, the father was only obligated to support his child but not the mother. Fathers with children by more than one mother often had different methods of supporting the children (for example, a father might pay child support for one and give informal support to another), depending on their relationship with the mother and the agreements they had made.

Parents also suggested that fathers could meet their financial obligation through either direct or in-kind support. Furthermore, these contributions need not be in the form of child support payments. In fact, as we shall see in chapter 7, child support may sometimes indicate a breakdown in voluntary contributions by fathers. Both mothers and fathers argued that men should make a sincere effort to provide monetary or in-kind support for their children, but they realized that a father's efforts might be undermined by low wages and unemployment. According to parents' accounts, fathers had the responsibility to "do the best they can to take care of their kids." In the following exchange, Ishadeema, a mother who received welfare and worked through a temporary agency, talked about alternate ways fathers could take care of their children financially:

> Well personally they don't have to give me no money. You could just buy him anything you think he needs. You can walk into a store and say "Maybe my baby needs this, let me get that." Or, "This is cute, I'll get this." But they don't actually have to put money in my hand. I'm not a greedy person. . . . If I was working and you're not working, I feel the best thing you could do is keep the child while I work.

Other men who worked full-time jobs or made higher wages were expected to provide more financial support for their children. One mother said she understands when fathers are not working, "but if he can do something, do it." As these examples suggest, parents defined fathers' obligation for support in relation to what fathers could provide.

At the same time, this flexibility did not diminish mothers' concerns about receiving some economic support from fathers or their belief that fathers should provide according to their ability. If mothers believed that men were making an effort to support their children, they said that they did not usually take issue with the amount of money fathers provided. However, dissatisfaction arose when mothers believed that fathers showed little effort to support or be involved with their child, when they spent money on themselves instead of on their child, when they had to be asked repeatedly to buy things, when they did not provide things in a reasonable amount of time, or when they supported someone else's child but not their own. Fathers acknowledged the legitimacy of the first two objections, particularly when a father spent money on such things as drugs or alcohol rather than supporting their child.

To illustrate this point, Denise explained that even though her former partner contributes from the money he receives from disability, it upsets her that she has to ask for the money each month and that the father is typically late with his payments. To make matters worse, he gives her children $100 each month, but he recently bought a $300 television for himself and his girlfriend.

Despite these common objections, mother and fathers typically did not believe men should be evaluated primarily on their economic contributions. Rather, parents said that spending time with their child also dramatizes fathers' altruism more than economic provision. Yusef explained:

> You can't base how much you love your child by what you give them. You know what I'm saying? It's not how much you make or whatever. Regard-

less [it's] how much time you gonna spend with them. Like I was telling you how time-consuming it is now. As far as this child right here, 'cause she would call sometimes, she be like, "Daddy, daddy, daddy this; daddy that." You know, "I want my daddy." . . . You take time and you sacrifice your time [to] be a good father.

Some parents, like Salaam, actively resisted equating a good father with a good provider. In fact, Salaam suggested that lower-income fathers usually tried harder to take care of their children, given their financial constraints. By distinguishing themselves from other men who simply provide for their children, fathers derived a positive sense of their own capacity to be good fathers.

A real good father can come from all different categories. 'Cause a father could be a doctor and be an excellent father. A father could be a doctor and be a bad father. And I feel as though most of the good fathers is the ones that don't have nothing, but still insist on raising and taking care of their kids. That's where you find all the good fathers at. Just because you made it—you're a lawyer, you're a doctor, you're a judge, and your kids got everything they need—that doesn't necessarily say that you're a good father. You's a good provider, but half of the time these people don't even get time to spend with their kids. So I feel as though a good father is somebody that's out there trying to make things work.

Although Salaam had been out of the work force for a long period of time, he was "getting money best way he knows how" to support his children. Because he had given up selling drugs after repeated arrests, "the best way he knows how" usually meant trying to win money in dice games.

Kareen distinguished himself from the men in his own neighborhood who had money (that is, drug dealers) rather than from professional men. Kareen said that these men with money were "livin' the fast life. . . . They all about objects—gold rings, brand new cars and beepers and stuff." Although these fathers might "throw ten or twenty dollars" on their children every time they saw them on the street, Kareen suggested that handing children money is a way of avoiding children and of skirting the real challenge of childrearing.

Parents who were more financially stable also were reluctant to reduce fathers to a source of income, sometimes disapproving of fathers who supported their child economically but not emotionally or socially. Jean, who lived with her children's father, said:

I'll say my boyfriend's a good provider. I can't say he's a good father . . . my kids are never hungry. But a good father is one who puts individual time aside for each one of the kids. Or does things that's just, "mine and daddy's day." I have all week to amuse them. All day until he gets home. But he comes home; he's tired from work. Falls asleep about eight o'clock, and he's grouchy on the weekends. And he doesn't want to be bothered.

Although many parents believed that fathers might substitute money for forming an attachment to their child, research tends to indicate a complementary relationship between nonresident fathers being in contact with their children and providing child support (e.g., Seltzer, Schaeffer, and Charng 1989).[16] Scholars have suggested that economic constraints experienced by African American fathers are related to paternal absence (McAdoo 1988). Some examples from both classic (e.g., Liebow 1967) and more contemporary studies of low-income African American fathers (e.g., Anderson 1989) also indicate that a father's feelings of failure as a provider causes him to withdraw from his children.[17]

Several fathers talked about the strain they felt when they were not able to provide more economic support to their children. However, only a few fathers said that this inhibited them from having contact with their child. One father who had withdrawn from his children struggled to reconcile his feelings about not providing for them with collective ideas about involved fatherhood:

> Once I get where I want to be at, I can spend the time I want to spend with [my son]. Do the things I want to do with him . . . if I have nothing to give to my kids I don't really want to be all up under them. 'Cause I mean, I want to be able to give them something. . . . They say the best father is to be able to just spend time with your kids. That's a good father. But see, I'm stubborn. And with me, maybe my father gave me a lot in life, I want to do the same for my kids. And [when] I have nothing to give them, I feel funny being around them.

As we shall see in the next chapter, however, fathers sometimes said that they limited contact with their children because of the mother's reaction when they showed up to see their child empty handed, or because of their problems with the child support system, rather than their own feelings as failed providers. When fathers had strained relationships with mothers, the causality between involvement and support could also run in the other direction. Some fathers said they were hesitant to give money to the mother for their child's support when they were prevented from spending time with their children.

In general, fathers denied that their own lack of income prevented them from establishing an emotional connection with their children. Joe, an unemployed father of three, reflected the views of many parents:

J: [A good father] is someone that's there for their kids when they need them most. In all aspects, not just financially. Because anybody can give somebody money. I'm talking about somebody who has some time to love their kids the way they should be.

M: What does "being there" mean?

J: Whenever they need to talk to you or whenever they just want to see you. Take them to the movies. You know? Just little stuff that shows them that you love them and that you care about them. Most important is just the love. That's the most important thing.

When I asked Joe if he ever felt bad about seeing his children when he does not have money to give them, he said that he tells them "money ain't everything." At the same time, Joe considered competing models of paternal responsibility simultaneously in his response, talking about involved fatherhood in dialogue with breadwinning—a model of fatherhood that retains an important, if increasingly attenuated, place in contemporary American culture. In doing so, he also responded to possible critiques of not providing much financial support to his children.

It's hard 'cause you want to do so much for them, and then when you can't, you feel so bad. You know what I mean? But as you get older, you get over that. You realize you gotta be there even if you ain't got nothing.

Some previous studies have noted that low-income mothers and fathers accept "mainstream" ideas about fatherhood but lower their expectations for financial support. By minimizing their expectations, fathers can turn their failures into successes (e.g., Liebow 1967; Rainwater 1970). Like other writers, I found that parents' expectations reflected the fact that unmarried fathers, like mothers, were often living in poverty. While sometimes downplaying the significance of economic support, parents emphasized paternal love and guidance. This emphasis may reflect a generational shift away from the provider model toward more involved models of parenting.[18] In fact, the FFCW survey suggests that both married and unmarried parents rank emotional involvement and guidance above economic support.[19] Involved fatherhood might also take on increased importance in situations in which many parents are living apart and there is an absence of male role models in the community.

Given that these fathers have less control over providing for their children than they do over offering love or guidance to them, monetary support was not the primary criterion upon which to distinguish "good" and "bad" fathers. Rather, fathers were expected to maintain a strong emotional and social connection to their child regardless of their financial situation and were evaluated on the basis of emotional and moral criteria. This model of fatherhood, which combines contemporary and traditional elements, provides ways for low-income unmarried men to accept responsibility for their children and to derive a sense of honor from fulfilling their responsibilities.

* * *

Unmarried parents argued that men have an unconditional obligation to their biological children in part because they could have chosen not to become fathers. If fathers choose to ignore this obligation, they do so to the serious detriment of their children and themselves and risk losing respect as men. Mothers also argued that because fathers share biological responsibility for reproduction, they should share equally in children's upbringing.

When describing this obligation, parents used widely available models of fatherhood, but they interpreted these models in relation to their experiences with childrearing in difficult social and economic conditions. Drawing on the involved father model, parents emphasized emotional involvement as a primary component of paternal responsibility. In addition to stressing the importance of communication and spending quality time with their children, parents argued that children with absent or neglectful fathers would experience emotional harm. The parents I spoke with mentioned guidance as another important component of paternal responsibility, invoking conventional ideas about fathers as teachers and disciplinarians and more specific ideas about paternal role models for young black males in urban communities. This model was also tied to beliefs about the needs of children for paternal involvement.

The parents I interviewed viewed economic support as a necessary form of paternal responsibility but not a sufficient one. Fathers were expected to provide in-kind or monetary support according to their ability, but they were evaluated primarily on their effort to do so. Although parents may have downplayed economic support because of fathers' economic constraints, they placed a high value on fathers spending time with children to provide love and guidance. These beliefs may point to a generational shift toward more involved fatherhood and may attain more significance in conditions in which many fathers are living away from their children.

Rather than representing a disorganized culture deviating from a system of mainstream values, unmarried parents articulated consistent standards of paternal responsibility as they blended new ideas about involved fatherhood with more conventional ideas about discipline and economic provision. These collective beliefs diverge from the "good provider" model (Bernard 1981; Schwartz 1994) and connect ideas about masculinity with non-economic forms of paternal responsibility, particularly guidance. Although parents articulated shared standards of paternal obligation, these standards were often difficult to achieve. In the next chapter I explore unmarried fathers' departures from collective beliefs about paternal responsibility.

CHAPTER FIVE

Departures from Paternal Responsibility

She uses my son as a weapon toward me. . . . The judge said I have to give her twenty-four hours' notice or I can't pick him up. I mean, I have no driver's license. . . . So, she gets all mad at me and stuff. And she's, like, "Oh, well, if you don't pick your son up . . . you're not gonna see him for this long." Or then she'll tell my son . . . like, he'll get on the phone, and he'll say things like, "Daddy, you don't want to see me because you want to hang out and go party with your friends." It's, like, where's my son getting that? He's not saying that right off the top of his head. And it's not even like that. I gotta work. It's not even like I'm going out partying with my friends. . . . My son don't know that. He's five years old. (Jared)

Despite the convergence in their views about what constitutes a good father, the parents I interviewed acknowledged that men often diverged from these standards. Some fathers considered themselves to be inadequate or uninvolved parents, and many mothers expressed dissatisfaction with the fathers of their children. In this chapter I investigate how unmarried parents described and explained variations in paternal behavior.

In the first section I examine how parents used collective standards when fathers evaluated themselves, when mothers evaluated the fathers of their children, and when both evaluated other fathers. I also compare parents' views of maternal and paternal responsibility. The second section of the chapter examines how mothers explained, and how fathers justified, a father's lack of involvement with his children. In particular, I consider parents' vocabulary of motives in terms of paternal disengagement, or the socially constructed ways they explain fathers' motivations for noninvolvement. Like interpretations of fatherhood, these explanations are drawn from a culturally available repertoire and are developed in response to specific situations. Fathers' explanations about their own lack of involvement are also constructed in dialogue with actual and potential critiques of their behavior (Mills 1940).

In this analysis, I do not judge the validity of parents' claims. Rather, I investigate the modes by which fathers justified their actions and mothers attributed motives to fathers' behavior to better identify the points at which parental relationships break down. In later chapters I document strategies mothers used to influence fathers who they believe have illegitimate motives for not spending time with or supporting their children.

Evaluating Fathers

During the interview, I asked men to evaluate their performance as fathers and women to evaluate the behavior of their child's father. When parents had more than one child, I asked them to talk primarily about their parenting experiences with their youngest child. The responses of both men and women can be divided into three general categories: the first consists of fathers who were considered, or who considered themselves, to be "good" or much better than other fathers; the second, "satisfactory" group is made up of fathers who gave themselves, or received, a mixed evaluation; and the third group includes fathers considered to be "bad" fathers, or those who were absent from their children's lives. When parents described themselves or their child's father as average but described the average father as being either extremely good or extremely bad, these fathers were assigned to the high or low group, respectively.

Perhaps not surprisingly, the number of men who considered themselves to be good fathers was larger than the number of women who assessed the father of their child in this way. Because I did not generally interview mothers and fathers of the same child, I cannot look at the consistency of their responses. Also, as noted previously, this study may have selected more involved fathers. At the same time, some research shows that nonresident fathers report higher paternal involvement than do mothers (e.g., Seltzer and Brandreth 1994).[1] Although I consciously tried to be nonjudgmental in the interviews, the effect of being interviewed by a woman may also have encouraged men to overstate their own participation.[2]

Self-Evaluations

The majority of men I interviewed described themselves as good fathers, a slightly smaller group identified themselves as satisfactory or average fathers, and only three men described themselves as bad or absent fathers. Those men who characterized themselves as good or above-average fathers explained their self-assessment in reference to the image they held of a typical father and according to the standards of responsible fatherhood described in chapter 4. Consistent with these standards, parents evaluated fathers primarily in terms of the time fathers spent developing emotional bonds and providing guidance to their children and the effort they made to support them.

Self-identified good fathers reported that, in general, they spent more or better-quality time with their children and made more of an effort to fulfill their paternal duties than other fathers did. They also talked about particular moral characteristics, such as altruism, dedication, and dependability, which set them apart. Arthur enthusiastically stated:

> I do everything I think a child should have as a father. And I made sure, when my girlfriend and I thought about it, I knew exactly how I wanted my child to be raised and like how I was gonna treat her and everything. And that's what I'm doing. I'm doing the best I can. That's really what a good father is—someone that does the best they can. Not someone who does a half-assed job taking care [of] the kid and let the kid go off. I'm always there for my daughter. Always. Except when I'm working.

Similarly, Robert considered his effort to be greater than other fathers:

> I think I'm a better father than other men my age due to the fact that I spend more time . . . I teach them more. I show them more. Just spend more time with them. . . . If you don't spend time with them, you never really know them. You never get to know your child until you sit down and you listen to her side of the story. She's, well, "Daddy, why is this?" When she starts asking a question, you explain it to her, and she doesn't understand it. You try to break it down a little further for her. I read to them. . . . These are two very special girls. I mean, they require a lot of attention. If they don't get it, they will be just out of hand. . . . She [the mother] comes to me when these girls get out of hand; she'll call me. If it got that bad, she would call me and tell me to come and get them. 'Cause she knows I can deal with them. She can deal with them, too, but it's just that they listen to me more. They've always been like that. They daddy's little girls.

Some fathers cited situations in which they believed they responded exceptionally. Anthony described a circumstance in which he actively pursued visitation rights to his child, knowing he would incur a legal child support obligation in the process. He thought of his behavior as atypical and noted that the judge at his hearing told him that most fathers would not go through this process voluntarily. Likewise, Bucky believed he was exceptional in committing to stay with a disabled woman after finding out she was pregnant with their child. Comparing himself with other fathers, he asked, "Who's gonna be around a pregnant woman or a lady in a wheelchair with a baby? Who's gonna actually admit up to that?" He proudly described caring for both the mother and their daughter in addition to paying child support.

Those fathers who considered themselves to be average or satisfactory fathers described some ways in which they fulfilled collective expectations for fatherhood and other ways in which their involvement and support were insufficient (either generally or at specific times). One father, for example, said that he "always tries to be there for his children" but considered himself to be a "part-time" father because he did not want to spend as much time parenting as the mother did. Another father explained why his sister called him a "holiday dad" during a period when he rarely saw his son:

> Because I didn't see my son as much [before]. Like when I didn't see him for like a year and a half. That's when she started calling me a holiday dad. Christmas, Easter, birthday . . . that's when I'd see him. . . . Like my son's mother and I, we used to get into arguments. And she said things like, "You'll never see your son again" and I'd be like, "Good, good." . . . There were times when he'd come over and the whole time he's with me he'd cry. You know, he wanted his mother or whatever.

A small group of men I interviewed considered themselves to be inadequate or absent fathers. Although some men said that their lack of financial resources discouraged them from seeing their child, few fathers suggested they were bad fathers solely because they had difficulty supporting their child economically. Those who described themselves as inadequate or absent fathers offered justifications for why they did not attempt to support or have contact with their child. Their motives, and those of other fathers, are reviewed later in this chapter.

Mothers' Evaluations

When evaluating the fathers of their children, the mothers I interviewed responded by almost evenly dividing the fathers among the three categories (good, satisfactory, and bad). Mothers who characterized their child's father as a good father expressed no dissatisfaction and generally reported high levels of paternal involvement and effort. Mothers also suggested that exceptional fathers made as much effort as a mother would. For example, one mother said that she considered her children's father to be a good father and "a good mother, too." She explained that she had been living with the father for the past few years and that he was taking care of the children full time while she was going through a drug rehabilitation program.

> He's like the best person I know. I commend him for what he's doing now with my son. 'Cause he gets up at 4:30 every morning. He gets up and dresses them 'cause he has to be at work at 7:00 and he commutes to work. So he has to get up and dress them and get them ready for nursery school and feed them. And he does all that.

She added that the father could not offer much financial support, but he spent time talking with their son and being a "father figure" to him. In fact, she thought her son would probably "go insane [if the father left]. That's how close they are."

Mothers who gave their children's father a mixed evaluation frequently cited inadequate involvement as the reason for their dissatisfaction. In addition, mothers mentioned issues such as the father not taking his responsibilities seriously, acting immaturely, or having the wrong priorities. When mothers evaluated paternal behavior, they used their own involvement with their children as the standard by which to judge the father.[3] Diamond described her daughter's father:

> Her father's good in some ways, some ways not. Like I tell him it's an emergency, he won't think it's an emergency. He don't take everything serious, like I would take it. [That's] something he need to learn.

Diamond also disapproved of the fact that his parents took more responsibility for the child than he did.

In their assessments of their children's fathers, women were much more likely than men to use labels such as "bad," "way below average," or "absent." More mothers reported that their child's father had no contact with them than fathers reported being out of contact with their children.[4] Again, this may be an artifact of the sample. At the same time, the difference between mothers' evaluations and fathers' self-evaluations may reflect variations in the ways mothers and fathers used collective standards to assess fathers' behavior. What unmarried fathers view as a real effort to meet their responsibilities may be perceived as inadequate by mothers.

Most of the mothers who considered their children's fathers to be bad or below average reported that the fathers had been uninvolved in their child's life for at least a year or that the fathers had not claimed their child. However, a few mothers who reported that their child's father was absent did not consider them to be bad fathers, noting special circumstances such as imprisonment, military service, residence in another country, or psychological problems that legitimately prevented the father from seeing his child.

General Evaluations

To gain a better understanding of the general images that parents hold of fathers, I asked parents to evaluate fathers they knew personally and fathers in the community or the larger society. Using the three categories noted earlier, the fathers I interviewed tended to rate other fathers they knew similar to the way they evaluated themselves: they considered the majority of fathers to be either good or satisfactory fathers. However, when talking about fathers they did not know, particularly fathers in their own community, men tended to describe them as either satisfactory or bad fathers. According to Salaam, most fathers in Trenton did not take responsibility for their children.

> Out of a hundred, you might get eighty-five that don't care. As long as they out there selling drugs or making money or whatever. They be, like, "I'll bring my kids something when I get ready." Or tell the parent [mother] that I'm gonna bring it and never take it. Or he just don't [bring] it at all. "Look, I'm tired of buying these kids something. How I know they mine's anyway? Give me a blood test." Or, "That baby ain't mine, take that baby home. Get him away from me." That's how most men is right here in Trenton.

As this example suggests, fathers who evaluated themselves and their friends and family members as satisfactory often did so in comparison with fathers who they believe denied their children or did not try to take care of them.[5]

Perhaps because women's personal networks included fewer men, mothers spoke more often about young fathers in their community or in society than about male friends who were fathers. Both African American and white mothers said that many fathers were essentially unreliable. African American women were particularly forthcoming in their evaluations of men in Trenton, and their estimation of these men was overwhelmingly negative. In fact, only one African American woman regarded the majority of fathers in Trenton as "good," while the rest of the African American women I interviewed identified men in the community as bad fathers, more typically labeling them as "dogs" or "no good." To explain this view, mothers suggested that many fathers in Trenton were drug dealers, did not have jobs or an education, only wanted sex from women, and left them after getting them pregnant. Suggesting a ratio similar to the one Salaam mentioned, Crystal said: "I say out of a hundred, it's like 10 percent good dads, because you can't find too many good fathers." Because of a lack of good men in the community, mothers also felt their choices for finding a partner capable of being a "father figure" were limited:

They [men in Trenton] ain't no good. This is our [she and her cousin's] New Year's resolution. The very next time we get pregnant or have a baby—I got it guaranteed because I'm on Norplant. If I ever have a baby by someone, it's gonna be a father. It ain't gonna be none of these sorry, low-down men in Trenton either. He gonna be worth something. He gonna have a job. You know, he gonna really be worth something. He gonna be a father figure. If he ain't, I ain't having any.

Mothers gave more positive evaluations of the fathers of their children than they did of other fathers in their community. Furthermore, when they were around their female friends, African American mothers spoke more negatively about fathers than when they were in the private interview setting.[6] For example, some women I talked with on the street in Trenton made comments like, "We've got some bums for you," or "I don't know where my baby's father is; I never see him." When I talked to women privately, they offered more mixed assessments of men, sometimes criticizing them and sometimes giving them credit, but almost always using a more balanced tone.

Similarly, men assessed themselves more highly than they did other fathers and often seemed to embrace negative representations of low-income unmarried fathers. These reactions suggest that parents restated negative ideas about poor fathers that are held by society, even as they made careful distinctions among fathers that they knew personally. By distancing themselves from these public images, fathers derived a more positive sense of themselves as parents.

Maternal versus Paternal Responsibility

As we saw in the last chapter, parents said that fathers play a critical role as disciplinarians and role models. They also emphasized the significance of fathers creating an emotional bond with their children but talked less about providing direct care for them—a task traditionally associated with motherhood. When asked whether mothers and fathers should have different responsibilities in caring for their children, parents initially tended to minimize distinctions and argued that these duties should be shared.

Sometimes you could play two different roles, but the most important thing is that you play the same role, not as a mother, not as a father. Okay.

Y'all made it together, but she birth it and now it's your part to blend in with it, to take care of it together. One wash up, one get the clothes out. Or one feed and one cook, like that. (Daniel)

Like other parents, Daniel said that fathers should be involved in the day-to-day work of child care and rejected the idea that they should be excused from certain tasks such as changing diapers, bathing, or feeding children. The blurring of the gender distinctions in direct care, at least in the way men express their willingness to participate in tasks previously assigned to mothers, suggests a generational shift to a an involved father model. At first glance, the association of direct care, nurturing, and emotional involvement with motherhood seems to be attenuated in parents' accounts. However, when I probed further about differences in maternal and paternal involvement, parents typically acknowledged that mothers assumed more responsibility for children's care and rearing than men do. Furthermore, when tasks were shared, they were not shared equally.

Lamb et al. (1987) use the terms engagement, accessibility, and responsibility to identify three primary types of paternal involvement. According to these authors, engagement involves direct interactions with children (such as direct care and play), and accessibility refers to indirect activities and the potential for interaction (such as cooking in the kitchen while the child plays). The term responsibility, as it is used by these writers, refers to taking ultimate responsibility for children's care and welfare.[7] A review of recent studies shows that married fathers spend approximately 44 percent as much time as mothers being directly engaged with children and approximately 66 percent as much time being accessible to them. Although these figures point to important increases in recent years, fathers continue to be much less involved in taking ultimate responsibility for their children's care (Pleck 1997).[8] Research also indicates that mothers' engagement usually involves caretaking, whereas fathers' involves playing with children (Davis and Perkins 1999; Lamb 2000).[9]

In my interviews with unmarried parents, fathers often accepted and naturalized differences between maternal and paternal responsibility, whereas mothers attributed these differences to fathers' lack of effort. Because many fathers believed mothers have a "natural bond" with children, they said the ability to care for children came more easily to mothers. Consequently, fathers often showed a willingness to be involved in the same way as mothers but not at the same level. Because most parents in this study were not living with their child's other parent, fathers had less opportunity to be involved with their child than resident fathers had. But consistent with research on married parents, these interviews suggest that fathers were more likely to be engaged with and accessible to their children than to take ultimate responsibility for their welfare.

Daniel, the father who said that men and women should take on the same role for raising children and share child care tasks, conceded, "Can't nobody raise a baby like a woman" because children become "more attached to a woman than a male. They gave birth and they breastfeed." He believed for a man to raise a child by himself he would have to be "real good at it." Fathers said that this attachment also created stronger emotional bonds with children. Joe observed, "The mother's love is unconditional . . . because the baby came from the mother. So there's more love there." But, at the same time, he agreed that if a father raised a child alone, he would probably develop this kind of love for the child.

Like other fathers, Michael said he was willing to perform nontraditional child care tasks for his son, but he acknowledged that he could only take care of his son for a few hours each week and believed that women naturally had more patience to perform these tasks:

> I consider myself a good father. I can take him. I bathe him. I change his diapers. I do everything I have to do, but I know that it would drive me crazy to do it every day and not work and spend all day with him. I can push him around. I walk him when he's at my house. I enjoy the one day I get with him. You know, I walk him around the neighborhood. He plays. I got certain toys at my house for him. I got a crib in my room for him. But after a while it would get to me doing this every day. I think there might be a little more bonding when you give birth to this child. Whereas, being a father, the child is there and is handed to you.

Fathers with varying levels of contact with their children used the mother–child bond as rationale for why they spent less time with their children than their mothers did. According to Salaam, a father who has regular contact with his children: "A mother is somebody there every day, not taking no break." When I asked him whether fathers should be there every day as well, he replied, "If it's possible, yeah. But if it's not possible, you can't help that. I mean you try to do your best. You know, nobody in this world's perfect." Similarly, Yusef, who sees his child on an irregular basis, explained that fathers have more discretion about how much time they spend with their children because they do not have the same kind of parental bond as mothers: "[To be] a good mother is like automatically time-consuming. That's what [being] a mother is. . . . A lot of men don't want to spend time with their child like that."

As custodial parents, the mothers I interviewed spent more time with their children than the fathers did, and often they preferred this arrangement. Some mothers, in fact, distinguished themselves from other mothers who were not willing to accept full-time responsibility for their children and "threw their children off on other people" to care for them. However, they objected to fathers who did not make an effort to share childrearing duties with them. Most of the mothers I interviewed said they wanted the father to be highly involved with their children, but often they took on the bulk of responsibility when help from the father was inadequate.

Because custodial mothers had a disproportionate share of the responsibility for children, they said they had to be concerned with all aspects of the environment in which their children were raised. Crystal thought that both the material and emotional environments in which children live reflect women's ability to be good mothers.

> If I was close to being a perfect mother, I wouldn't be living here. If I had the option of living here and living in a nice beautiful house with nice surroundings, I would choose that because the environment plays a big part in how your children grow up—what you're teaching them, what they're learning day by day, what the atmosphere's like, what's going on in the household. They pick up a lot; they take in a lot. That's why I never had an abusive relationship.

The accounts by custodial mothers also referred to the emotional and physical demands of taking care of children much more than did the accounts by men.[10] Because Lynn's former partner had psychological problems and was absent from their lives, she acted as the sole provider and caregiver for their three children. Lynn said that she, like many women, learned as a child that mothers did not get time off. Noting that she had gone out with friends only a few times during the year, she explained:

> It's really hard. It's really draining. Sometimes you can't get off by yourself, and you really need that. That's probably the single hardest thing is that you need sometimes to kind of replenish yourself and that doesn't always happen. I mean mothers don't get a day off.

Almost all the mothers I interviewed acted as the primary parent to their children, and most were concerned with the difference in efforts between mothers and fathers in fulfilling their parenting obligations. In fact, about two-thirds of the mothers I spoke with thought their child's father could do better (most of these mothers were no longer in a relationship with the father). If fathers continued to be involved with their children, mothers sometimes said that fathers put less care and thought into parenting than mothers do. One mother discussed the amount of time she spends picking out her daughter's clothes and making sure her bows, socks, and barrettes match. When her daughter visits her grandparents, the mother makes sure that her daughter has extra clothes, creams, medicines, and anything else she may need. In contrast, she constantly has to remind her daughter's father to take care of these kinds of details, noting that the difference between mothers and fathers is that "moms really put their heart and souls into it."

Although some mothers did not want their child's father to take their children overnight when they were newborns, mothers criticized fathers' unwillingness to spend more than a few hours with their older children. One mother observed that because "he's not with her twenty-four hours a day, he knows my child good, but not good enough like I know her." Therefore, she felt he was not familiar enough with their daughter's needs or how to satisfy them. Similarly, Debra said her children's father takes them to school almost every day and provides support but that he has "never been a real parent" and "doesn't know how to be one" because he has not cared for them on a daily basis.

When fathers were much less involved in their children's lives, mothers' cited stronger and more basic objections to differences in maternal and paternal effort. As noted in the last chapter, mothers were dissatisfied with fathers when they did not make an effort to support their child, when they spent money on themselves instead of on the child, when they had to be asked repeatedly to buy things, when they did not provide things in a reasonable amount of time, or when they supported someone else's child but not their own. Evette said she asked her son's father numerous times to get him the bike he wanted for Christmas. After many requests, the father eventually bought another, much cheaper bike, and she was left to purchase the bike her son wanted. This was just one example of the father's lack of effort to support their child. She explains:

> I say James [their son] need this, he need that. He always holler all right I'm gonna get it, I'm gonna get it. He don't never get it. When James come around he give him ten or twenty dollars but that's not enough. That's nothing to me. . . . When I really get on my feet and everything . . . I'm gonna make James give it back. And I'm gonna tell him, your little chump change and stuff you're giving him, you think that's all right, that's not all right. . . . I buy shoes, I buy clothes, and everything, I buy food, I buy everything. And all you can give him is give him a little ten or twenty dollars here and there and thinking that's all right. You know, that's not all right, you know. But I take it now because it helps.

Mothers with uninvolved fathers lamented the lack of equity in parental responsibilities, but they were often resigned to the fact that they were raising their children alone or with the help of a new partner. Laquana explained that her daughter's father denied paternity and has not tried to contact her:

He's no good. He seen her one time since she was born. He been in jail ever since. So, I don't even consider him as a father. Her father is my boyfriend. So, she don't need her daddy when he comes out of jail. He gonna see his girl upset and saying I don't have a daddy.

Rather than seeking ultimate responsibility for their child, Laquana described herself as accepting it by default.

Motives for Noninvolvement

What motives did parents cite as explanations for the divergence between ideal and actual paternal behavior? In particular, how did mothers make sense of fathers' decisions not to take sufficient time or make sufficient effort to participate in their children's lives? And how did fathers talk about their own lack of involvement?

A large body of research shows that departures from paternal responsibility occur when parents' romantic relationships end in a divorce or breakup (e.g., Furstenberg and Cherlin 1991). Some studies have documented justifications that nonresident fathers offer for not seeing or supporting their children in these situations (Hannerz 1969; Furstenberg 1992, 1995; Arendell 1995).[11] Furstenberg (1992, 1995, 2001) suggests that in low-income communities, unmarried parents' claims about why fathers do not support their children can be understood in terms of a "culture of distrust," as noted in chapter 2. According to Furstenberg, young men and women articulate and play out particular cultural scripts that reinforce negative views of the other gender. These scripts include expectations that women will be unreasonably demanding of men and that men will not keep commitments to their families. Women frame their experiences in terms of these expectations, and men anticipate and respond to women's disappointment and criticism.

Furstenberg finds that low-income fathers justify noninvolvement by denying paternity or claiming that another man has taken their place with his child, that the support is not going to the child, that they do not have the money to support the child, and that the mother does not let them see the child. In contrast, low-income mothers counter these arguments with their own explanations for fathers' nonsupport: men are spoiled and immature; men are unable to accept the responsibilities of fatherhood because of such things as fear, selfishness, or laziness; and men often had children before they were ready (Furstenberg 1992, 39–41; 1995, 133–136).

Arendell's (1995) research on divorced, higher-income fathers provides a useful comparison with Furstenberg's research on low-income parents. Although the parents with whom Arendell spoke were older, had all been married previously, and had more financial resources to support their children, they offer similar justifications for noninvolvement. Arendell examines how men draw on a "masculinist discourse of divorce" to justify their lack of involvement and to manage their emotions.

Like low-income fathers, these men report that their dissatisfaction also stemmed from specific conflicts with the mother of their children when they believed the mother hindered access to the children, denigrated the father in front of the children, instigated conflict, was uncooperative in legal matters, demanded additional money sometimes in exchange for access, and squandered the child support payments she received (Arendell 1995).[12] In a study of divorced mothers, Arendell (1986) finds that women often attribute decreased paternal involvement to changes in the father's personal and social life, particularly remarriage.[13]

Common Explanations

I asked mothers who reported limited paternal involvement and fathers who were dissatisfied with their involvement or were uninvolved to account for these outcomes.[14] Although mothers and fathers identified many common motives for noninvolvement, they often interpreted these motives from different perspectives and attributed blame to the other parent. I discuss parents' explanations for disengagement separately, but many of the problems they describe overlap and exacerbate each other.

Father Wasn't Ready to Have a Child

The parents I interviewed considered that not being ready for marriage was a legitimate explanation for staying single. After becoming a parent, however, it was unacceptable for mothers or fathers to say they were emotionally incapable of taking care of the child. Both mothers and fathers explained men's disengagement by saying they were unprepared or were immature when their child was born. However, fathers tended to talk about this retrospectively and not to characterize themselves as immature at the time of the interview. A twenty-three-year-old father who now considered himself responsible explained his motivations for noninvolvement at age eighteen:

> I guess it was the fact that I was young. Didn't want to get tied down too much. Still wanted to run around. And the fact that I was scared. You know,'cause I had no clue about what to do. Had no clue of my responsibilities or nothing like that. Had no clue that the baby depended on me, and, you know, just didn't know. I was scared, so I ran.

This father said he was ordered to participate in a responsible fatherhood program when he failed to pay child support. The program may have helped change his orientation toward fatherhood. Also, he may have tried to present himself in a good light during the interview by comparing his current involvement with his previous actions.

Julie's explanation, like those of other parents I interviewed, indicates that some men are inherently unable to accept the responsibilities of fatherhood. Mothers sometimes suggested that this inability was the result of a fundamental emotional deficit. Julie talked about how she came to terms with his incapacity to be involved with their daughter.

> I've had to take a long [time] to put the bitterness [behind]. I separated my personal life with him as opposed to her. He's not a father. He didn't choose to be a father. He tried, and I give him credit for that. He did make an attempt, and it wasn't him. And she was very uncomfortable with him, because it wasn't what he wanted. He loves her in his own way, but he can't do it. He's not cut out for it. . . . He's told me, "I love her. She's my child." But he can't be a father. He knows that [my boyfriend] is in her life now. And he knows that we have plans where he's going to adopt her. . . . I have told her natural father, "You're more than welcome to call me to see how she's doing." . . . He has not seen her since her second year. . . . He's made no attempt. He hasn't asked or called.

Although Julie's anger toward the father emerged a few times during our discussion, she used an explanation at hand—he wasn't cut out for fatherhood—to help her make sense of the father's behavior. The fact that her boyfriend acted as a father figure to her daughter and planned to adopt the daughter may also have helped her come to terms with the father's absence.

More often, mothers denounced the behavior of fathers who they believed were too immature to accept responsibility for their child after an unexpected pregnancy:

> I didn't feel him emotionally there for me, with this whole thing going on. . . . I don't think it seemed real to him yet, 'cause I wasn't really showing a lot. He never told his parents. And he's thirty-one years old. . . . [When she was born], my mom called his parents to let them know. And they came to the hospital the next day to see her. He never came . . . not a card. No. Just nothing from him. . . . I always just thought he would just help. Even if he didn't really want to see her and stuff, he would just help out and whatever. But, I don't know. He's a chicken. Like, he's very, very immature and very cowardly.

Some mothers said that fathers' actions showed they were not ready for parenthood even though they wanted recognition as a father. Rather than spend time with their children, these fathers preferred to spend most of their time with friends, running the streets, and seeing other women.

[My son] don't get to spend much time with him. He only get to see him once in a blue moon. My son always asking about him. And it more like the only thing I really could say to him is that, "We can call your grandmother and tell your grandmother to tell your dad this." . . . T [the father] is nice. T's not a father figure. [He's] not ready. He'd probably act like he was ready. Act all big, bad, tough like, daddy, daddy, daddy to his friends about his son or whatever. But as far as little T wanting to go live with him and having a chance to do all that—he don't have time. He's a street man. He like the streets a lot.

Parents Are in New Relationships

Both men and women said that paternal involvement might decrease if one parent became involved with a new partner. Men explained that their obligations to children in different households limited the amount of time and support they were able to offer each child and that mothers had difficulty understanding this complication. Situations such as these were especially problematic if one mother thought that the father showed favoritism toward a new child.

It's hard financially. And then with so much going on, it's hard to really spend time with them. And then it's the fact that I have three children by three different girls. You know what I mean? It's not like I'm with one girl, and we have a child, and I can be around that child every day. And this and that, this and that. So, it's kinda hard. It gets frustrating at times. Especially when the mothers don't want to act right and have a attitude about one thing and that carry over to the relationship between me and my kids. . . . One of them, she has two kids now, and one on the way. So, I guess she would love to have more financial support. And more of me being around my son. . . . My youngest son's [mother], she has four kids. So, she definitely would like more financial support and for me to be around him more. And it's, like, I tell them I have a family myself now. You know what I mean? I have a brand new daughter. So much of my time is with her. And they don't get too happy about that. (Joe)

In chapter 4, both men and women argued that fathers are obligated to their children, even when the mother or father starts a new family. However, putting these ideals into practice was often complicated when fathers were overwhelmed with responsibilities. From Joe's perspective, the mothers of his older children should accept that he has more to offer his baby who is living with him, while acknowledging that he is making a good faith effort to be involved with all of his children.

Some mothers said that fathers who start new families often forget about their prior obligations, leaving the mother to accept a disproportionate amount of responsibility for the child. Jean believes the father of her older two children who "just up and left" should be responsible for their support. She explained, however, that men feel they can walk away from their responsibilities when they get involved with someone else: "They're not the ones who carried that child around for nine months. They're not the ones who went through it alone. You know, they just found another girlfriend. And so be it."

According to the mothers I interviewed, fathers could also be resentful of mothers' new relationships. In these situations, fathers sometimes began withdrawing from their children and withholding support when they were jealous of the mother's new partner. Some mothers suggested that men used this as a strategy to "get back" at them.

> When I was pregnant, he bought all [the baby's] bottles. He bought lotion, powder, all that newborn stuff. You know, he bought that. He bought him Pampers. He bought him clothes. That was when [the baby] was first born, like the first month. After that he bought him a couple of outfits here and there. This is when . . . he lived right down the street from me. You know, he was doing a little here and there. But, when I got my friend, he really slowed down. But we wasn't going together then. And then I needed somebody to talk to. And my friend was there for me.

Policy Rules Discourage Involvement
Fathers reported that child support regulations prevented them from seeing their children because the laws exacerbate conflicts between parents. For example, some fathers who were trying to repay a large child support debt felt they did not have time to see their children. Brian said he had to hold down two jobs to pay his child support obligation. When he began seeing his children less often, the mother became angry and began to restrict access to them. He explained: "I'm not there to be with the kids the way I wanna be. And I'm more into worrying about what's going on with welfare. And that's what's really on my mind."

Mothers agreed that policy rules, particularly child support enforcement, sometimes encouraged the father to withdraw and withhold financial support. Beth said she had been unsure about pursuing child support because she was afraid the father might file for custody so that he would not have to pay the award. At the same time, she believed the father had an obligation to pay and should not "get off scot-free." When the child support order was initiated, the father cut off contact and informal contributions:

> My mom's opinion is, that maybe that's why he did that [cut off support]; so, he could be, like, "Well, I didn't have anything to do with her because [he was unsure of paternity]." And he was scheduled on the eighteenth of August to go [to court]. And I just found out a couple days ago that he's been rescheduled 'till the fifteenth of September. And I don't know why. So my mom's, like, "Well, maybe he's trying to get out of the country or something."

Fathers also explained that formal visitation and custody agreements prevented them from having more contact with their children. Men often believed that these agreements were biased toward women. In fact, some fathers who wanted custody thought that to be granted this request they would have to prove the mother unfit. Jared described his constraints on visitation:

> She had to go on welfare. I had to pay . . . child support and stuff. Then she took me to court, and it was [for] visitation. I get him every other weekend. She gets him all the holidays. She asked for all the holidays and everything. Judge gave it to her . . . the system nowadays is totally, totally gung ho for the female on this. . . . She took me to court. It's terrible. [Laughs] Every other weekend I get him.

Jared explained that legal restrictions on contact are compounded by the mother's tendency to become angry and restrict access to his son when he has problems complying with the visitation schedule.

Father Is Unsure of Paternity

Some parents said that uncertainty about paternity contributed to fathers' lack of participation in their children's lives.[15] Jake explained that he was seeing a woman casually when she got pregnant. Because she was receiving welfare, he was ordered to pay child support. Although Jake spoke to the mother occasionally, he had no relationship with the child because he doubted he was the father.

> It was kind of a torrid affair, you know? I was just whoring around myself, and she was, like, sleeping around. And we didn't even know, I still don't know, if it's my son . . . but, needless to say, she moved away anyway. And she always wanted to have my baby. So, I think she just picked me. You know what I mean?

Jake said it was "totally irresponsible" of him not to take a blood test to determine whether he was the father. When asked whether his relationship with the boy would be different if he knew it was his son, Jake replied indignantly, "Of course."

Alicia was dating her son's father for more than a year when she became pregnant. According to Alicia,

> In the beginning, when I first told him I was pregnant, he didn't want to believe that [it] was his. . . . And I said, "Look, when she's born, we have a blood test." And he was, like, "No, no, I believe it's [ours]." But deep down I know [he's] saying it just to shut me up, 'cause I was just going off.

Alicia thought that the father raised questions about paternity to justify his decision not to be more involved with their daughter. As long as he refused to take a blood test, he could hold on to his doubts and use them as an excuse for noninvolvement that would be legitimate to himself, his friends, and his family.

Fathers' Explanations

Fathers offered reasons for disengagement that were distinct from those of mothers. Typically, these explanations attributed a father's lack of participation to a mother who assumed a gate-keeping role, which, they believed, obstructed access to their child. Other fathers, however, simply explained their access problems as a result of living apart from their child.[16]

Child Lives in a Different Household

Many fathers who lived apart from their child talked about problems scheduling time with them. Men often described a no-win situation. Sometimes mothers were not home when the fathers were scheduled to pick up or drop off the child, but these same mothers did not tolerate the fathers being late. Some mothers complained when fathers did not take their children enough and also when fathers took their children too much. William, who had been living with the mother and their daughter but recently had moved out, described how his new living arrangements prevented him from spending time with his daughter:

> I argued with her [the mother] today because I wanted my daughter, and she said yeah. And at the last minute, it's like: "No, I'm not bringing her out there to you." She just didn't want to right now. And she said I could come get her later or whatever. I said: "Look, I want her now. I want more time with her." 'Cause she like to bring her to me, or if I go get her she says

[to] bring her back by a certain time—which'll be like two or three hours. You know, I'd like more time with her.

Other fathers explained that they were constrained from spending more time with their child because they were living with other people in crowded houses or apartments. These fathers hoped to become more involved when they could afford housing that had space for a child.

I wish it could be a little better. I wish I had my own place. If I had my own place, then I could really, I'd be all right. Then I could spend time, and he could stay with me as much as I want. You know? I'm not saying my grandmother don't let him stay there or nothing like that. But, it's better, you know, [being] together. A man and his son sitting around in boxers all day. You know what I'm saying? It's just like men. Their bond. You know what I'm saying? That's something I can't do with him.

Mother Restricts Access When She Is Angry
Another reason fathers often gave, in addition to that of living apart from their child, was that they had difficulty being more involved because the mother was angry at them and trying to retaliate, because the mother was playing games with them, or simply because the mother had an "attitude problem." Andre, whose extended account of why biological fathers have a responsibility for their children was quoted in chapter 4, explained the reason he was out of contact with his youngest child. During his relationship with the mother, the couple had lived together and Andre had assumed responsibility for watching their child while the mother worked. However, since their breakup, they had had an antagonistic relationship. He explained:

She's still being ignorant and disrespectful. . . . From the time we went together to the time we broke up, all I been trying to do is communicate. Look, I told her, "Just because we got a problem between me and you, [you should] let my son get to know me. Let him get to know who his father is so when he come up he has someone to look up to." She just didn't want to hear that, 'cause, like I said, last time I spoke to her was about a month ago. I asked her could I see my son. She told me no. Hung up the phone on me.

Andre said that the mother may also be trying to "get back at him" for cheating on her: "But all it doing is hurting my son." He also acknowledged that he "snapped on her one time" and began choking her when he saw her boyfriend holding his son. Although he quickly "came to his senses," he said that he intentionally stayed away because he was afraid of his own response. At the same time, he attributed his inability to control his anger to her behavior.

So I just stay away from her. Don't think I'm a woman beater or nothing like that. It took a lot to get me angry with her. She already reached my point. She stopped me from seeing my pride and joy, which is my son. And she know how I feel when my son was born. I was there, I seen my son come out. Nothing is harder on a man when I saw my son [being held by another man].

Andre said the mother ignored the three letters the court had sent to schedule mediation. Although he held the mother responsible for not letting him see their child and said he does not want to send money to her if he doesn't know how it's being spent, Andre's account suggests that he has had a hard time reconciling his behavior with his idea of responsible fatherhood.

In a few extreme cases, fathers were completely out of contact with their children and did not know where they lived. Sonny, for example, saw his children from a previous marriage regularly but had no contact with his two children born outside of marriage, one of whom he had never seen. (Sonny did not acknowledge that he had any children born outside of marriage until midway through the interview.) Sonny presumed that the mothers and their families did not want to see him and used this belief to justify noninvolvement. The responsibility he assumed for the children he had fathered while married allowed him to put his obligation to his nonmarital children out of his mind. In response to my question about whether he planned to contact his nonmarital children in the future and whether it was difficult to be out of touch, he explained:

I go through things in cycles. I'll attack things for a while then I'll lay back for a while. So possibly if I sit down one day and I'm really not doing anything, and it really starts bugging me, yeah perhaps I may. But until [then], I'm not gonna disappoint myself. . . . It's been hard to a point and then again it's not. Because, you know, I have four other kids. And when you're working, taking care of a house, taking care of four kids, you really don't have time to think about anything else. It's hard enough to remember that I have to do laundry on Saturday, that I gotta go out and buy fifteen boxes of cereal to feed these animals. . . . You don't have time to think about a whole lot of other things in your life.

Mother Restricts Access When the Father Doesn't Have Money
Some fathers explained that their child's mother required them to bring money or gifts whenever they wanted to see their child. Fathers who could not regularly provide these things said they were prevented from seeing their children. According to these fathers, mothers blamed them for not providing enough support but often did not understand the financial constraints.

I don't see my youngest son as much, because me and his mom don't get along. . . . She wants money every time when she see me. She want money. She want money. She want money. If I don't have no money, I can't see him. I can't deal with that. So, it's like, I see him when he goes to school. I give him a hug, and I chat with him just before he goes in the school. And I say, "Dad is right down the street." And that's as far as I can go until she straighten out. As long as she acting like she is that, it stop me from being around him.

Fathers said that women sometimes pressured them to come up with money immediately or demanded more than they could provide. Furthermore, several suggested that mothers not only are "petty" and "immature" but also often imprudent in their requests.

I don't know how the judge feels it's gonna work, but the way it works around here [is] if you don't buy your kids nothing, you gonna be hearing from their mother all day. It's gonna be like: "You don't care about your kids."

Salaam argued that mothers did not understand how difficult it was for men to get a job and that when they worked, their wages were garnished for child support. At the same time, he thought that women were often spending the welfare and child support money they received on themselves instead of on their children: "Most females around here with kids that lives in the 'hood, all they worry about is theyselves. I get me dressed up, worry about the kid later." Claiming that he knows whether or not the mother of his child has legitimate requests, he said:

If the child happen to run out of Pampers or baby food, wherever I'm at, she either come find me and be like "the baby need food" or "the baby need Pampers." But at the same time the baby really don't be needing. She just be wanting me to push the money off on her, so she can do what she want with the money. And it get to the point where as though I have to walk off sometimes or say I'll be over to bring it. And she might say, "Well you ain't got to bring it. Just give me the money and I'll go get it." Then, right then and there, you know really the baby doesn't really need [it].

The Mother Deceived the Father

A small group of fathers explained their behavior toward a child by pointing out their lack of control over how the pregnancy had been resolved, especially when they believed the mother had deceived them. Stanley had had an affair with his child's mother while he was engaged to another woman. Although he now had an emotional relationship with his son, Stanley acknowledged that he had not had contact with him for a period of time and still did not pay child support. He thought his resistance to paying child support was justifiable because he had been deceived by the mother and forced into parenthood.

> It was, like, forced upon me. I live close to the housing projects. A lot of my friends live around there. And being around them and seeing my family, like at home. I see where a single parent goes through a lot. And then, no matter what anyone says, it's hard growing up without a father. And I always wanted not [to] have a child until I got married. Or at least know that we'll be together for the rest of our lives. And [she] stopped taking her pills. She got pregnant, and I wanted her to get an abortion. I was gonna take her to get one. And then she said her sister was gonna take her. So, I gave her the money and she ran away. . . . [When] she came home, she was seven months' pregnant. So, you know, it was sort of like thrown upon me.

He also appealed to a more conventional, middle-class sensibility by implying that having a child with a woman from the projects had destroyed his plans to form a family with his college-educated fiancée.

*   *   *

The men I interviewed seemed to derive their positive sense of themselves as fathers by comparing themselves with what they believed was the typical father, that is, someone who was uninvolved with or did not make an effort to care for his children. Because mothers evaluated fathers' behavior in comparison with their own, they regarded good fathers as those who put as much effort into parenting as they did. Although the parents I interviewed often held negative images of fathers in their community and in the larger society, they gave more positive evaluations to themselves, the fathers of their children, and other fathers they knew personally. This result suggests that parents may accept derogatory public images of unmarried fathers while at the same time making careful distinctions between them and men they are able to evaluate through personal experience.

Both mothers and fathers often endorsed some differences in parental duties. Fathers, however, often naturalized imbalances in maternal and paternal responsibility, whereas mothers attributed this imbalance to a father's lack of effort. Similarly, mothers and fathers often identified similar motives for paternal disengagement, but they interpreted these motives from different perspectives. Parents' accounts suggest that many of the problems they described overlap and exacerbate one another. Some of the common motives that parents cited to explain a father's lack of involvement include the father not wanting a child or being unready for the pregnancy, the mother or father starting a new relationship, conflict caused by child support and visitation rules, and uncertainty about paternity. Fathers said that their involvement was also constrained by living apart from their child and by mothers who restricted contact with the father or demanded money in exchange for access. Other fathers chose to limit their involvement with their child because the mother had deceived them about the pregnancy. Parents' attempts to make sense of their experiences mirror a larger vocabulary of motives used by resident mothers and nonresident fathers. These explanations resemble both the cultural scripts that Furstenberg documents among low-income men and women and the masculinist discourse of divorce that Arendell describes among higher-income fathers.

As I illustrated in previous chapters, the mothers and fathers in this study value paternal involvement. They also hold strong, collective ideas about paternal responsibility. As other studies show, departures from paternal responsibility occur when romantic relationships between mothers and fathers end. Because the mothers and fathers I interviewed had different expectations of how parental responsibilities should be shared and held negative beliefs about the other gender, they may have been less able to negotiate paternal involvement when their relationships eroded and when economic resources were extremely limited. The analysis in the next chapters examines the formal and informal strategies used to accept paternal responsibility and illustrates what happens when mothers deem paternal efforts to be insufficient.

CHAPTER SIX

Recognizing Biological and Social Paternity

A father is not the person who gets the [woman] pregnant. The father is the person who takes care of their baby, is there for the baby through all the emotional [things], through every little thing from changing diapers to buying whatever the baby needs. That's what a father really is. Anybody can have a baby, but to not be there—I wouldn't consider that person a father. If you're not there, then that's not your kid. Don't go saying that's your kid if you're not there taking care of the baby. (Stanley)

Previous chapters have documented how unmarried parents in New Jersey define collective beliefs about paternal responsibility and evaluate fathers on the basis of these standards. Chapters 6 and 7 turn to the practices by which these parents express these beliefs and apply their standards of evaluation. These chapters also consider how unmarried parents' collective beliefs and informal practices interact with formal paternity establishment and child support regulations.

These regulations emerged in response to sharp increases in nonmarital births, the high incidence of poverty among families headed by unmarried mothers, and the small proportion of these families who have a child support order. According to these regulations, unmarried mothers must establish legal paternity for their children before receiving child support. In an attempt to make more children eligible for child support, new federal legislation requires states to increase paternity establishment rates to 90 percent.

This large-scale effort to establish paternity for children born outside of marriage is a relatively new phenomenon.[1] To better understand unmarried parents' responses to legal paternity establishment and child support, this chapter examines informal methods these parents have developed to recognize biological, emotional, and economic relationships between unmarried fathers and their children, because these practices may predate and mediate recent governmental efforts in regard to paternity. The chapter also examines the significance of these extralegal practices, which are part of parents' cultural repertories. After examining cases in which men contested, and later resolved, questions of paternity, I describe practices by which fathers acknowledged their biological paternity and took social responsibility for their child.

Contesting and Resolving Paternity
Establishing Paternity in Low-Income Communities

> When it really gets rough, the guy can always say, 'How do I know it's my child?' And what can a woman say when she knows? It's different because she watches her stomach grow. It's the strangest feeling, to feel another human being inside of you. And a man never feels that. They never know. It's like a shoot of cum, and that's it. They never know that it's a part of them, like a woman does.

How typical is it for unmarried fathers to deny their children when things "get rough"? If paternity is denied, how is the identity of the father resolved? Previous qualitative studies indicate that the majority of poor fathers who live apart from their children informally accepted biological paternity. However, these fathers typically did not establish legal paternity through the child support system (Liebow 1967; Rainwater 1970; Sullivan 1989; Furstenberg 1995). Rainwater's (1970) research on family life in a St. Louis housing project, for example, illustrates how paternity establishment was a "collaborative endeavor" involving young mothers, fathers, their families, and their peer groups. Rainwater notes that fathers made small economic contributions to establish their paternity symbolically and to accept children into their kinship network. However, Anderson (1989, 66) suggests that paternity is commonly denied by young, impoverished, African American fathers and that their peers support this behavior.

When asked about the prevalence of denying paternity, the parents I spoke with disagreed about how frequently this happened. Consistent with most previous research, however, these parents agreed that acknowledging paternity informally (that is, to families, friends, or neighborhoods) was more common than establishing a legal connection between unmarried fathers and their children. Recognizing biological paternity was also more common than accepting social responsibility for the children, or social paternity. As Mariah pointed out, "most guys be proud of 'having a baby,' but you don't tell everybody [when] you ain't taking care of the baby."

The parents I spoke with described cases in which men denied paternity as well as those in which women falsely accused men of fathering their children. Joe said, "I've heard plenty of people say: 'You better tell your mommy to stop lying, I'm not your dad.'" When asked why this happens, he explained, "This is a cruel, cruel world. And Trenton, especially Trenton, it just takes your heart away. I mean, you become so hard and so cold living around here, because it's hard and cold around here period."

Parents speculated that paternity was more likely to be contested when men wanted to avoid responsibility, when women had many sexual partners, or when women wanted to "pin" paternity on men they thought would support their child. Women also described strategies to reduce the likelihood that their partners would deny their children. These strategies included staying in monogamous relationships, getting to know the father's family, and making sure they knew the last name, address, and (sometimes) the Social Security number of men they were involved with. Because parents gave conflicting assessments of how often paternity was disputed in their communities, I turn to parents' accounts of their own experiences to document how paternity was contested and resolved.

Evidence of Paternity

Approximately 5 percent of the parents I spoke with said their child's paternity was in question at the time of the interview. Another 22 percent of fathers, however, had initially questioned their paternity and had sought evidence to establish it firmly.[2] According to fathers, men who had doubts about paternity were strongly influenced by the quality of their relationship with the mother. In particular, if a man and woman were not in a committed and trusting relationship before the pregnancy, fathers said they were more likely to doubt the mother.[3] In these instances, fathers said they considered such factors as the number of sexual partners the mother had had and her possible motives for making a false paternity claim. Andre explained why he discounted a claim of paternity made by a woman with whom he had had a casual relationship and whom he did not know well:

A: I never denied none of my kids. I only have two. You know people claim they been pregnant by me and all. I'm like, "Get out of here. How can you be pregnant [if I'm] wearing a cap? It didn't bust." Well sometimes I didn't, I'm not gonna lie. But they were no more pregnant than [me] sitting here now.

M: So there was no baby?

A: Nah. She claim she got a little girl by me, which I doubt very serious, because she didn't show me no kind of proof—no proof in the world. I'm like, if you have a child by me, show me the birth certificate or show me a picture or something of the little girl.

Andre argued that, absent any type of physical evidence, he could not view the mother's claim as legitimate. When he asked mutual acquaintances to find out whether the child existed, he said that no one reported seeing her. Andre assumed the mother was lying about having a child and that her motivation was to extract money from him.

When there was real ambiguity about paternity, fathers considered other forms of evidence to assess the validity of the woman's claims. The main proof that parents looked to was physical resemblance between the father and the child.[4] Some fathers said that the resemblance between themselves and the child convinced them of their paternity. More often, fathers described resemblance as a constraint on denial, sometimes joking that the child "looks like me, so I couldn't deny him if I wanted to." Ashley described how her daughter's father responded to the news of her pregnancy: "He was, like, totally shocked, and he said it wasn't his. And I was, like, 'You, jerk-off!' But, we found out that it was, 'cause she looks just like him." African American parents in Trenton suggested that physical resemblance was also accepted as evidence of paternity in their neighborhoods, making it difficult for fathers to deny the biological connection to their children.

In the past, when juries in paternity cases assessed evidence of physical resemblance between the child and the alleged father, they considered whether a baby's features had "settled."[5] Similarly, parents I interviewed said resemblance may not be immediately apparent to fathers but that often it becomes clearer as the child grows older. One African American father stated that he had refrained from putting his name on the birth certificate until the child was one month old. The mother was seeing another man at the time of the pregnancy, and the baby had a complexion much lighter than his own. He explained, "I wasn't sure about it. Soon as he started getting a little darker, that's when I said 'Yeah, he look just like me.' Got the pictures of him. So I signed it."

For men able to come to terms with fatherhood, physical evidence might be highly convincing. However, men who were not ready for fatherhood might use a lack of physical evidence as a justification for noninvolvement. In one instance, James suggested that physical resemblance, coupled with other evidence, was convincing to him: "I didn't think he was mines. Then he was born; he looked just like me." In another situation, however, James did not accept paternity for an eleven-year-old girl. Although the mother said he might be the father, and he believed the girl bore some resemblance to his own father, he said there was no other evidence of his paternity. Furthermore, James explained that the man the mother lived with thought it was his daughter, and he did not want to "mess anything up" for them now by raising the question. "It's been so long, and she has a father," James concluded.

Parents usually regarded physical resemblance as compelling but not conclusive proof of paternity. Many parents warned that "appearances can be deceiving" and told stories of men who supported children who seemed to look like them, only to find out later that they were not the biological fathers. If men seriously doubted they were the fathers, they usually took a blood or genetic test to resolve a contested paternity.[6] Only three mothers I interviewed reported that the father of their child had denied paternity, but all said the father had requested proof in the form of a paternity test. Two of the three mothers reported that these fathers had been certain of their paternity but had taken the test in an unsuccessful attempt to avoid paying child support.

> I was really angry when the day actually came and I saw what she [the baby] went through. I was furious, and trust me, I let him know no two ways about it when he showed up for the test. Because he knew damn well that child was his, and he tried every trick in the book to say it wasn't. (Julie)

All of these women resented having to put their child through the turmoil of an unnecessary paternity test. The mothers who had gone through this experience had highly antagonistic relationships with the father and did not want him involved in their child's life.

Only one father I interviewed reported taking a paternity test, and he admitted he did so to escape a child support order. However, Jake, a respondent who was unsure of his paternity at the time of the interview, said he regretted having waived the opportunity to take a paternity test. As a result, a default order for child support was issued.

Acknowledging Biological Paternity

In contrast to fathers who questioned their paternity, about three-quarters of fathers immediately acknowledged it to their child's mother. In addition, fathers used widely recognized gestures and symbols to convey their biological connection to their children. Fathers could publicly acknowledge the child to their families, friends, and the community, put their name on the birth certificate, and give the child their surname. They could also legally establish fatherhood by voluntarily signing a declaration of paternity. Dramatizing their acceptance of paternity also implied a moral obligation for men to act as fathers and to be treated as such (Goffman 1959). My interviews with parents suggest that collective ideas about paternal responsibility gave parents ways to think about and coordinate informal strategies of establishing paternity (Mills 1940).

Public Acceptance of Paternity

According to parents' accounts, most men publicly accepted paternity during the mother's pregnancy by talking to other people about becoming a father, beginning to buy things for the child, or, in some instances, having sympathetic morning sickness. I first interviewed Anna when she was pregnant. She described how her boyfriend publicly acknowledged he was becoming a father: "When he sees one of his friends on the street, and we're walking, he's like, 'I'm expecting.' And I'm like, 'I'm expecting, not you.' They're like, 'Got a bun in the oven, huh?'" Another mother remembered, "My baby's father, like when I was pregnant, they knew I was pregnant, because they went through the symptoms. Like my youngest baby's father, he was sick; he went through the symptoms for me." She described the father as having frequent headaches and stomach pains and recalls, "I used to think it was so funny. [I] said, 'Uh huh, I'm not the only one going through this.'" Tricia described ways in which men displayed paternity after the baby was born: "[They're] always talking about 'my baby.' 'Got pictures of the baby.' 'I'm getting this for my baby.' 'My baby this, my baby that.' Taking them to the park. Hanging out with the guys with your baby. Sometimes [fathers] go a little bit overboard."

Fathers who did not publicly recognize paternity were typically indicating that they did not want to be involved in their child's life. Alicia said that her child's father initially rejected her claim because he was involved in another relationship during her pregnancy. Although she encouraged him to take a paternity test, he chose to withdraw from their daughter rather than recognize her publicly.

He's still got that thought that it's not his; so that's how come he's not doing much, not really taking an interest and coming by to see her. Or he didn't even bother to call on Easter. He didn't even want to let his parents know that he had a daughter. Everything was hush-hush, top secret. His co-workers didn't even know until I brought her in that day at work. (Alicia)

The Birth Certificate

Parents regarded the act of putting the father's name on the birth certificate as an important way of signifying the biological connection between fathers and their children and of indicating men's plans for future involvement. More than 80 percent of fathers in this study came to the hospital when their child was born, and about 70 percent of parents said that the father's name appeared on the birth certificate of their youngest child. In cases in which fathers did not appear at the hospital, parents indicated that they had either ended their relationship or the father was incarcerated. According to parents' accounts, when fathers came to the hospital but did not put their name on the birth certificate, all but one did so to avoid a child support order. In the FFCW study, approximately 78 percent of unmarried mothers said their child's father visited them in the hospital at the time of the birth, a figure comparable to my finding of 80 percent. But in the FFCW study, 86 percent of mothers said the father's name would be on the birth certificate (this had not yet happened when they were interviewed in the hospital), compared with my finding of 70 percent.[7]

The majority of fathers who put their name on the birth certificate thought they did so at the risk of incurring an obligation to child support.[8] When discussing the decision to put the father's name on the birth certificate, parents pointed to both the emotional and the practical significance that they believed a birth certificate has to children later in life. According to parents' accounts, the birth certificate satisfied children's need to know that the father was there at the time of the birth and was willing to claim them.

> Children today, they don't want to grow up not knowing who their real father is. Like I said before, the other children will be bringing their father up in life. Then when they can't respond, they feel bad. They just don't like it. It may upset them to the point some of them may get in trouble. Or they might just be rebellious to their mother all the time. (Robert)

Parents suggested that having the father's name on the birth certificate gave the child a sense of identity. They also pointed out that should the child be separated from his or her natural father, the name on the certificate would allow the child to find him later.

Furthermore, parents argued that putting the father's name on the birth certificate carried a moral message that the father was a responsible person. Commenting on how children might evaluate their father's character if his name were absent, Lisa observed:

Any child would want to look on their birth certificate and say, "Wow, my dad signed my birth certificate." I think it would hurt a child later to see in life that "Dang, my daddy didn't even have the decency to put his name on my birth certificate. Dang, I wonder what kind of dad I had?"

Parents also noted that this act represented the father's interest in sharing responsibility with the mother of the child. As one mother said, "I think if they willing to take that responsibility, they need to go through it all, just as I am going through it."

As shown in previous chapters, parents criticized fathers who denied paternity and frequently referred to fathers who knowingly did so as being "less than men." Larry agreed with this remark. Although he acknowledged that the birth certificate could create a problem with child support, he argued, "I wouldn't dare have 'unknown' on my son's birth certificate. Birth certificates are forever." Kareen began to question the decision to put his name on the birth certificate after he was jailed for nonpayment of support, but he believed that the decision was an important way of making a commitment to his child.

I see it as being more truthful with yourself. That's one of the first steps of being a father. Not that it plays a really important role, but it might later on in life. But for now I see it as being, just being more truthful with yourself. 'Cause in order for you to sign something saying that it's yours, you got to be willing to take that responsibility.

Naming

Giving the father's surname to the child was another way of fathers publicly recognizing paternity and making an early symbolic commitment to the child. As with the act of including the father's name on the birth certificate, parents said that this practice often indicated that the father planned to play an active part in the child's life.[9] Approximately two-thirds of fathers and half of mothers I interviewed reported that their youngest child had been given the father's last name. This figure is lower than that in the FFCW survey, in which 81 percent of unmarried mothers planned to give their child the father's last name when asked about this at the time of birth.[10]

In a conversation about how Bayshawn and his girlfriend chose to give their son his surname, he commented that the child "was getting that regardless. . . . It carries my father on, and it's carrying me on now, and hopefully he'll carry it on if he has a son." However, Bayshawn cautioned that men should not give the child their last name or put their name on the birth certificate without thinking about the implications: "When you sign your name, that's like signing your life, 'cause that's a part of you now." Many parents who decided to give their son the father's last name also wanted to give him the father's first name, so that firstborn sons would become "juniors." As with the birth certificate, parents suggested that the last name could have emotional significance for children. According to Daniel, "When they growing up and they realize what their last name is, it make them feel good, make them happy."

Among the majority of couples in committed relationships, giving the child the father's surname sometimes indicated that they intended to stay together and, possibly, marry. Anthony, who lived with the mother of his child, explained the decision to give their daughter his last name: "I wanted her to have my last name anyway, 'cause Ann gonna have my last name when we get married. So, the baby already have it instead of changing it over." Ann supported this statement and added that the last name may make their relationship closer. A small number of white parents also indicated that the notion that "the child has a name" conferred social legitimacy on him or her.[11]

Because parents often assumed that the last name carried legal weight, some women were reluctant to give their child the father's name because they believed this act would entitle him to gain custody of the child. In general, women who had unstable or antagonistic relationships with the father at the time of the birth chose to give the child the mother's last name. In a few cases, this decision created conflict with fathers who had wanted the child to have their surname. However, other couples with more amiable relationships, or couples less concerned about custody issues, decided to give the child the father's last name precisely because they believed that doing so facilitated the receipt of economic benefits from the father. Marion remarked:

> Keeping my last name is not going to make things any different to me. Them having their father's last name—if something was to happen to their father, they would get his Social Security. If anything happened to me, they'd get it anyway because I'm their mother. The three of them—their lifestyle could put them in a risk factor for being killed or being hurt permanently in some kind of way. So I think it was a good idea to go ahead and do that [give her children their father's last name].

Similarly, Janet explained that when the father of her oldest child was shot in gang activity, "Like, I wasn't expecting for my son's father to die. So, it's like, now he's gonna get taken care of for the rest of his life, and that name played a big part in it." This concern was not mentioned by white parents, who generally lived in less crime-ridden neighborhoods.

Establishing Legal Paternity

Paternity establishment can be accomplished voluntarily or by the state, and it is necessary if a mother is to obtain a child support order.[12] This legal relationship allows children born outside of marriage access to Social Security and medical benefits from their father as well as information about the family's medical history.[13] When I asked parents if they had established paternity, most indicated that they did not know what it meant to be legally recognized as the father and were not sure if they had gone through this process. In fact, parents typically thought "paternity establishment" meant taking a paternity test. Because paternity establishment was a prerequisite for issuing a child support order, all parents with an order had established paternity. Although this group constituted at least 45 percent of the sample, few of these parents understood this legal process or the rights and obligations it incurred. Anthony's response about whether he had established paternity during his visit to family court was similar to that of many other parents: "I signed a couple papers. I don't know what they were."

Before the welfare reform legislation of 1996, unmarried fathers were not required to sign a legal declaration of paternity in order to put their name on the birth certificate. Although some in-hospital paternity establishment programs had been created at the time of this study, my interviewees typically established paternity before a hearing officer in the process of setting up a child support order.[14] Parents were often receptive to creating this kind of legal relationship, but most believed they had done so by putting the father's name on the birth certificate or giving the child the father's last name. As one father explained, "I figure once you put that [his name] on paper, and once you establish that, then nobody can really take that away from you." Those fathers who came to the hospital and did not put their name on the birth certificate typically said they were trying to avoid a legal relationship that would incur a child support obligation. O'Shen advised other men, "If you do sign it, and she gets welfare, you in trouble. Bottom line. Your name is already in that computer." Fathers who chose not to put their name on the birth certificate to avoid a child support order typically did not give the child their surname.

Accepting Social Fatherhood

Although parents acknowledged that recognizing biological paternity was a necessary step for fathers to become involved in their child's life, they said that accepting social paternity represented a much higher level of commitment. Like other social roles (Goffman 1959, 15), the role of social father can be thought of as an enactment of rights and duties associated with men's status as fathers.

Paternity as a Reciprocal Process of Recognition

Parents described social paternity as a process of mutual recognition that was negotiated between the father and mother and between the father and child.[15] A man acknowledging social paternity had to *act* like a father to be recognized as such by the mother, his child, or the community. Unlike the case with biological paternity, which can be mandated through paternity establishment regulations, parents argued that acknowledging social paternity required fathers to make a voluntary commitment to care for their children. Because parents believed that social fatherhood derived from a father's love for the child or his sense of moral obligation, it represented a more authentic commitment than simply recognizing a biological connection to the child. It also implied a sustained agreement to be involved in the child's life, which, parents argued, cannot be "forced." When discussing this reciprocal process of recognition, parents distinguished between ascribed and achieved fatherhood:

> Just because you made a child doesn't mean you're a good father or a dad. . . . [A good father will] be there to tuck your child in at night or to pat your child on the back or to throw that ball to your son when he need somebody to throw a ball to them. Or if he want to play catch in the park, take them to the park. Or to just take them for a walk to the store. Or just be a man, show them how to use the bathroom. You know. Stuff like that. (Keisha)

According to the parents I interviewed, fathers initially sought the recognition of their child's mother. However, if men did not recognize biological or social paternity, mothers might actively withhold recognition in order to influence men's behavior. Chastity described how she negotiated recognition with her boyfriend:

> He says, "Is that my kid?" And it gets me to the point where I tell him, "That's not your kid," just to shut him up. And now he's the one arguing back. It's reverse psychology. He's the one who argues back, "That's my kid. Don't tell me it's not my kid."

She explained that she would not fully recognize her boyfriend as the father until he fulfilled her expectations: "I'm putting 'father unknown' on the birth certificate until the day I decide whether or not he's worthy enough to call himself a father." She continued, "The baby will have my last name. I said, 'If after two years I decide you're a good enough father, I will change it.' He didn't like that." She said that an alternate scenario would be: "The baby will have my last name until the day I get married, then whoever I marry will adopt my child. And he got mad, but he agreed." Because fathers suggested that the mother's recognition of them as the father was important to them, mothers could use it to negotiate informal support and visitation agreements.

Stanley described a similar kind of struggle for recognition from a father's perspective. Illustrating the reciprocal nature of paternity, he talked about what it meant for him to be recognized as a father who accepted responsibility for his son: "She tried to say it wasn't my son, which I knew it was, 'cause he look like my baby picture—if you take my baby picture and put it in color." He explained that his son's mother began to deny that he was the father and to insist that their son's last name should be changed back to hers. Stanley, in turn, argued that they take a paternity test to resolve the issue.

> Now I could have been just like one of those fathers and said, "Fine, no problem. He ain't mines. See ya later." But see, one thing always stuck in my mind. My mom always told me, if you mess up your bed, lie in it. And what she mean by that is, if you get somebody pregnant . . . take care of your problem . . . 'cause that was part of me. I didn't want nobody else taking care of my son besides me.

Parents observed that fathers must later win the recognition of their child to be considered a social father. Importantly, parents believed that fathers might be hurt eventually if they did not recognize their child because the child will one day return the favor by not acknowledging them. Many fathers describe their child's refusal to recognize them as a painful, but justified, attack on their character.

> If her baby's father came up there and heard that baby calling the other guy "daddy," it would cut him to the heart knowing that it's not. How is that gonna feel, just knowing that she's calling somebody else daddy. Just the feeling, you know? (Tricia)

Simone observed that men could not be forced to accept paternity but that "a good man will own up to his." She believed that when a father did not accept social paternity, it "makes him look stupid. 'Cause you got a child out there that needs you and depends on you, and you're not doing nothing for them. The child's gonna grow up to hate him." Supporting these accounts, Marion added that fathers have to be involved in their children's lives at an early age to gain recognition. After a certain point, she believed that it became "too late" to enter, and the child could refuse him.

> If he never sees him, he would probably hate him. He might hate him; but then again, he might love his father. But there will be a barrier where, "You can't just be my father now. I needed you back when, you know. And this is my stepfather."

Andre also described a situation in which a father "came back trying to be that figure. [The son] told his father, 'You ain't my dad. You ain't been around all this time. Who are you to take care of me?' And his father couldn't say nothing. And, see, I don't want to be in that predicament with my youngest son." Although Andre attributed his own absence from his child to the mother, he expressed a great deal of anxiety about not being recognized by his son as the social father:

> I had a dream one night that he [my son] said that to me. I had told him to come here. I had seen him, I'm like, "Come here, come here." And he, like, "No, no, no." And finally I got a hold of him. I said, "Why didn't you come when I told you to?" He said, "You ain't my dad." I'm like, "Oh yeah?" It's a dream though. I said, "Why you say that?" He said, "'Cause you wasn't there when I needed you." And I looked at him and it hurt me. And I started explaining it to him, and then I woke up. I explained that, "It's not my fault, it's your mom's fault. Your mom took you away from me. I didn't leave. I didn't run away." (Andre)

Indicators of Social Fatherhood

As discussed in previous chapters, a father's commitment is evaluated according to the time he spends with his children providing love and guidance and by his effort to contribute to their support. In the remaining section, I look at some concrete indicators of these practices. Because I was not able to observe quality of time or effort in interviews with parents, I used their reports of contact and support as an informative but limited gauge of a father's interactions with his children.[16] This information also allows me to make comparisons with other studies. Parents' combined reports indicate that approximately 75 percent of fathers had had some contact with their child in the previous year, with close to half of these fathers seeing their children weekly. Approximately 40 percent of African American mothers said that their child had visited the father at least once a week, and 65 percent of African American fathers reported seeing their children that often. Approximately 20 percent of these mothers and 5 percent of these fathers indicated that there had been no contact in the last year. White parents indicated lower levels of contact: 31 percent of white mothers and 44 percent of white fathers reported weekly visits with the father; half of these mothers and one-third of these fathers said there had been no contact. These differences in paternal contact by race could be the result of sample selection. However, African American fathers in this study also lived in closer proximity to their children than did white fathers, thus facilitating access.[17]

Looking at reports of paternal contact by gender, we see that approximately 58 percent of fathers said they saw their children weekly (or lived with them) and 28 percent reported no contact. In comparison, approximately 36 percent of mothers reported that the father had weekly contact (or lived with them), and a similar percentage reported no contact in the last year. The higher level of contact that fathers reported compared with mothers could, again, be due to sample selection: five women said their children's fathers were in jail, whereas none of the men I interviewed were incarcerated. The study also could have selected for more involved fathers who volunteered to participate. Because mothers and fathers were sampled separately, I cannot directly compare their responses. However, it is possible that subjective evaluations of parents differ. For example, a few of the fathers I spoke with counted seeing their child in the neighborhood as contact, whereas mothers tended to describe more substantial interactions as contact.

In general, my respondents' reports resemble those of parents interviewed in national surveys. Lerman and Sorensen (2000, 148) found that approximately 52 percent of the fathers in the National Longitudinal Survey of Youth (NLSY) who had had a child outside of marriage between 1979 and 1992 and were still unmarried reported seeing at least one of their children about once a week or reported living with these children. Approximately 20 percent had no contact with their child. In comparison, approximately 42 percent of unmarried mothers reported that the father lived with them or visited any of their children born outside of marriage once a week and that about 30 percent of fathers had no contact with their child.[18]

According to parents' current and retrospective accounts, the type of interactions fathers have with their children seems to differ primarily with the children's age and the father's residential status. Because unmarried fathers are more likely to live with their children when the children are young, these factors tended to co-vary. When talking about these interactions, parents again drew from collective ideas of paternal responsibility.

Like custodial mothers, unmarried fathers who were living with their child when I spoke with them, or who had done so when the child was an infant, talked about the time and effort they spent providing direct care. Bucky explained why caring for children demanded sacrifice on the part of parents.

> You got to get up and fix bottles at 2:00 A.M. in the morning, and you're dead tired . . . and not too long ago got home from work and went to sleep. You got the doctor appointment, you got the screaming and hollering, you got the temperatures and the shots to deal with. You got the cut another teeth to deal with. If the baby got diarrhea or she's constipated, you got to deal with the doctors. You usually get WIC—got to run back and forth there. You got so much responsibility of being there for them, raising that kid. 'Cause I know at times I be so tired. I was so tired one day [that] I just couldn't do anything about it but let her cry because I was so tired. I just got home from work, and she was just screaming and hollering; she was yelling her head off. And I was, like, "Oh please God, let me sleep. Let me sleep, I'm so tired, I'm so tired, I'm so tired, let me sleep." She screamed and hollered the rest of the night, and I sat up with Hefty ten-pound bags under my eyes. But, that's the sacrifice you make. And being a father or mother or parent or whatever they call it, that's the sacrifice that they make. 'Cause there's just some things you just gonna have to give up for the sake of your kid.

As their children grew older, men expressed social fatherhood through different types of interactions. Daniel, who lived with his daughters when they were young, explained, "I stayed with her [the mother] and I put her [his daughter] to sleep. And I would make a hot, warm bottle and change her diapers and all that." When Daniel's children were older and he no longer lived with them, he provided less direct care, but he took his children on outings: "I take them to Asbury Park. I take them to the movies. Take them downtown for pizza." He also explained that the teaching component of his "job" as a father became more prominent.

> What I like most about being a father is teaching them the right from the wrong. And care and loving them. Hugging them, you know. Just, just spending time with the kids. 'Cause I know most fathers don't spend time with their kids. But I know that's something that I have to do. That's my job. You know, that's what I like doing. Well, right now [I'm] teaching them, [when] I turn the TV shows—I watch the news mostly with them—and my oldest daughter, she ask me why did that man shoot that man and all a that. And I say well, that's violence, wherever you go, there's violence. . . . And I teach them, you know, [how to put] their own clothes on, and sometime they don't be matching, but you know they just get them

and put them on. . . . Sometime they learn how to fold their pants and stuff. I teach them that. . . . It feels so good to me to teach my kids to have something that I didn't have, you know what I mean? It just feel good.

When fathers stopped living with their child, they were more constrained in their interactions and had more difficulty demonstrating their commitment to the child. Since moving out of the home, William felt frustrated in his attempts to spend time with his daughter.

The hardest thing [now] is, well, I'm taking care of my daughter but, I'm not really taking care of her the way I want. Because I know how it is to grow up without a father, without parents in the house. And I don't want her coming up without me being in the same house. . . . I'd just rather have her with me. . . . I can get my daughter and stuff now, have her for a while [but] I want custody where she's with me.

The second indicator of social paternity was demonstrated by fathers' efforts to support their children. Turning again to some concrete measures of support, the parents I interviewed said that approximately three-quarters of fathers gave some kind of economic support to their children in the past year, either formally through the child support system or informally by making direct contributions to their children. Similar to parents' accounts of paternal contact, a greater proportion of African American parents reported providing or receiving economic support from the father in the last year. Approximately 80 percent of African American mothers and 95 percent of African American fathers reported receiving or giving economic support compared with 50 percent of white mothers and 66 percent of white fathers. As the figures indicate, the same fathers who failed to provide support for their children also failed to have contact with them during the last year.

Parents placed a high value on both in-kind support and direct monetary contributions. The parents I interviewed said that fathers provided in-kind support such as diapers, clothes, food, car seats, toys, medicine, bottles, bassinets, shoes, baby lotion, baby powder, cribs, walkers, and strollers. Some fathers also supported the mother through child care, transportation, and rent or other bill payments, particularly when they were living together. Marion explained that her child's father did not contribute much financially, but she appreciated the help he gave her with child care and housework before he went to prison:

When he was here, he'd help out. Especially help out around the house. Washing dishes. After I'd wash the clothes, you know, before we'd put them away. He fold them and help me put them away. Making the beds. Getting up in the morning and getting the kids washed and dressed. He would do that. He cut all their heads, all the boys' heads, so I didn't have to go out to a barbershop. He would cook dinner . . . clean up behind me and the kids. I wouldn't have to take my plate off the table. He would wash the dishes. He would clean the whole kitchen—that includes mopping the floor, everything. Dust, clean, everything I wanted done, he would do.

Other fathers provided monetary contributions either directly or through child support payments. Jason said, "I was giving her $35 a week [informally] and the court made it $50. . . . I've been supporting my daughter ever since she was born." A third group combined in-kind and monetary support. For example, O'Shen gave his son's mother $150 each month for her rent. In addition, he and his mother bought things for the children:

I buy him something every week. He gets something every week. Like tomorrow, I'm gonna go buy him a couple of outfits. My mom went and bought him like six outfits Sunday. We gonna get his pictures taken this weekend and his sisters and what not. So, when I go shopping tomorrow, I'll probably buy him a pair of sneakers, T-shirt, and a sweat suit.

Parents suggested that financial support also had a strong emotional and moral component. In fact, parents said that social fatherhood was better demonstrated by the sacrifice and effort fathers made to support their children than by the absolute value of the contribution. Again, William explained that he was trying to be a social father in his effort to provide for her as well as to see her:

I'm there for my daughter, if she needs anything. There's a lot of time that when I was working or whatever I'd be going through my lunch money for that week, and I found out my daughter was running low on Pampers. I'd go spend my lunch money. I wouldn't ask anybody for anything. I'd just spend, you know. I mean I'd go out my way for my daughter, and I still do it now. I'll try to do anything for her just to make her have what she needs for her to be happy.

In sum, parents said that fathers' interactions with their children and their effort to support them were important indicators of social fatherhood. This expressive behavior allowed mothers and children to evaluate evidence of paternal commitment and provided an opportunity for fathers to dramatize collective ideas about paternal responsibility.

My interviews with unmarried mothers and fathers suggest that parents developed an extra-legal system to assign responsibility for children. Although this system of establishing paternity was based in part on formal processes, it was fundamentally grounded on informal, reciprocal gestures and symbols of recognition among the father, mother, child, and community. Supporting the results of previous studies (Liebow 1967; Rainwater 1970; Sullivan 1989; Furstenberg 1992), my results showed that the majority of fathers acknowledged their biological connection to their children through informal practices. About three out of four fathers immediately acknowledged paternity to their child's mother, and almost all questions of paternity were eventually resolved. However, a minority of fathers turned to evidence such as physical resemblance and blood tests to firmly establish their paternity. The majority of parents I interviewed said that in addition to publicly claiming paternity to family and friends, the father had put his name on the birth certificate of their youngest child. Most parents also reported that their children had been given the father's surname. Both the birth certificate and the father's surname indicated men's initial intention of being involved in their children's lives.

Although recognition of biological paternity was a necessary step for fathers to become involved in their children's lives, parents' accounts suggested that establishing social paternity, or becoming the social father of the child, represented a much more meaningful expression of paternal responsibility. Social paternity required fathers to dramatize a voluntary, sustained commitment to their children by spending time with them and making an effort to contribute to their support. Parents' accounts indicated that the performance of these roles was assessed through collective standards about social fatherhood and paternal responsibility. As such, parents described social fatherhood as a reciprocal process: not only did fathers have the option of recognizing their children, but these children and their mothers had the option of acknowledging them.

Almost half of the parents had a court order for child support and therefore had established legal paternity. However, parents typically did not understand this process or the rights and obligations it entailed. The next chapter presents more information about parents' perceptions of formal paternity establishment and the child support system.

CHAPTER SEVEN

Reconciling Formal and Informal Systems of Paternal Support

I feel like if you're with the mother and you're taking care of the kids, you shouldn't have to be made to pay [child support]. But that's going through the system. That's welfare doing that. So, that [money] is not hers. Some people feel if it's like that then I shouldn't have to take care of the kids [informally], I shouldn't have to give her no money. She shouldn't ask me for nothing. . . . 'Cause if you're making two hundred dollars a week and they take eighty dollars out your check and you're still taking care of your child, I'm not making nothing. (Carl)

The collective beliefs and informal practices of unmarried parents documented in this study come out of a larger social and political context. Significant legislation has been passed over the past few decades to ensure that parents who live apart from their children contribute to their financial support. As we have seen, unmarried parents considered economic support a necessary but insufficient expression of paternal responsibility and believed that this economic support could be provided in various forms. They also established informal systems to recognize paternity and care for their children. However, participation in the formal child support system is mandatory for all parents whose children receive welfare. Furthermore, policy efforts have been directed toward increasing the number of legal child support orders in place and standardizing these agreements.

Child support policy serves several important goals, including reducing poverty and financial insecurity among children and custodial parents, preventing single-parent families from entering the welfare system, helping families leave the system quickly, and reducing public spending on welfare. It also affirms the principle that parents are obligated to support their children financially. Despite considerable efforts to improve the child support system, however, this policy has often been ineffective, particularly for low-income unmarried women. In 1997, only 59 percent of custodial mothers in the United States had a child support order, a figure that has remained nearly constant since 1978. For never-married mothers, the chances of having an order were only 47 percent. In 1997, approximately 45 percent of never-married mothers with child support agreements or awards who were supposed to receive payments did not (Committee on Ways and Means 2000, 527–528; U.S. Census Bureau 2000, 6–7).

Because child support legislation was mainly developed for families with divorced fathers with regular employment, it often does not match the social and economic situations of low-income unmarried parents.[1] Furthermore, this legislation assumes a provider model of fatherhood that clashes with unmarried parents' ideas about paternal responsibility. In this chapter I identify points at which my respondents reported that the child support system broke down for families headed by low-income unmarried parents. I also document why many of the unmarried mothers and fathers were reluctant to participate in the child support system and how they reconciled collective ideas about paternal obligation and informal support practices with welfare and child support requirements.[2]

Historical Overview of the Child Support System

Early U.S. law adopted English precepts of establishing paternity and support for children born outside of marriage. These laws were designed to protect legally recognized families and keep children born to unmarried women off the public dole (Grossberg 1985).[3] Although these laws also reflected society's moral interest in discouraging nonmarital births, the "bastardy proceedings" that resulted emphasized financial support from the child's father and were largely criminal in character (Grossberg 1985; Melli 1992). Women faced penalties for failing to name the father of their child or to appear in court. The hearings favored conviction for men, particularly lower-income men, who could be arrested, indentured, and lose property as a result of these hearings. In many cases, wealthier men could avoid these hearings altogether and settle out of court (Grossberg 1985, 199).

In 1922, the Uniform Illegitimacy Act proposed by the National Conference of Commissioners on Uniform State Laws made establishing paternity a quasi-criminal process. Such criminal procedures as issuing a warrant, posting bail, and holding a hearing to determine probable cause still appeared in the proceeding (Melli 1992, 34–35). In 1973, the Conference put forward the Uniform Parentage Act for state adoption, which supported equal rights for all children, buttressing a series of U.S. Supreme Court decisions that conferred a new set of rights to children born outside of marriage. It also set up presumptions of paternity and promoted using civil procedures for identifying fathers—a process that had begun a decade earlier. The use of scientific blood testing techniques to demonstrate a biological relationship between the father and child also significantly changed paternity proceedings, with genetic tests eventually limiting the need for other evidence of paternity (Melli 1992, 36–41).

Major federal involvement in the last decades of the twentieth century grew out of important social changes during the 1960s that continued through the 1990s. Increases in rates of divorce and nonmarital childbearing have led to rapid growth in the proportion of children living in single-parent families. Because many of these families have been poor and have received welfare, wide concern has developed about the adverse consequences for children growing up in these circumstances. A better child support system has come to be viewed as a major part of a national strategy for reducing poverty and use of the welfare system.

The child support system itself generated other demands for reform. Before 1975, child support policy fell under the jurisdiction of each state's family law code, and it was largely local judges who determined whether a noncustodial parent would be required to pay support, what the amount of the award would be, whether the amount would be modified as circumstances changed, and how support obligations would be enforced. The uneven results of this system led some to conclude that it was capricious and inequitable. Partly in response to these problems, federal policy moved in the direction of rationalizing the system (Garfinkel 1992).

The modern era of child support policy began in 1975 with the Title IV, part D amendment to the Social Security Act. Since 1975, child support legislation has increasingly sought to reduce administrative discretion, improve equity and compliance, and coordinate enforcement across states. The IV-D amendment established the partnership between federal and state governments that remains the basis of current child support policy. A main part of this partnership involves the Office of Child Support Enforcement, which provides national leadership and assistance in developing and managing child support policy. The states, in turn, retained responsibility for finding noncustodial parents, establishing paternity, and establishing and enforcing child support orders. To qualify for federal welfare funds, states are required to implement child support programs that meet federal standards. The federal government then pays most administrative costs of each state's child support enforcement program (Sorensen and Turner 1996).

Congress has revisited child support policy several times since 1975.[4] The Child Support Enforcement Amendments of 1984 require states to adopt expedited procedures for establishing paternity and support orders, develop guidelines for setting support levels, establish income withholding for noncustodial parents, and offer enforcement services to nonwelfare families. The Family Support Act of 1988 strengthened these amendments by requiring states to withhold wages in all cases, to use guidelines for establishing support orders, to adhere to federal standards for paternity establishment, and to track cases through an automated system. In the 1993 Omnibus Budget Reconciliation Act, Congress required states to develop a simple administrative process that allowed unmarried fathers to declare paternity voluntarily. States were also required to make the process available in hospitals so that unmarried parents could conveniently establish paternity at childbirth.

Although best known for its changes in welfare policy, the Personal Responsibility and Work Opportunity Reconciliation Act (PRWORA) of 1996 also introduced approximately fifty changes to child support enforcement.[5] Consistent with the history of U.S. child support policy, PRWORA maintained both an economic interest in collecting support from the fathers of children receiving welfare and a moral goal of encouraging private responsibility among unmarried parents and reducing nonmarital childbearing.[6] As in the past, higher-income families can establish private support agreements and avoid the child support regulations applied to families receiving state assistance.

How the Child Support System Works

When a custodial parent starts to receive benefits from Temporary Assistance for Needy Families (or TANF; formerly Aid to Families with Dependent Children, or AFDC), the designated state (or county) agency automatically opens a TANF child support case. Special rules apply for TANF cases:

- Welfare recipients must cooperate with the state in locating the noncustodial parent, establishing paternity, and obtaining support payments.[7] PRWORA states that failure to cooperate in establishing paternity will result in at least a 25 percent reduction in aid and could lead to removal from the TANF rolls.[8] The agency can approve a "good cause exception" in "the best interest of the child." Although rare, in such instances a case will not be opened.
- The custodial parent must assign to the state all rights to child, spousal, or medical support up to the amount of aid received. This assignment includes all current and past-due support, and it continues as long as a family is receiving cash assistance. If the applicant will not assign rights, then welfare and Medicaid benefits for the parent are dropped. The children will still receive cash assistance and Medicaid benefits, but the check will be sent to a payee rather than to the custodial parent.

- Most of the monthly support payment is used to reimburse state and federal governments for welfare payments and does not help increase the family's income. After 1984, custodial parents were allowed to keep up to $50 as an incentive to cooperate with child support regulations. PRWORA allowed states to eliminate the "pass-through" payment, and the majority have done so.[9]
- No credit is given for in-kind payments made directly to the custodial parent (for example, for clothes, food, diapers, medicine, and toys).

When the child support agency opens a case, it asks the custodial parent to help locate the noncustodial parent. When an "alleged" father is located, the child support agency brings him before a court or administrative agency, where he can either acknowledge or dispute paternity.[10] If he disputes paternity, an order for blood and other scientific tests is requested. If the "alleged" father denies paternity despite contrary test results, a court decides paternity. States are now required to administer in-hospital voluntary paternity programs. Since 1996, unmarried fathers cannot place their names on the birth certificate if they have not signed a declaration of paternity.

After paternity is established, a support order sets the amount that the noncustodial parent is to pay in child support.[11] In some states, support obligations are high percentages of fathers' incomes. If a noncustodial parent is in arrears, up to 55 to 65 percent of his income can be withheld (Committee on Ways and Means 2000, 492). In general, past due payments cannot be forgiven, even if the noncustodial parent is unemployed, in jail, or otherwise unable to earn income. Although this provision is intended to protect custodial parents from reductions in the amount of child support owed by the noncustodial parent, it can make it more difficult for fathers to pay child support if substantial arrearages accrue during these times.

New Jersey Parents and the Child Support Process

Mothers interviewed for this study typically began the process of initiating a child support action at the time they applied for welfare or Medicaid benefits.[12] First, the mother's caseworker asked for information that would facilitate locating the father. After the child support enforcement office located the "alleged" father, he was notified that he was being sued for paternity and must appear in family court for a child support hearing. If the man was personally served and did not appear at the hearing, a default order for child support was established. Alleged fathers who had not been served but had received notice by mail could be issued a bench warrant. New Jersey's child support system used hearing officers to expedite the child support process. Consequently, fathers who appeared in court typically did not meet with a judge but instead with a hearing officer, who reviewed the case, prepared a written determination of paternity, and recommended a child support order based on state guidelines. A judge then reviewed and signed the order. The alleged father could request an immediate rehearing with the judge if he objected to the officer's recommendation. If the man contested paternity, a genetic test to determine paternity was ordered.

After the award was set, the Probation Department monitored, collected, and distributed support payments. The state kept all but the first $50 of the child support payment (that is, the pass-through payment) to offset the costs of welfare. If arrears began to accrue and wage withholding could not be initiated, the father received a notice to appear at another hearing at which withholding, liens, and incarceration could be ordered. Fathers who failed to appear at the hearing could be issued a warrant for noncompliance with the child support order (Probation Child Support Enforcement Services 1990, 23–25).

Negotiating Child Support and Welfare Regulations
Distinguishing Deadbeat Dads from Responsible Fathers

The unmarried parents I interviewed held collective beliefs about paternal responsibility and practices of caring for children. Fathers were expected to spend time establishing emotional bonds, providing guidance, and acting as role models to their children. Parents also believed fathers should make an effort to provide financial support to the extent they could. Although parents typically endorsed the principle of child support, many believed that formal child support was not appropriate when parents lived together and the father shared expenses or when fathers reliably met their responsibilities.

Jacqueline described the circumstances in which she thought pursuing a formal child support order would be appropriate:

> I think I would say go to court for child support if [fathers are] not willing to help you. If they're not willing to even be there. If like the mother and the father of the child were having a relationship, and they just cannot get along, so the father doesn't do something for the child 'cause the father doesn't like the mother. I don't think that's fair to the child. If she has to go to court or he has to go to court for child support, then they should do it. 'Cause, like, with my son's father and I, if he didn't have the money and I needed something, I understood, 'cause he was, you know, he was struggling. But at least if he would be there and come visit him. Just come over and take him for a walk to the park. Just have some type of participation in his life and that's it. But if they don't want to participate at all and just being jerks about it, then yeah, you should go to court.

Although Ann, who lived with and planned to marry her child's father, did not want to pursue child support, she felt she had little choice. When asked whether she received child support, Ann replied, "We're in the process of doing that right now, but I really didn't want to go through that because he's been doing everything. I mean, if she needs something, he'll go get it." At the same time, Ann firmly believed that the state should crack down on deadbeat dads like her own father who had offered no support to her or her mother as she was growing up. She characterized child support as the minimum a father should offer his child if that father did not participate in the child's life: "I mean, if you're not spending time with your kid, at least give him something."

Because the child support system did not honor parents' informal child support agreements or reflect their beliefs about paternal responsibility, the system often conflicted with parents' sense of justice.[13] Fathers maintained that the system pursued men indiscriminately and refused to acknowledge the degree of effort they made. Yusef, for example, recognized the necessity of child support. At the same time, he did not believe that fathers who tried to care for their children should incur a formal child support obligation just because the mothers of their children receive welfare.

I say it's a catch-22 situation to me, okay? In a way, if the father's not doing for the child, then I think that it is a necessity. If it come to the point where I think they have to have some kind of law to force them to pay, I think they should. But then again, like I was telling you before, if I'm doing for this child and I'm seeing the child, me and the mother is on good terms, you know what I'm saying? And I'm doing for this child, and she's on welfare. And because she's on welfare, they still looking for me. And I have to still pay, and I'm still doing for her. I think that's wrong. I think that's totally wrong.

Child support policy is intended to encourage fathers to behave responsibly toward their children by making support payments. Although the unmarried parents interviewed for this study distinguished between responsible and irresponsible dads, they did not necessarily believe that fathers who paid formal child support were more responsible than those who contributed informally.[14]

A lot of dads are deadbeat dads. A lot of mothers are deadbeat mothers. But they call them deadbeat dads because they're not paying child support to the establishment. You know, a lot of people, a lot of people don't like paying child support. A friend of mine just got out of jail day before yesterday. Spent ten days in jail for child support, and he does everything in the world for his son. He just doesn't like the idea of [them] taking the money. (Larry)

The majority of unmarried parents in this study expressed a preference for informal support; however, about one-third of the mothers I spoke with actively pursued a formal order, largely because of problems with informal support. All but one of these mothers had a strained relationship with the father of their child. For example, Debra said that even though she was bothered by the fact that her children's father pays $70 a week in child support and she receives only a fraction of it, she did not trust him enough to work out an informal arrangement: "He says, 'Get off welfare, and I'll give you $400 a month for the kids.' I don't trust him to give me no money out of his own pocket. I say no, just keep paying child support." She cautioned other mothers: "The child needs help—help that the father may not always give, you know, or be there. At least the state will make him take care of his child. A lot of fathers need to be made to take care of their kids."

These mothers, however, typically sought child support after the father had shown himself to be irresponsible in their eyes:

[A good father] is gonna be there for that child. Somebody that's gonna be there for them, through the ups and downs, that they can rely on. Not just financial—emotional, everything. A friend to talk to and everything. . . . It's not just all the money. True it does help. There was some time when, like, with my daughter's father, if he never gave me a penny for her I would scrimp and scrape, but I think that if he loves her and he spends all his time with her doing this and that, I wouldn't even press the issue as much as I do. I wouldn't even took him to court. Because if he can't do it, it'd be something different. (Tracy)

Despite the previous examples, most of the parents I interviewed were disinclined to participate in the child support system. The remainder of this chapter illustrates why resistance to the child support regulations was so strong among these parents, given that they believed fathers were obligated to support their children and that they endorsed the principle of child support.

Problems with Mandatory Cooperation Rules

Parents often objected to the requirement that women receiving welfare must sign over to the state their rights to child support.[15] The close connection between welfare and child support policy created by these special rules were an important reason for the parents' reluctance to cooperate with the official child support system. Parents argued that a father's child support payments did not increase the child's standard of living and that the child's needs were not met with the "pass-through" payment. Joe observed:

> The money doesn't go to the kid. It's not like you're buying the kids something. The money goes to them, because they pay that girl some welfare. So all it is nothing but a payback situation. You know what I mean? You're giving us money to pay back what we had to give her. It's not like you say, "All right, I know this $35 will buy my son some Pampers." It ain't like that.[16]

Although, in general, parents understood that the father's payment was used to offset the costs of welfare, they did not consider the regulation fair. For example, Janet received very little economic support from the father of her youngest child, but she believed he did his best to make a contribution.

> I mean I could see if he wasn't doing anything; I mean, that would be a big difference. But he is doing something for them, and for them to judge how much of what he gives me, when he does, and then to take it out of my monthly income. I don't feel as though that's fair. But that's what they will do.

The financial disincentives facing a low-income father can be substantial. If a father pays $200 per month, yet his child gains only $35 as a result of his contribution after food stamps and Medicaid are reduced, the effective "tax rate" is 82.5 percent. Even if the father pays only $100 per month, the effective tax rate is still 65 percent. A strong economic disincentive also exists for a mother whose child's father might make direct contributions greater than $50 a month. Several parents indicated that before a child support order was in place, the value of the father's in-kind support or direct cash payments equaled or exceeded $50.[17]

> I'd give them triple the amount. . . . I mean I might buy a coat that cost $50. You know what I'm saying? Sneakers cost $50. You know, if I just say, I'll just pay up and don't get them nothing, then she coming out or my son coming out, with the bad end of the stick. 'Cause he might need some sneakers and a jacket. How you gonna get sneakers and a jacket with $50? (Kareen)

The economic disincentive created by assigning child support rights to the state led many mothers and fathers to work out cooperative arrangements to circumvent this financial penalty. Fathers often gave priority to their children's concrete needs for such provisions as clothing, diapers, and food rather than to child support payments. Pointing to his children's material needs, Yusef referred to child support payments as a "waste":

> You wind up doing for your child anyway. Why you have to pay somebody to take care of your child when you still have to take care of your child anyway? You know what I'm saying? You think that I pay the city so much amount, like $200, $300 a month, but I still have to get shoes and clothes and stuff.

Many fathers indicated they could not make regular child support payments and contribute directly to their children. Some fathers made sporadic payments to the state in an attempt to provide for their children's needs while keeping child support enforcement at arm's length. Others decided that when they had extra income they would give things directly to their children rather than paying any child support to the state.

Mothers also resisted child support regulations in order to continue receiving financial assistance directly from the father. Approximately 15 percent of parents said that they or their child's mother had withheld the father's name in the welfare intake interview or review process so that they could maintain informal parenting arrangements. Denise explained these economic motivations:

> If they start taking money from him, then we wouldn't have anything to live on. . . . I thought they would go after him for money and he would have to give money to the state that we would never see again. So, instead of giving money to the state that we would never see again, we really needed it, because, we were like on our own. So I told them I didn't know who the father was.

Kathryn Edin (1995) reports that about half of the mothers she interviewed engaged in "covert noncompliance" by lying about the father's identity or giving misleading information to child support officials to avoid establishing a support order. Edin notes that the majority of mothers who received "covert" cash or in-kind payments from the father did so because they could receive more through informal support.[18]

Most of the parents I spoke with did not withhold the father's name or lie about his identity but attempted to evade the system in other ways.[19] For example, some mothers supported the father's decision to withhold his name on the birth certificate, to ignore notices to appear in court for a hearing, or to make informal payments. Mothers sometimes forgot to bring or said they didn't have such information as the father's address, place of employment, or Social Security number with them at the time of the intake interview, even though they were in contact with the father and could presumably obtain this additional information. When mothers sought an award, however, they would report this information to child support.[20] By withholding some information about the father, mothers could satisfy the formal requirements of the child support system while not actively seeking an order.

If parents were no longer in a romantic relationship, providing informal support required a father to be willing and able to come to a friendly agreement with the mother. It also demanded that the father make an effort to see and support his children. Ishadeema described how she and her former boyfriend came to an informal agreement during her pregnancy: "Well, I used to always make out these papers for him, and he used to sign them. Like little agreements: 'I, Timothy, agree that I'll always take care of my child no matter what. Whether we're together or not.' . . . He sign and I sign." She later sent these written agreements to the father's parents as a back up. She believed they now gave him money to support their child based on these agreements.

Because I interviewed parents with young children, they may have been more optimistic about negotiating informal support than were parents of older children. Generally parents acknowledged that these informal, voluntary arrangements could be difficult to maintain. To establish an informal arrangement for support, a mother needed to be convinced that the father was making a serious effort to cooperate with her and to contribute financially. Parents' accounts suggest that the mother's and father's individual assessments of the father's efforts to support the child could differ. If the mother felt that voluntary agreements had broken down, she was often willing to use the child support system. The formal system of child support gave a mother more power in negotiating with the child's father, even if she did not establish a formal support order. A mother who believed a father was being irresponsible or uncooperative sometimes used the threat of reporting him to the child support authorities as a "negotiation tool" (Edin 1995). With this leverage, mothers could garner informal support, induce fathers to be more responsible, and thereby bypass the formal system. Liza explained:

> I would give that man an alternative—either you're going to help me with my child without going to court, or we can go to court and take it from there. So I would advise women that are having it hard and feel that the fathers are not doing anything to take it to court and get that child support. But for the women who are having the fathers help them, I would suggest that they continue having that understanding with the father.

To avoid a child support order, the father of Liza's youngest child did not put his name on the birth certificate. When they began to argue about whether he would support the child, she decided to pursue an award:

> We weren't getting along that great then and he called my bluff. And you do not call my bluff. You do not tell me that you are not gonna help me with your kids. He called my bluff, and I took him up on it. And I went and filed the child support papers against him.

Several mothers said they had changed their minds about child support after they saw that the father was not willing to take care of their children in the way they had expected. For example, Alicia said that initially she did not want to tell her caseworker that she knew who the father was because she did not want to "get him in trouble." But when he did not offer support or visit their daughter regularly, she reconsidered. Her mother had also advised her to think about the future, when her daughter would need more expensive things. Alicia considered how her daughter would feel if she wanted to locate her father one day but paternity had not been established. A child support caseworker suggested to Alicia that the father was trying to control the money. After considering all of these factors, Alicia decided to seek child support:

> I'm gonna tell them everything he did. I'll tell them, "Yes, your Honor. Every time I need help I have to get on the phone and call him. It's not like he's giving me money out of his pocket every week or anything like that. I mean the majority of the clothes, the bottles—it's all coming out of my pocket. The only thing he bought was a bassinet, your Honor, car seat, a couple bottles. Everything else you see on her back is from me and money in my pocket."

Despite her intention to pursue a child support order, Alicia advised other mothers to use the child support system only as a "last resort."

Men recognized and took seriously the fact that women had the power to pursue child support.[21] Salaam observed that mothers who withheld information at first could contact their caseworker at any time to pursue child support:

> You know, if you don't live up to your expectations from the agreement that you and this lady made, first thing she gonna do is run down there and say, "I know so and so. I know where he work at."

Another important reason mothers wanted to avoid formal child support in a few cases was that they believed this process would encourage contact with the father that could be detrimental to themselves and their children. For example, Lynn said she initially had withheld the name of the father because they had had a marriage-like relationship in which he supported their family. But when the father became an alcoholic, began abusing her, and was sent to prison, she continued to withhold information because she did not want contact with him when he was released.[22]

Although the formal system allowed mothers to exert leverage against fathers, this process could aggravate relationship problems. Joe explained that some men interpret being called into court for child support as a hostile gesture on the part of mothers.

> [Mothers] don't know that once you do that, that puts a whole distance between you and the baby's father. Now the baby's father say, "So, you want to go that route? Okay. Then I'll give them $35 a month, but you can't get another dime from me for nothing." Now you never know, this guy might come across this amount of money doing this or this amount doing that. Instead of giving it to you and your child—well here's your $35. You know what I'm saying? So sometime the girl don't know and it hurts them more than it helps.

Parents suggested that child support rules could pit mothers against fathers and create or exacerbate conflict in their relationships.[23] These conflicts made already difficult parenting arrangements more antagonistic and could lead to their dissolution.

The welfare system requires mothers on welfare to establish paternity for their children. It also requires them to initiate the process of collecting support from low-income fathers. These requirements appear to limit mothers' discretion and perhaps reduce interpersonal conflict with fathers. However, conflict seemed to develop for several reasons, based, in part, on inadequate information and previous feelings of distrust between parents.

First, fathers might blame mothers for applying for welfare and thus creating their obligation to the state. Similarly, mothers might attribute their reliance on welfare to the failure of fathers to adequately support their children. Second, parents sometimes did not know the amount of the child support payment and how much of it was retained by the state. As a result, some mothers believed that fathers were making smaller payments than they were, and some fathers believed that mothers were receiving larger payments, which they spent on themselves. Third, fathers were often aware that mothers had room to maneuver within the child support system and could decide how vigorously to pursue child support. In fact, they may have believed that mothers had more power to evade child support than they actually did. Fathers also had discretion in how they responded to a child support order—a fact that mothers were well aware of. When faced with such an order, fathers could choose to withhold support entirely or to restrict contact. Finally, the economic demands placed on poor fathers by child support payments could add additional strain to relationships.

Problems with Formal Support Orders

Parents recognized in-kind contributions, such as diapers, food, and clothing, as valid expressions of paternal obligation. According to parents' reports, many fathers made informal monetary or in-kind contributions. Parents stressed that gifts had much greater meaning to children than a child support check that mothers received in the mail. Children had difficulty comprehending child support, particularly when it was an add-on to the mother's welfare check. Although the father made gifts in the form of both in-kind support and "gifted" money, parents suggested that children appreciated these direct contributions more than they did child support.[24] In fact, parents thought children might believe their father was not giving them anything when he paid child support. In addition to suggesting that children might benefit more financially from informal support, parents described strong emotional grounds for this preference. Because parents said fathers should provide support out of a sense of love and responsibility for their children, formal child support represented a "forced" payment rather than an authentic expression of paternal love.[25]

> It would be a whole lot better for the kid, for the dad, for the mother, if the money was coming straight from him. . . . The child would understand, 'cause eventually the child as it gets older knows what child support is. Knows that his father ain't been around. So it's like, "Damn. My father don't buy me nothing, but he pay child support." Who wanna say that? What kid wanna grow up knowing, "Well my father pay child support, but he don't buy me nothing"? . . . A child would rather have his father bring him five pair of jeans and some sneakers and some shirts than a check in the mail. . . . The material stuff, [at] a child's age, is a whole lot more than paper. . . . It would show more love. (Joe)

Fathers also said that when they were making formal child support payments, they could not afford to buy things their children needed. Salaam described his dilemma: If he paid child support, he could not buy things his children requested. Therefore, he felt guilty and avoided spending time with them. But if he provided in-kind support instead of making child support payments, he risked arrest. He said he had already been arrested three times for failure to pay support. Recounting a conversation with his mother and sisters about this, he explained:

My mom and them are like this: "Why don't you stop buying them stuff? The courts can handle that. Whatever you decide to buy them, take that money down there to the courts." But it still gets to the point of: what about my kids? 'Cause, you know, kids can talk. Kids can walk up and say, "Dad can you buy me this?" And they know if I can afford it, they know I'm supposed to get it for them. But then if I be, like, "Uh uh, I can't get that. Your mom's supposed to take care of that," . . . then the kid be kind of upset and then it distracts you. It makes you feel bad to tell one of your childs [that] when you know you can get it for them.

Men who considered themselves to be responsible fathers often resented the fact that child support prevented them from showing their love and being responsible for their children. These fathers used an antigovernment rhetoric to express opposition. Yusef asked, "Why do I need the government to tell me that I should take care of my child when I know for a fact that I need to?" And Darren explained, "If I know I got a child I got to do things for, ain't no need for them to tell me I got to pay such amount. Because I know what I got to do, and that's my job to do it, you know."[26]

Some women agreed with this assessment of child support. For example, mothers sometimes regarded "forced" child support as both tainted and unreliable because it did not derive from an emotional bond. According to Tricia, when several people had tried to encourage her to initiate child support proceedings before she reluctantly agreed to do so, she responded:

But that's my baby. And when I do that, I feel as though I'm forcing [the father] to take care of his child, forcing him to love his child. And I'm not going to force him. I got love for everybody for that girl. And for me the way I feel to go through the system to force him to take care of his child is like he don't love her.

In-kind support is important among parents who have romantic or amiable relationships with one another. Some parents jointly sought to avoid participating in the formal system because of their belief that child support enforcement undermined their efforts to establish cooperative parenting arrangements based on emotional commitments. Mothers sometimes worried that child support would introduce animosity into their relationship with the father, and their child would risk losing the emotional involvement, guidance, and care the father provided. Marion lived with the father of her child before he was sent to prison, and she planned to marry him when he was released. After describing the kind of work he had done around the house and his substantial involvement with their children, she said:

> [In many cases] it's a good idea. But in many cases, it's not a good idea 'cause it will cause a conflict between you and the baby's father. Right now welfare is trying to take him to court for child support. But what it all boils down to is if he's going to be here with me, I'm getting more out of him being with me. It might not be exactly financially, but as far as raising the kids, you can't put a price on that. So, I'm getting more out of him being here, than not being here and trying to pay child support.

In-kind payments were also preferred by fathers whose relationship with the mother was antagonistic; such payments gave them the feeling that they were more in control of the situation.[27] Many fathers expressed uneasiness about how mothers spent the formal child support money. But they said that with in-kind support, they had assurance that their contributions benefited the child. Some fathers believed that the mother would spend the money on herself rather than their child, whereas others felt she would not spend it wisely. These attitudes toward paying monetary support again reflect general feelings of distrust between the men and women.

Not surprisingly, this issue also arose among fathers who believed the mother had a drug problem. James commented, "[The] thing with child support, you know, they don't investigate. You're giving child support to a woman that's got your kids. You don't know what they're doing with that money. You know, they could be drugging it. . . . I'd rather buy it myself, that way I know it's going toward them." Vincent, a father who has contact with one child but not another, described the mother of his youngest child as a "pot-smoking hippie" who went on welfare to support her drug use. When asked about his view of paternal support to children, Vincent responded: "What if the mother's on drugs, and she spends the money on drugs? It doesn't matter how much you give these drug heads." When asked what he would say if the mother were not on drugs, he falls back on gender stereotypes: "The mother's not on drugs? Well then hopefully she's not gonna throw the money up in the air. And there's some mothers not on drugs, but they buy jewelry or they buy frivolous things that have nothing to do with healthy living."

Formal child support orders often foster resentment and distrust that are directed toward the other parent instead of toward the state. Tricia described how her daughter's father had begun to direct his resentment about child support at her by withholding informal contributions. Although Tricia did not want to pursue an award, she felt she had to. After child support enforcement contacted the father, he began to distrust her. As a result, when he was ordered to pay less to the court than he had given informally and when she asked him for the difference, he refused.

Although not all mothers experienced a real economic loss, others mentioned that securing support through the formal system could create conflict when the father began paying child support and stopped doing the "extras" for their children. Andre explained why he stopped buying things like clothes and shoes for his son when he was ordered to pay child support:

> I pay child support for him. And I told her, "I'm paying child support [and] that's all you're gonna get from me is child support. Now if you would have did what I asked you to do, you would of got a lot more." If she would have did what I asked her to do, just go get WIC and not welfare, then my oldest son would get a lot more than child support. You know, the little extras and everything. But she want me to give my son extras and to pay child support.

Problems with Enforcement Practices

After low-income parents became involved with the formal system and a support order was established, concerns about how the system enforces support orders emerged. Mothers often perceived the enforcement practices as ineffective. They expressed frustration about the trouble they have communicating with child support caseworkers.[20] As Beth explained, "It's one of those numbers you can never get in touch with. Like you call and it's busy." Mothers also complained about how slow the process of setting up a child support award could be:

> Child support really lollygags you around a lot. They send you a letter. Tell you they're going to [do] this, and they never take any action. They send my daughter's father a whole bunch of letters saying that "If you don't get down here before this day, we're going to put out a warrant for your arrest." No. He doesn't go. And then what are they going to do?

Fathers also became frustrated with the system's insensitivity to their changeable economic circumstances and its use of criminal sanctions to enforce compliance. It is likely that these perceived problems with the enforcement process contributed to the reluctance of parents, particularly fathers with limited financial resources, to participate in the formal system in the first place.

Insensitivity to Poor Fathers' Economic Circumstances

Fathers suggested that a major problem they faced was the system's inability to recognize or respond to their economic circumstances. Many fathers of children receiving welfare have low skills, lack stable employment, and may not have sufficient income to pay child support without further impoverishing themselves or their families (Sorensen and Turner 1996; Garfinkel, McLanahan, and Hanson 1998; Mincy and Sorensen 1998). Because child support legislation was developed on the model of an employed, divorced father, enforcement assumes that all noncustodial fathers can pay child support. Fathers' descriptions of their economic circumstances raise serious questions about the validity of this assumption.

Fathers talked about problems with paying regular support when they had irregular employment. Furthermore, because their jobs were often part time, temporary, or low paying, they found it hard to make child support payments while meeting their own basic expenses. Some fathers also had obligations to more than one family. Fathers who were unemployed said the system is least understanding of their circumstances. For these fathers, awards may have been based on imputed income that assumed full-time work at the minimum wage.[29] When they had orders that were set beyond their ability to pay, many fathers were deterred from participating in the child support system at all. Yusef commented on what he and his friends think about this situation:

> A lot of fathers are just getting fed up with the situation. They be like, boom, if I'm still looking after my kids and I still have to pay the government so much money a week and still support myself, you ain't gonna do it. . . . How can you, on a simple job out here, how can you support yourself plus pay for your kids that way, plus still have to do for your kids and maintain yourself in this kind of environment?

In many cases, fathers faced large arrearages as well as the interest that accrued on these arrearages. These fathers were incredulous that they could accumulate a substantial debt during periods when they were unable to pay, such as while they were unemployed or incarcerated. Unemployed fathers asked rhetorically, "How are you expected to survive?" In the course of a four-hour interview, Salaam spent much of the time talking about his frustration with the job market.

> They don't understand that you have to pay rent or you might have to find somewhere to eat or sleep. . . . This is a big problem; I don't see where they coming up with making us pay child support [without a job]. I mean, give

us something to do. Give us a program or something to get into. That way we could learn and work at the same time. . . . Give us something to do, there's plenty to do if they take the time out to allow us to do it. I mean, everybody that's out there on the street doesn't want to be out there. And everybody ain't bad. But just by standing out there long period of time, you get a tendency of falling into trouble. If we was at work eight hours a day, I'm pretty sure we would be so tired we would go into the house, sleep, and wait until the next day of work. I would love to have a job.

Most states establish retroactive orders for child support that may reach back several years before an order is established; therefore, fathers may already be in arrears when they begin paying formal support.[30] At the same time, an award usually does not take into account direct, informal support given to the child before the award had been set or the father's income at that time (Sorensen and Lerman 1998; Roberts 1999). Some fathers have child support debts for periods that they were living with the child's mother and helping to support the household (Roberts 1999). Cohabiting fathers could also accrue new debt.

Interviews with fathers suggest that child support enforcement practices that assumed fathers were absent from the family could undermine relationships between unmarried couples. O'Shen had been working a night shift at a local hospital when he was arrested on an outstanding warrant for child support. He subsequently lost his job. Describing the hearing, he said:

Do you know that judge stood in front of my face and told me, "I don't care where you live at, you better move back in with your mom, 'cause I'm taking half your money." He got no right to tell me that. You know what I'm saying? If I'm living with my kid's mother, I got a roof over my kid's head. You should have said, "Damn, if you're still with her and you're living with her and helping your kids out, well, okay," . . . 'cause you're not making no money like a doctor or lawyer so that somebody can take half your net pay. Heck no, come on man.

O'Shen explained that he had fallen into arrears during a time when he was living with his children. Most of his income at that time had gone to purchasing things for the children and to paying for household expenses.[31] He added that he eventually moved back in with his mother.

As the interview with O'Shen suggests, some fathers claimed that the enforcement process could cost them their jobs. Jake said that when child support began to enforce wage withholding, his employer did not want the hassle, and so he was fired: "When it first started getting strict, I had a job at a body shop, and they called the people and told them they were gonna garnish my wages. I lost the job just like that." Although it is against the law to fire a noncustodial parent because of wage withholding, Jake, like other fathers, believed this commonly occurred.

Fathers also objected to the inflexible enforcement practices of the child support system during times when they were out of work. If fathers had informal arrangements, mothers could be more understanding about when fathers made payments, particularly if fathers were trying to maintain a relationship with their children in other ways. Many fathers did not know how to modify their child support orders or had difficulty doing so. For example, Jason explained that after losing his job, he had difficulty meeting his child support payment of $50 a week. He was temporarily homeless, moving from one low-rent hotel to another, and supporting himself with a string of under-the-table jobs. He explained that before his child's mother had gone on welfare, he had regularly given his daughter $35 a week or in-kind support for seven years. If he had missed a week of payment, he said the mother understood. Now that the mother was on welfare and he had lost his job, the character of the situation had changed from cooperation to coercion. Despite his economic situation, he believed it would be too difficult to return to court for another hearing. Like other fathers, he did not know how to modify an order and did not think he would be successful at it:

> If I don't [pay], they, they threaten you. They say, "If you don't do it, we'll put you in jail." Deadbeat dad. I know that's what they say. And I say I'm not a deadbeat dad. I try to do my best. I try to earn as much money as I can. And I try; I love my daughter with all my heart. But I can only do what I can do. I can barely support myself as it is.

In response to enforcement of regulations they perceived to be inflexible and unfair, fathers often said they would advise other men in this situation to pay just enough to avoid harassment or incarceration. A response of some fathers who felt intimidated or overwhelmed by child support enforcement was to ignore the child support orders and accumulate substantial arrearages. Fathers also tried to generate more income to support their child, whether formally or informally, by participating in the underground economy through under-the-table jobs, selling drugs, and gambling.[32] Other studies document how some fathers quit their jobs when they discovered how much of their wages were garnished or in response to other enforcement practices (see Furstenberg 1992; Johnson and Doolittle 1998; Johnson, Levine, and Doolittle 1999).

Criminal Sanctions and Heightened Enforcement

Another objection voiced by fathers to the enforcement process was that they were treated like criminals if they fell behind on their payments.[33] Almost one-quarter of fathers I interviewed said they had been arrested on child support charges. However, Doolittle and Lynn (1998) note that many noncustodial fathers held in jail on charges related to child support were actually picked up for other violations.[34]

Fathers believed that heightened enforcement practices ignored their efforts to support or be involved with their children. In fact, they often believed that the system was more likely to penalize involved fathers working in the regular economy than those who had gone underground. African American fathers' perceptions were also influenced by the extensive involvement of other African American men with the criminal justice system. Some of these fathers believed that child support enforcement targeted low-income African American fathers for imprisonment.[35] Robert, a father who previously had lived with his children and had a cooperative parenting arrangement with their mother when I spoke with him, resented being pursued for formal child support, saying, "It's ridiculous . . . I wouldn't say they cracking down on these fathers that are not supportive. They cracking down on the fathers that are supportive."

Vincent, a father who was recently released from prison, remarked:

The jails are full of these guys for child support, and it's the craziest thing. And it's counterproductive, because you have these guys—they're practically living on nothing. You lock them up for child support. These guys who are already living on the edge, living in a terrible neighborhood, working a horrible job. And then they get put in jail because they fall behind on their child support.

Fathers also noted that if men did not have enough money to come up with a payment sufficient to keep them from going to jail, then they certainly would not have the money after serving time in prison. Furthermore, these men would accumulate more arrearages during their time in jail. Fathers who had not been able to make their support payments said they faced the choice between getting money illegally or going to jail. Kareen's somewhat hyperbolic statement illustrates how child support can have the unintended effect of pushing fathers into the illegal economy:

It's hard to get a job, you know. But these [child support] people still saying, "You got a child, you got a child, you got to take care of them, you got to bring us such and such money a week." Where you gonna get that money from if you ain't got no job? Then you got to turn around and rob and steal and kill. You know what I'm saying? Taking this money keep your behind on the street. You know what I mean? That's like squeezing blood from a turnip, water from a rock. How can you do that?

Kareen added that he has been picked up on outstanding child support warrants six times, and "I keep telling these people: 'Look, I ain't working nowhere. You keep locking me up, then y'all ain't never gonna get the money.'" He attributed his problems with getting a job to economic changes in many northeastern cities, including high levels of unemployment for men without a high school diploma and a decline in jobs for lower-skilled workers in inner city neighborhoods.

According to fathers' accounts, child support magnified employment problems and put men like Kareen in a nearly impossible bind:

It's crazy. You got 5,000 men and only 1,000 of them got jobs. . . . That's entrapment, if you ask me. You know he gonna come back to jail 'cause he ain't got the money to pay you. He might get himself locked up, and then he might get out. Within a couple months he gotta come right back. 'Cause, like I told you, the job market is slow. Certain jobs want certain skills. And obviously you got the record, the record gonna look bad.

Exacerbating these problems was the fact that many low-income fathers were unfamiliar with child support regulations, did not have legal representation, and did not feel that they had "had their day in court" (Furstenberg 1992; Sullivan 1992; Achatz and MacAllum 1994; Johnson, Levine, and Doolittle 1999, 97–98). Jared described the lack of power he felt as a noncustodial father when dealing with the child support system:

The system's totally out for the female. I wasn't working . . . and I called up my probation officer. I was talking to him . . . telling him I can't afford it. And he was like, "Well, it's not my problem. You gotta pay it." . . . [The arrears] just kept building up and building up. I didn't have a job. . . . I couldn't get no assistance from nobody. I didn't have a driver's license. And like I said, I don't got too much of an education. I can't read or write so well. So, I couldn't get a job, no good-paying job anyway. I mean, I worked a couple jobs here and there, minimum wage, but that wasn't paying the bills. I'd work all week long, forty, fifty hours a week, then pay my child support, and then I got twenty dollars left. I couldn't do it. No way I could possibly do it. . . . Back then I was paying $77 a week. . . . They based it on my old income. . . . When I went into court, I didn't know what was going on. I didn't have no lawyers. She had lawyers from the state and everything. I was in there totally blind. Didn't know what was going on.

Brian's Experience with Child Support

One case in particular portrays how several features of the formal child support system interacted with the situations of low-income unmarried fathers and with welfare requirements to place these men in very difficult circumstances. Brian explained that he lived with the mother of his child the first year after his son's birth. During that time, he paid for most of the family's expenses. After they broke up, he was called into family court and discovered that the mother had been collecting welfare at her own mother's address. As a result, Brian had unknowingly accumulated arrears for child support during the time they had lived together. A child support award was also set for his older child. Although he said that he had tried to explain that he had been paying the expenses and that he now gave both mothers $50 per month, the court disregarded evidence of support such as copies of bills he paid and money orders:

> They said they didn't care nothing about that. That wasn't court ordered. . . . I had everything stapled together, like I had them in a big box. And I took the shoebox up to the guy, and I had all the receipts in it. He said, "That's not court ordered. I don't care anything about that."

As with other fathers who had assumed that the court would recognize contributions to children, particularly documented contributions, Brian was shocked to find that his support was irrelevant in the eyes of the court.[36]

Brian felt that child support enforcement was more likely to catch the fathers who worked in the formal economy because the system could identify them through their Social Security numbers. He pulled out his pay stubs to show that half of his paycheck was being garnished for child support. After he recently lost one of his two jobs, he said that he went back to court to modify an award. However, he was told that he was responsible for losing his job and that his request would be denied. Without legal representation, Brian raised his voice in court, and he was also jailed for contempt.

> Then the guy told me that the reason why I lost my job was my fault; I shouldn't have lost it. You know, I was working two jobs, two full-time jobs. I didn't have enough time to sleep between each job, so I always had a cold or something. When I was trying to explain that in court, he cut me off. And he said, "That's not our problem; that's your problem."

If Brian and the mother had opened a child support case when their child had been born, his difficulties might have been avoided or minimized. Many parents believe, however, that informal agreements better meet their family's needs. In Brian's case, the formal system's refusal to count informal and in-kind support, its insensitivity to his precarious economic status, its use of criminal sanctions, and its refusal to modify his order led to an intolerable situation. Unable to pay his rent, Brian said he was being threatened with eviction. He felt he had few options and had considered trying to get fired, changing his name, or selling drugs. He said that in desperation he had even considered suicide. As tension between him and his child's mother increased, Brian began to withdraw from his children's lives.

* * *

In recent years, social policies have attempted to encourage unmarried fathers to behave more responsibly toward their children by establishing paternity and paying child support. Yet my interviews indicate that child support policy is often at odds with the perceptions and experiences of low-income parents. The parents I spoke with did not necessarily characterize men who paid child support as responsible fathers, nor did they characterize all men who did not make payments as deadbeat dads. Rather, parents distinguished between fathers who made a voluntary effort to support their children and be involved with their lives and those who did not. In general, parents endorsed the idea of child support but believed it was appropriate only when an informal agreement could not be maintained. To preserve informal relationships or avoid participating in the system, many parents engaged in strategies to circumvent child support regulations that they perceived to be unfair, counterproductive, or punitive. Mothers typically sought an award only when their relationship with the father had broken down and when his commitment to their child had waned.

My interviews with low-income parents indicate that welfare and child support regulations often interacted to create adverse effects for their families. Many parents objected to signing over to the state their rights to child support. Parents indicated that child support payments did not increase their children's standard of living. They also noted that their children's needs were not met with the pass-through, or the amount of monthly child support that they actually received. Both fathers and mothers favored informal support arrangements, including in-kind payments, although fewer mothers than fathers supported this setup. In addition to believing that their children would benefit financially from informal support, parents described strong emotional grounds for this preference.

Many parents avoided participation in the child support system because they believed that enforcement generated conflict and undermined efforts to establish cooperative parenting arrangements based on emotional commitments. Some mothers also worried that formal child support would reduce or eliminate the emotional involvement, guidance, and informal support that fathers provided for their children. Fathers identified two additional problems with child support enforcement. The first was the system's inability to recognize or respond to a father's unstable economic circumstances. Fathers of children receiving welfare often lacked steady employment and sufficient income to pay their child support orders. The second was the practice of treating fathers as criminals when they failed to make payments. Fathers often believed that heightened enforcement practices ignored or even impeded their efforts to support or be involved with their children.

The unmarried parents I interviewed endorsed the principal of child support and held collective beliefs about paternal responsibility. However, their experiences and beliefs clashed with the assumptions of child support policy. These interviews suggest that unmarried parents would be more willing and better able to follow welfare and child support regulations if the regulations were more attuned to the parents' socioeconomic situations and shared ideas about paternal responsibility.

Conclusion: Fatherhood, Poverty, and Public Policy

This volume has documented the ideas and practices unmarried parents use to define and express collective beliefs about paternal responsibility. In general, I found that unmarried mothers and fathers held similar ideas about the importance of paternal involvement and the general obligations of unmarried fathers to their children. When describing these obligations, most parents embraced the involved father, teacher, and role model images of fatherhood but interpreted and modified these models in ways that made sense within their circumstances. Drawing on ideas about the importance of paternal affection, communication, and quality time, these parents believed that children with absent or neglectful fathers would experience long-term emotional harm and would act out these feelings in negative ways. They also emphasized the importance of paternal guidance and discipline, particularly when describing the challenges of childrearing in low-income environments in which drugs, crime, and other risks were prevalent and in which many fathers were living apart from their children. In African American families, parents also used a specific language about the importance of male role models for teaching sons how to become men in these difficult economic and social circumstances.

Parents characterized economic support as a necessary but insufficient expression of paternal responsibility and suggested that this support could be provided in various forms. Parents also evaluated fathers on the basis of their effort to provide for their child instead of on the absolute monetary value of their contributions. Men gained recognition as social fathers by dramatizing this effort to take care of their children and by participating in their lives.

Rather than adopting an incoherent set of values that deviated from mainstream culture, unmarried parents used widely shared ideas about fatherhood to articulate consistent standards of paternal responsibility. These standards blended contemporary expectations for emotional engagement with more conventional ideas about discipline, role modeling, and economic provision. Although these standards responded to the inability of unmarried fathers to offer substantial economic support to their children, they also signaled an acceptance of newer beliefs about involved fatherhood. This model of paternal obligation provides ways for low-income unmarried fathers to be connected with children and to derive a sense of honor from fulfilling these responsibilities.

Even as parents shared the conviction that unmarried fathers have an unconditional responsibility to their children, their accounts indicated that fathers' behavior often diverged from collectively held standards of paternal responsibility. Because women evaluated their children's fathers by comparison with themselves, many suggested that fathers' attempts to take care of their children were insufficient. However, men often derived a positive sense of themselves as fathers by comparing themselves with other men they considered to be inferior fathers.

Both mothers and fathers accepted some differences in parental tasks, but mothers attributed imbalances in childrearing responsibilities to a father's lack of effort, whereas fathers attributed imbalances to natural differences between mothers and fathers. Similarly, mothers and fathers identified many of the same reasons for paternal disengagement, but they often interpreted these motives from different perspectives. Their accounts mirror a common set of explanations that higher-and lower-income parents use to make sense of their own behavior as nonresident fathers or that of their former partners.

Interactions with the Child Support System

Historically, legal paternity establishment and child support laws have been used not only to establish children's legal rights but also to protect the economic interests of taxpayers and the moral interests of the state in promoting childbearing within marriage. The modern child support system developed as a response to the growing number of single-parent families, many of which were raising children in poverty and turning to the welfare system for help. This system arose at a time when single parenthood was primarily the result of divorce rather than nonmarital childbearing. It also emerged at a time when the breadwinning model of fatherhood had greater cultural currency. Because child support policy promotes private, economic responsibility for children, it approaches noncustodial parents as potential providers and requires them to fill this role. Only recently have policymakers encouraged the emotional as well as economic involvement of fathers in children's lives by providing some support to community-based programs for low-income noncustodial parents.

To address the sharp increase in nonmarital births, child support legislation now includes significant provisions mandating legal paternity establishment—a necessary step to securing child support. Although many parents were receptive to the idea of creating a legal connection between fathers and their children, they typically did not understand this process or the rights and obligations it entails. My interviews with unmarried mothers and fathers suggest that many parents developed an unofficial system to accept paternity and evaluate paternal responsibility that was outside the compulsory, legal system of paternity establishment. This unofficial system of establishing paternity was based in part on formal processes (for example, birth certificates, naming, and genetic tests), but it was fundamentally grounded in informal, reciprocal practices of recognition among the father, mother, child, and community.

Parents said that fathers must go beyond basic recognition and demonstrate their sustained and voluntary commitment to their children to be considered social, not just biological, fathers. Indicators used to evaluate men's performance as social fathers included the quality and amount of time fathers spent with their children and the degree of effort they expended to support them economically. Through these and other symbols and gestures of paternal recognition, unmarried fathers dramatized collective standards of paternal responsibility and, in turn, received recognition as social fathers.

In general, the unmarried parents I spoke with endorsed the concept of child support and held strong collective beliefs about paternal responsibility that emphasized children's need for paternal love and guidance. However, these parents often felt that participation in the current child support system detracted from their children's well-being, exacerbated conflicts between parents, unduly burdened poor fathers, and punished them indiscriminately. As a result, many parents preferred informal support arrangements and evaded child support regulations. At the same time, mothers were aware that informal support arrangements could be difficult to maintain, particularly after a romantic relationship with the father ended. Mothers therefore evaluated a man's performance as a social father when deciding how actively to pursue a child support order.

Child support policy assumes particular social and economic situations of fathers as well as a particular model of paternal obligation that are often at odds with the experiences and beliefs of many low-income unmarried parents. This mismatch often puts parents caught at the intersection of welfare and child support policy in an untenable position. Fathers said they faced a tradeoff between providing for their children's needs directly and making child support payments to the state. If a father followed child support regulations, he felt he could not increase his children's standard of living or provide the kind of support that was emotionally meaningful to them. Although fathers preferred to make direct contributions to their children, these payments were not recognized by the child support system. In addition, many low-income fathers could not afford to make child support payments consistently; as a consequence, they fell into arrears. Given the irregular nature of a father's employment, these arrears could be overwhelming. Fathers who circumvented child support regulations, or who were unable to pay support, could be incarcerated. Both unmanageable arrears and incarceration undermined a father's economic stability and his connection to the formal labor market. In addition, these enforcement mechanisms could further reduce a father's incentive to make formal payments and could exacerbate conflicts with the child's mother.

Unmarried mothers also faced a difficult situation. If they participated in the child support system and it worked as planned—that is, if they were able to leave welfare for stable employment, if their child's father was able to secure a steady income, and if he paid child support regularly—then mothers had a chance to better their financial situation. By actively participating in the child support system, however, unmarried mothers risked losing informal support from the father, which could create greater economic hardship for their family in the short run. They also risked alienating the father from the family and undermining the chance of a long-term emotional and economic relationship. If they did not cooperate with child support regulations and instead received direct support from the father that they did not report, mothers could have their grants reduced or face charges of welfare fraud. Furthermore, informal support arrangements could break down over time, leaving a mother without a legal support order.

Unmarried Parents and Public Policy

Policymakers have attributed the welfare dependence of unmarried mothers to a father's absence, irresponsibility, and unwillingness to support his children. In this study, most parents said that they or their child's father had been in contact with and provided some support for their child in the last year, but a significant minority did not. This research indicates that the problem of paternal absence and nonsupport was not that most fathers lacked a sense of obligation to their children. Rather, economic instability, antagonistic relationships between parents, and child support, welfare, and visitation rules interacted to undermine a father's involvement with his children. Furthermore, fathers' beliefs about gender provided cultural justifications for their absence. Fathers could more easily disengage from their children than could mothers, and they were more likely to do so when the romantic relationship or friendship with their child's mother fell apart. In the end, many unmarried mothers had the principal responsibility for children, and with limited income from employment or support from the state, they experienced economic hardship.

Child support policy represents a public response to the widespread problem of nonresident fathers withdrawing from their children and supporting them inadequately. Although parents I spoke with typically preferred private support arrangements, the current policy was introduced in part because private arrangements proved inadequate. At the same time, heightened child support enforcement ignores the fact that many unmarried fathers are unable to pay child support. It also overlooks the economic and emotional importance of direct support from unmarried fathers to their children. Furthermore, it emphasizes a father's role as economic provider at the expense of other types of paternal involvement.

Child support policy distinguishes responsible fathers from deadbeat dads on the basis of whether they satisfy formal child support obligations. However, the parents I spoke with did not necessarily characterize men who paid child support as responsible fathers, nor did they characterize all men who did not make payments as irresponsible. Rather, parents distinguished between fathers who made a voluntary and concerted effort to support and be involved with their children and those who did not. In general, parents endorsed the idea of child support but believed it was appropriate only when an informal agreement could not be maintained.

Although most mothers and fathers I spoke with were no longer romantically involved with their child's other parent, the relatively high level of involvement that mothers and fathers reported and their optimism about working out informal parenting agreements may have stemmed from the fact that they typically had young children. Because parents' informal arrangements often erode over time, the formal child support system constitutes an important safety net for unmarried mothers and their children. Establishing a fair and effective child support system would likely encourage more low-income mothers and fathers to participate.

Child Support Policy Options

Because states are required to make paternity establishment nearly universal, to increase child support collections, and to move families off of welfare quickly, they are under more pressure to improve their child support programs.[1] Findings in this study suggest that the child support system would gain greater legitimacy in the eyes of low-income parents if it were perceived as beneficial to their children, supportive of their efforts to negotiate cooperative economic and parenting agreements, and consistent with their ideas about paternal responsibility.

Policymakers now have the chance to rethink the goals of child support policy following fundamental changes to the welfare system, given the close links between these programs. It is also an opportune time to consider whether the goals of child support conflict with each other, particularly whether the goal of recouping welfare costs may actually make families less stable. The following child support reforms are being implemented or considered in states across the country. As a result of the complexities of these problems, no single option is likely to be a panacea for the child support program. But a thoughtful combination of these and other options in a program that recognizes informal economic relationships and collective beliefs in low-income communities may enhance the well-being of unmarried parents and their children.

General Changes
Increasing the Pass-Through

Parents believed that a father's child support payments did not increase their child's standard of living and that the child's needs were not met with the pass-through payment. Unmarried parents also believed that the child support system did not adequately recognize fathers who were making an effort to support their children through participation in the formal economy. The majority of states have decided to eliminate the pass-through altogether, so that children do not receive any of the child support contribution paid on their behalf. This measure is likely to increase resentment among low-income parents and to decrease their willingness to participate in the formal system. Such policies may actually reduce the amount of TANF funds recouped from noncustodial parents.[2]

The system would encourage more cooperation if it gave tangible rewards to fathers who made formal child support payments. Following Wisconsin policy, states could pass through all of the support order collected from a noncustodial parent and disregard it when calculating the welfare benefit. This policy would both increase parents' incentive to participate in the formal child support system and reduce the incentive to engage in under-the-table payments. Early results from the Wisconsin experiment show that implementing a full pass-through has not only increased the amount of child support received by children but has increased the amount of child support paid by fathers, with little cost to the state (Meyer and Cancian 2001).

Passing-through the full amount of the father's child support payment would represent a significant change in child support policy goals. Enforcement would de-emphasize recouping TANF costs from noncustodial parents and instead would focus mainly on reducing poverty and improving the material well-being of low-income custodial parents and their children. With TANF's five-year limit on welfare receipt, the cost to the state of complete pass-throughs is lower now than in previous years, and the long-term benefit to families of establishing a child support agreement is higher.

Supplementing Parents' Child Support Payments with Public Funds

The federal government or individual states could provide other incentives to supplement formal payments from fathers. For example, states could match support payments made by low-income noncustodial fathers and phase out matching funds at higher-income levels.[3] Both child support payments and matching payments could be passed through to the family and disregarded when calculating welfare benefits and eligibility. Like a full pass-through, supplementation would help reduce poverty among low-income custodial parents and their children by increasing their income.

Establishing Child Support Assurance

Child support assurance would guarantee a publicly funded minimum support payment each month for all children for whom paternity has been established. This measure would help stabilize the incomes of unmarried parents and their children (Garfinkel 1992). The promise of a stable income for children would be particularly valuable for mothers who are close to reaching or have already reached their time limit on TANF or whose co-parents fall behind on payments because of irregular employment or financial emergencies.

A child support assurance system would almost certainly be less stigmatizing than welfare, particularly if it were a universal program and not targeted only toward welfare recipients. As the system stands today, parents whose children do not receive welfare have much more discretion regarding child support than do other parents. Eliminating this two-tier system would increase the legitimacy of the child support program for low-income parents. A field test in New York of targeted child support assurance resulted in net government savings because the cost of public assistance benefits dropped more than administrative costs grew (Hamilton et al. 1996).

Helping Noncustodial Fathers Find Employment and Navigate the System

Parents' Fair Share, Partners for Fragile Families, and other community-based programs attempt to increase both the earnings of noncustodial fathers and their involvement in their children's lives (Doolittle et al. 1998; Johnson, Levine, and Doolittle 1999). Many programs provide the following kinds of support:

- Employment and training services
- Peer support sessions that help men deal with the challenges of fatherhood and of establishing sustainable co-parenting arrangements
- Information on how the system works, including guidance on establishing paternity, avoiding or managing arrearages, modifying orders, and setting up visitation agreements through separate processes
- More intensive case management

Although these programs sometimes embrace differing visions of responsible fatherhood, their increased funding and political support reflect a growing consensus that fathers (and not just mothers) of children on welfare need help to achieve economic security for their families. Effective programs might bring new fathers into the system early, helping them avoid large arrearages. Programs might also connect fathers to other available services, such as legal, health, drug rehabilitation, and domestic violence programs. Evidence from the Parents' Fair Share demonstrates some success in increasing formal payments but not in increasing fathers' employment and earnings (Doolittle et al. 1998). Because a clearly successful program design has not yet been identified, states and community organizations need to experiment with alternate program models.

Specific Changes
Setting Awards as a Realistic Percentage of Noncustodial Parents' Incomes

The support payments required of low-income fathers can often represent a high percentage of their income. Unable to make full or even partial payment because of low wages, unemployment, or reduced work hours, many fathers said they built up overwhelming arrearages. They often did not know they could modify awards to take account of declines in their income. Those who did know about this possibility had difficulty acting on it without adequate legal knowledge or representation. By falling behind on payments, they sometimes faced the threat of imprisonment. Setting the amount of the child support order at a realistic percentage of a father's income and modifying that percentage automatically would help with these problems. Although initial payments might be low for many young fathers, their incomes (and thus their payments) would probably grow over time. Moreover, fathers would be more willing and better able to maintain their payments if the amounts were quickly adjusted to reflect changes in income. This change would also decrease the likelihood of fathers accruing substantial arrearages and would reduce the threat of criminal sanctions.

Forgiving or Limiting Arrearages

Because fathers identified large arrearages as a key deterrent to participation in the child support system, the state could offer a one-time amnesty to fathers who have accumulated large debts to the state. Amnesty would be contingent on future compliance with support orders. Alternatively, the state could limit the size of arrears and thus preclude the need for amnesty (Roberts 1999). In particular, states could cap the amount of arrears that a low-income noncustodial father could accumulate, suspend accumulation of arrears whenever he is incarcerated, cancel arrears when he reunites with his family, or limit the amount of a retroactive award when a support order is first entered or when a noncustodial father first receives notice of his support obligation.[4]

Recognizing Informal Support

Fathers sometimes arrived at court with receipts showing proof of in-kind or monetary payments to the mother for support of the child. Others said they had lived with the mother and had paid such major expenses as rent. In cases for which such contributions are well documented, the court could use the amounts to offset arrearages accrued before formal orders were established, or the court could consider these contributions when determining current orders. Given the changes that have occurred in family formation since the child support system was first created, particularly the increase in cohabitation, greater consideration could be given to fathers' participation in these informal unions. When fathers are living with their partner and child and are contributing to their support, a child support order should not be established. Similarly, if parents move in together after an order is set, the order should be suspended. Although parents may be reluctant to admit they are living together if they believe their welfare, medical, or food stamp benefits will be reduced or eliminated, the effective implementation of this policy, coupled with increased knowledge of the benefits available to cohabiting couples, may encourage more parents to reside together and thus promote their child's well-being.

Addressing Domestic Violence Issues

Some evidence indicates that welfare recipients experience high levels of domestic violence.[5] Heightened enforcement of child support could increase contact with abusive fathers and trigger more incidents of violence (Allard et al. 1997; Raphael and Tolman 1997). My interviews and other research suggest that some mothers do not want child support because they wish to avoid contact with an abusive father, whereas others want child support but need protection from the father. Mothers who do not want to establish a child support order should be clearly informed that a "good cause" exemption exists, and they should be given adequate opportunity to claim this exemption. For mothers who seek an award, procedures should be put in place to ensure that contact with the former partner is minimized and that the mother's personal information is kept confidential from the father (National Women's Law Center and the Center on Fathers, Families, and Public Policy 2000).

Other Policy Options

Child support now represents an important source of income for poor children who receive it (Sorensen and Zibman 2000a). Even if child support payments increased, however, many families would still have incomes insufficient to support their children. Unmarried mothers often turn to welfare because they cannot pay for some of their children's basic expenses on the earnings and benefits offered by low-wage jobs. Short of universal health insurance and child care programs—which have received less political support in the United States than programs that target poor families—employment, income, and other supportive services could be expanded to cover more parents, including those parents who have incomes that are low but that do not fall below the official poverty line. Programs that promote work and enhance earnings have gained political favor under a system of public assistance that mandates employment.

Some states and counties have attempted to make work and income support services more widely available to low-income families. Examples of these efforts include (1) providing child care, transportation, housing subsidies, and other supportive services to families; (2) ensuring that low-income families receive benefits such as Medicaid and food stamps for which they are eligible; (3) expanding health coverage for children and their parents; (4) providing educational and training opportunities to help families advance economically; and (5) offering an earned income tax credit at the state level and a higher state minimum wage to increase the earnings of low-income workers (Lazere, Fremstad, and Goldberg 2000).[6]

In recent years, more low-income single mothers have been working, and fewer have been receiving welfare.[7] However, many of these working parents and their children have remained poor. Work-based strategies will have limited effects if the wages of less-skilled workers continue to be low, and they may be inadequate when unemployment increases as a result of economic downturns (Ellwood 2000).[8] New policy should make the reduction of poor families, rather than a reduction in the number of families receiving welfare, its primary goal. For example, the United States could follow the United Kingdom in attempting to cut child poverty rates in half in the next decade (Primus 2001).

Although some states offer employment and training services for low-income nonresident fathers, significantly more resources are offered to help custodial mothers receiving welfare to enter the workforce. It is critical to retain these resources for mothers. Like custodial mothers, many noncustodial fathers have low incomes and face significant barriers to employment, such as low levels of education, lack of work experience, health problems, and substance abuse. Some fathers have additional barriers as a result of being incarcerated (Johnson, Levine, and Doolittle 1999; Sorensen and Zibman 2000b, 2001). Because poor fathers are expected to pay child support, many of the employment and work support services available to mothers could also be made available to fathers, thus allowing them to stabilize their income and better support their children (Sorensen and Zibman 2000b, 2001). States could also consider providing jobs for unemployed fathers who have a child support obligation.

Approximately half of unmarried parents are living together at the time of their child's birth and another third are involved in romantic relationships but are not living together, indicating that early commitments between parents are strong. However, these relationships are highly vulnerable to dissolution over time. Services could be designed with the goal of helping unmarried parents maintain and strengthen their relationships and of keeping fathers connected to their families. (This objective should only be pursued, however, in situations where paternal involvement would not be detrimental to mothers or their children.) Rather than assuming these families consist of a single parent and absent father, programs would treat unmarried mothers, fathers, and their children as a family. For example, programs offered at or near the time of birth could assess the needs of all family members and refer them to available services (McLanahan, Garfinkel, and Mincy 2001).

In some states, welfare policies or practices favor one-parent over two-parent families—including two-parent families made up of unmarried parents who live together—with the possible effect of discouraging cohabitation and unmarried fathers' presence in the family (McLanahan, Garfinkel, and Mincy 2001). Eliminating any restrictions on welfare eligibility that make it more difficult for two-parent families to receive TANF and increasing access to cash and in-kind assistance (such as health care, food stamps, and housing) for cohabiting parents would help parents establish a stable household together (Sorensen, Mincy, and Halpern 2000). Welfare regulations also encourage parents to live apart (or falsely report that they are living apart) because eligibility for welfare is calculated on the basis of household members' income. By counting only a portion of the father's income when determining eligibility and benefits, disincentives to cohabitation would be reduced (McLanahan, Garfinkel, and Mincy 2001). Because some parents do not know they are eligible for benefits when they live together, efforts could also be made to increase their awareness of program rules.

These steps to help unmarried mothers and fathers in the low-wage labor market achieve greater economic stability and to help couples stay together might make it more financially possible for parents to marry. At the same time, marriage should not be viewed as a primary or universal solution to poverty, given the significant changes in family formation in contemporary society and the complex socio-economic challenges that low-income unmarried parents often face.[9]

* * *

As nonmarital childbearing and nonresident fatherhood have become more prevalent, concerns about paternal absence and nonsupport have also grown. Many of these concerns are warranted; however, some are motivated by the perception that unmarried fathers lack any sense of paternal responsibility. My findings indicate that unmarried parents share collective beliefs about paternal responsibility and commonly establish informal arrangements of paternal acknowledgment and support. Unfortunately, these arrangements often break down over time. Furthermore, they are often invisible to legislators and consequently are ignored by the courts. By building on these beliefs and practices and helping fathers meet their financial obligations to their children, policymakers can design more effective child and family support policies even as they increase the long-term stability of relationships between unmarried parents and their children.

Methodological Issues

In this appendix I reconstruct my experiences over two years of fieldwork, the methodology I followed in this study, and the ways I chose to represent the men and women who participated. In the spirit of this genre, I have attempted to reflect on the responsibility that comes with imposing order on complex events and to acknowledge some of the emotional and ethical issues I encountered while conducting this research. During this research and fieldwork, I faced the task of describing other people's experiences and feelings— ones that sometimes contrasted sharply with my own but at other times were quite familiar. In this appendix I hope to provide a window into my successes and failures, and the unknowable ways in which my interactions with the men and women I met affected their self-representations, elicited emotional responses, and recast their perceptions. In addition, I hope the appendix reveals how these conversations prompted me to look at the contours of race, gender, class, and my own identity in new ways.

After spending more than two hundred hours interviewing people about their lives, albeit around specified issues, I have done my best to represent their accounts in an honest way and do justice to the richness of their narratives. At a minimum, I made every effort not to misrepresent their accounts. However, as a researcher telling a coherent, sociological story, I have had to emphasize patterns within data. In the process of doing so, I was mindful of Burke's (1989) insight that in using language to reflect reality, we also select and deflect reality. I was also aware of Clifford and Marcus's (1986) discussion of the partiality of ethnographic interpretation and writing. I do not claim to reflect parents' experiences in their totality; this book presents my interpretations of people's self-representations of their experiences. Both my interpretations and their self-representations employ linguistic conventions that order complex events and facilitate communication. The accounts I present probably could be (and have been) told differently by the people I interviewed. I made choices at every step of the interviewing process, from what questions I asked to editing and revising the material for presentation. Furthermore, I have faced limitations in my ability to articulate the scope of this material. Although readers do not have full access to the transcripts, I hope they will interpret the excerpted segments in ways that enrich and challenge my own reading of the interviews.

False Starts and Gaining Entrée

Ethnographies often begin with stories of arrival and initial contact with the "natives" (Abu-Lughod 1993, xv). However, because all of my interviews took place within thirty minutes of my home (with one interview conducted in my apartment complex), my study began in a rather unromantic way. Because my initial plan was to contact unmarried parents through community organizations that serve low-income families in Trenton, my fieldwork began in my apartment as I leafed through the Yellow Pages looking for voluntary and social service agencies. This quick investigation led me to meet with a volunteer coordinator at the United Way, who provided me with a list of all the nonprofit agencies in the Trenton area and offered to distribute some information about my study. After trying out many different versions of a flyer, I designed a "Help Wanted" flyer that would convey some basic information about my research, capture potential interviewees' attention, and sound legitimate but not overly scientific. It noted the topic of the interview, my phone number, and the $20 monetary compensation.[1]

I realized that some social service agencies might not distribute my flyer if I did not have a personal contact at the agency. Therefore, I decided to contact agencies such as day care, job training, family planning, and drug rehabilitation centers that served low-income parents directly. But before I started making my calls, a flood of questions entered my mind: Do I present myself as a researcher at Princeton University (which may carry negative connotations in Trenton) or as a graduate student (in which case I may have less legitimacy)?[2] How do I describe my research project in a way that seems relevant to the agency? Can I offer the agency anything in return? As a white middle-class woman who does not live in the community, how do I convey my sense of responsibility as a researcher, my concern about poverty among unmarried parents and their children, and my sensitivity to their clients?

How do I convince myself of my own legitimacy, given that I had never done a project like this before?

Because most of the people I contacted were receptive to my project, some of my concerns about self-presentation turned out to be less important than how to reach agency directors with extremely busy schedules. I usually had to wait days or weeks for return calls. Because the people at the agencies were doing me a favor, I was unsure of how persistent I should be in following up the initial contact. After I reached the appropriate people, they often asked for a letter about the project and for verification that I had received approval from the "human subjects" committee at Princeton. So I mailed out this information and continued waiting for my real research to begin.

After numerous delays, these initial efforts began to pay off. Soon I was meeting with social service providers all over the city. I also spoke at a community center and to General Equivalency Degree (GED) classes. During the same period, I posted flyers in Trenton's convenience stores, laundromats, grocery stores, and thrift stores in low-income neighborhoods. Although the flyers helped publicize my study, only a few people responded to them. Finally, I took out a classified ad in the local newspaper that specifically requested interviews with fathers. Unfortunately, this information and my home phone number were mistakenly placed in the personals section near ads that sought partners of various physical and sexual descriptions. (Thankfully, no one called.) I had more luck with the child care centers at which mothers and fathers received information about my study. The major problem with sampling from child care centers quickly became apparent: only a small number of women receiving AFDC and attending work programs placed their children in these centers. Furthermore, I could not effectively reach noncustodial fathers through these agencies. Although after months of contacting agencies and distributing information I had found only a few important contacts, I had gained a much better sense of the city. Unfortunately, I still did not have an effective sampling strategy. It seemed I was back to square one.

During the time I was seeking potential interviewees, I set up a meeting at the Child Support Enforcement (IV-D) office. The purpose of this meeting was to find out how welfare (IV-A) and Child Support Enforcement (IV-D) offices coordinated location, paternity establishment, and enforcement of child support from fathers of children receiving welfare and to get their take on parents' reactions to the child support system. Some of the information I received at this meeting, however, was different from what I later learned from many parents. I was told stories of men rounded up in a paddy wagon and arrested for nonsupport who then miraculously came up with a large "purge payment" in order to be released from prison. They also described men—influenced by the fathers' rights movement—who threatened child support workers. Although I had asked specifically about parents of children on welfare, these stories seemed to describe the experiences of higher-income fathers.

A turning point in my research came when I met two people well connected to social service agencies in the community. The first was a female minister of a church in Trenton at which a Head Start program, a food pantry, and a Women, Infants, and Children (WIC) site were located. By a stroke of good fortune, her administrative assistant also worked at another church with a WIC site and took it upon herself to talk with the woman who headed the WIC program in Mercer county. After meeting with the WIC director and explaining the project to her at length, she generously offered me access to clinics throughout the county.[3] A second key connection was with a young African American man who worked as a social service provider in Trenton and who introduced me to several unmarried mothers receiving welfare.

The Interview Experience

As I began setting up interviews with parents, I alternated between feelings of excitement about beginning the project and of apprehension about intruding on people's lives. I primarily struggled with whether my distance from the men and women I planned to interview (in terms of my identity and social location) would prohibit me from understanding their experiences and whether my research objective justified intensive contact with them. After discussing these issues with women in my pilot sample, my reticence dissipated but never quite disappeared. Throughout this project, I tried to sensitize myself to the power dynamics of qualitative interviewing and to the issues my particular research would raise. Although I attempted to minimize these imbalances and to incorporate reflexivity into each step of the research process, I did not want to ignore the authority I had assumed as an interviewer, interpreter, and writer. I typically initiated contact with parents, set the agenda for the interview, asked the majority of the questions, and interpreted their responses. Although I found many points of commonality, had meaningful contacts, and developed some friendships with my interviewees, my experiences differed in undeniable ways from those of the men and women I interviewed.

Before talking to parents, I designed an interview schedule that was structured around some general topics and that asked interviewees for specific demographic and background information. Within this structure, however, I asked mostly open-ended questions that allowed parents to elaborate on their responses.[4] I also modified my questions in response to issues raised by respondents. The interviews typically began with questions about a parent's experiences in his or her family of origin and current family life. I then moved the discussion toward more "cultural" questions about childrearing, about how parents distinguished good fathers from bad (both in the abstract and through specific examples), and about how they evaluated themselves and their child's other parent. The second half of the interview attempted to draw out narratives about an interviewee's relationship with the other parent(s), the experience of having a child outside of marriage, the participation of the father (or of the interviewee as father) in a child's life, and a parent's interaction with the child support system. During this part of the interview, I included scenarios to which I asked participants to respond, hoping to explore their general views about how unmarried parents should behave in specific situations. These scenarios encouraged parents to state their beliefs about marriage, reproduction, and paternal and maternal responsibility in relation to each other. Finally, I solicited their views about the governmental programs for unmarried parents and their children.

In my early interviews, I followed this schedule of questions closely and proceeded in the order I have just described. However, as I became more comfortable with my skills as an interviewer and with the topics I wanted to cover, I would ask parents general questions and prompt them with other questions that had not yet been answered. I also encouraged parents to establish a narrative flow and to introduce other issues that I had not mentioned. As my research proceeded, I was able to hear more nuances in what parents were telling me. Therefore, I varied the order of my questions, modified my interview schedule, and added different questions as I got a better sense of which issues were most salient to parents. Usually I met with parents only one time for the interview, which would usually last an average of two to three hours.[5] However, some interviews were as brief as ninety minutes, whereas others lasted for more than four hours.

After first meeting the interviewee, I usually spent some time chatting to help put both of us at ease. When I interviewed women, I would often bring a dessert or a toy for their children. Because interviews with men were usually held in restaurants, we ordered a drink or food and began talking before beginning the interview. To lessen the formality of the event, I dressed casually and used everyday language. In all of my interviews, I found humor to be a tremendous help in establishing rapport. Conversations began and were punctuated by frequent laughter. After talking for a short time, I would paraphrase the human subjects consent form, which told parents that interviews were confidential, that they could stop the interview at any time and still be compensated for participating, and that they could refuse to answer any of my questions. I also asked for permission to record our conversation.[6] Before we both signed the form, I gave them their payment for participating and asked them to pick a pseudonym for the written report.

Convinced by feminist arguments that an "impartial," blank-faced interviewing style often exacerbates power differences and coveys unintended, negative messages to research participants (Oakley 1981; Frankenberg 1993), I attempted to use a conversational and dialogic approach to interviewing.[7] In practice, this meant telling interviewees that they could introduce new topics for discussion, ask me to clarify or rephrase a question, or ask about my experiences with and interest in a topic. I also shared my thoughts and experiences when I felt they were relevant and appropriate.[8] However, I tried to be sensitive to how much each person seemed to want me to talk and made comments accordingly.[9]

In an article on feminist interviewing, Ann Oakley (1981) questioned the ethical position of withholding important information and advice from interviewees to maintain interviewer objectivity. Although I was obviously not qualified to give psychological or legal advice, I did bring a list of referrals with me and sometimes called parents after the interview with these numbers if they asked for assistance.[10] I believe this interviewing style not only helped to minimize power differences but also to explore more sensitive issues, such as when men were sure of their paternity or when parents were avoiding the child support system. One white father, in fact, did not acknowledge he had two children outside of marriage until well into the interview, when he presumably felt more comfortable with me. This style of interviewing also helped me to clarify the meaning of questions with parents and to obtain more reliable responses. For example, a fifteen-minute discussion with one father was necessary to establish whether or not he paid child support, during which time he changed his answer a few times and eventually acknowledged that he was unsure about what child support was.

The interviews varied according to interviewees' personalities, their interest in the issues raised, and how much time they had to spend with me. For example, one shy, young, white father told me he was afraid he would not be able to say enough during the interview because he talks so little to his coworkers and had trouble speaking to his lawyer. He had to struggle to keep his voice at an audible level and was pleased with how much he had to say. However, another young African American mother with a very outgoing personality asked me to bring extra tapes to her interview, came with a clear idea of what she wanted to talk about, resisted my efforts to keep her on track if she had not completely finished a story, and offered advice about how to describe certain issues. Incidents like this reveal points at which interviewees contested my power to set the agenda and to interpret their words and experiences. Although I remember only one occasion in which someone said they did not want to answer a question, there were other instances in which parents seemed to evade or deflect questions I posed to them.

Recording the interviews was less intrusive than I had anticipated. On some occasions parents would say something interesting after I had turned off the tape recorder. Before they got too far, I simply asked if I could turn it back on. Some respondents would pick up the tape recorder and talk directly into it when they wanted to emphasize a point. A few times, respondents would ask me to stop recording momentarily (for example, when they were talking about illegal activity).

The men and women I interviewed reacted to me in various ways, and none of these reactions fell neatly or simply along race or gender lines. Although white parents and I shared some experiences that were shaped by membership in the same racial group, white women were generally more reserved than other respondents and sometimes seemed distrustful of me. Because of the sensitivity of talking about race, some African American parents may have had reactions to my being white that were not directly articulated, despite my attempts at times to inquire about these reactions. From my perspective, gender had more obvious and consistent effects on the substance of the interviews and how parents related to me. I did not necessarily have better rapport with women because of my gender, but the reactions from men and women did differ. After reviewing my tapes and field notes, the difference appeared most obvious in the informal conversations before and after the interview. Women seemed to relate to me as a young, single, heterosexual woman and as a student. For example, women made comments to me such as "You're single. You must know how hard it is to find a good man." Some of the women I interviewed attended educational or other training programs through welfare and compared our common status of being out of the labor market and in school. Some women also expressed an interest in developing a friendship with me.

Both men and women remarked that in some way it had helped them to talk during the interview. However, men more often characterized the interview as a chance "to get things off their chest" and suggested that they did not have people that they could talk to about these issues. Perhaps because they were unaccustomed to having professional contacts with women or opening up emotionally to a woman they were not dating, or perhaps because of the emotional ambiguity of an interview situation, men more often thought of me as a potential girlfriend than as a potential friend. This reaction to me may have affected men's self-presentation in the interview. However, even men who expressed interest in me revealed sensitive information about themselves, such as nonpayment of support, their facing of charges of domestic abuse, strained relationships with women and with their children, criminal activity, unemployment, drug use, homelessness, and imprisonment.

The reactions of parents ranged from questions about my life to requests for job referrals. The interviewees expressed surprise that I was (in their words) young, nice, concerned, busy, brave (and perhaps naive), that I was conducting interviews at housing projects, and that I was speaking with men. Common questions posed to me by both men and women were about whether I had children, a boyfriend, family in the area; what I was studying in school; why I was interested in these issues; and when the book would be finished. In response to my answers, parents alternately expressed sympathy or congratulated me for not having children at my age.[11] Parents sometimes commented on the fact that I was a student, a *Princeton* student, a writer, or a sociologist. They also talked about where I lived and about my physical appearance.[12] Some parents called to thank me for being empathetic during the interview. A few parents seemed annoyed because I was difficult to reach by phone. Some parents complained about the length of the interview and about my request for a referral to their child's father. Two parents thought the sexual content of their interviews might shock me. One of these was a man who was self-conscious about telling me about a physical fight he had had with his girlfriend. He said he hoped I would change things around, "like some writers do." At times parents seemed to hope that I could fill a therapeutic, legal, or advocacy role. Others viewed me as a potential employment contact, as a connection for obtaining governmental resources, or as someone who could advise them on child support.

My reactions to the men and women I interviewed, as well as to the circumstances in which we talked, also had effects on my interviewees' perceptions of me and on the research process. I laughed a great deal with many of the parents I spoke with. I also expressed admiration and empathy for parents, particularly women, who struggled to take care of their children in extremely difficult circumstances. With tremendous pain in her voice, one woman I interviewed in a condemned house described her experiences of physical abuse from her parents and ex-boyfriend, her loneliness and depression, and her frustrated efforts to better her family's financial situation. It was around this time that I realized the interviews had taken an emotional toll on me. Experiences like this motivated me occasionally to debrief with someone who had mental health training and to seek her advice about how to reply appropriately to parents' emotional disclosures.

Although I did not respond dispassionately to parents' stories, I did try to respond responsibly and sensitively to them. However, my sympathetic feelings sometimes turned to discomfort. After listening empathetically to a man who gave a nonchalant and detailed description of recently killing another person (in self-defense, as deemed by the court) while his seven-year-old son sat next to us laughing, I felt greatly disturbed. And although I tried to appreciate the severity of parents' economic problems, I had a few uncomfortable situations in which people showed up unexpectedly at interviews or at other locations to ask for money.[13]

I did not have an individual office telephone and sometimes worried that I had made myself too accessible by giving out my home telephone number. Therefore, in addition to developing strategies of emotion management, I also developed tactics for responding to the contexts in which I conducted interviews. For example, I became much more careful about where I met potential interviewees. After I became more familiar with Trenton housing projects, I scheduled interviews for the morning or early afternoon, when drug dealers were less likely to be outside. I also learned more about safe areas to park and about the location of unmarked buildings. I decided to meet fathers at fast food restaurants, rather than smaller, neighborhood restaurants whose managers seemed uncomfortable with having an interview there. After interviewing a man in a neighborhood restaurant while his ex-girlfriend circled the parking lot, I decided to conduct interviews in restaurants slightly outside the interviewee's neighborhood. Some situations, however, were more difficult to control, particularly when a parent lived in a small residence with other relatives who could not leave during our meeting.[14]

Analysis

All interviews were recorded and transcribed. I used the written transcripts to create a database that recorded demographic and other background information I collected about interviewees. I also used a qualitative data analysis program to organize and classify the massive amount of interview data. After I developed a coding scheme, this program allowed me to assign codes to segments of the text that varied in length from a single sentence to multiple paragraphs. For example, I assigned general labels to all segments in which parents talked about paternity establishment and more specific labels to those segments to identify practices of establishing paternity. With these codes in place, I could then search for labels across interviews, allowing me to organize files around specific topics that emerged either spontaneously or in response to my questions and to compare discursive statements systematically across interviews. I also analyzed interview transcripts individually to examine narratives and themes that emerged, to see the relationship between themes, and to examine the internal consistency of responses. My analysis was inductive in that I synthesized findings to develop "grounded theories" (Glaser and Strauss 1967) and interpretations. I also analyzed information deductively, drawing on theories proposed by other researchers and from previous empirical studies (Burawoy 1991). Finally, I compared how accounts varied with the race and gender of respondents.

Writing

In recent years, many qualitatively oriented social scientists have emphasized the importance of writing as part of the research process. Although earlier scholarly works addressed the style, rhetoric, and conventions used in academic writing (e.g., Burke 1989), discussions about how social scientists represent the information they have gathered in the field are now perhaps most lively among anthropologists. In Clifford and Marcus's (1986) edited collection on writing, contributors called attention to practices of representation within social science and to the editorial and interpretative dimensions of this process. Clifford's introduction about writing notes explained that "the fact that it has not until recently been portrayed or seriously discussed reflects the persistence of an ideology claiming transparency of representation and immediacy of experience" (1986, 2). Because ethnographic accounts come from the specific, socially located perspective of the writers, Clifford also observed that any written representations are better viewed as "partial truths" than as a simple mirroring of research experiences. In my written account of the interview material, I also chose which statements to present and emphasized commonalties in responses over divergences. And like all interpretations, I consider my perspective to be both partial and specific.

Although I did not hesitate to use innovative sampling and interviewing methods to help reduce power differentials and to optimize the quality of the information I collected, I followed standard sociological conventions, with some caveats, in writing this account. In particular, I extracted statements from parents' interviews and did not present their full narratives. I chose this style of representation, with some reluctance, to further other research objectives: because my focus was on the language parents draw upon to talk about fatherhood, I wanted to present both the consistency and the diversity of responses across interviews. In comparison to other areas of sociological inquiry, debates about poverty and family have been particularly contentious and politicized. Therefore, I felt it was important to provide substantial evidence to support my claims. Although I obviously selected which segments of text to present, by using multiple interviews I believe there was somewhat less risk of presenting idiosyncratic interviews that best support a position and ignoring less amenable accounts. I hope the diversity of voices also allows room for multiple interpretations of my evidence by the reader.

Having said this, I also take seriously Abu-Lughod (1993) and other writers' suggestion that breaking up narratives may discourage the reader from sympathizing with research subjects and keep him or her from seeing the complicated nature of people's lives. By collapsing experiences and imposing coherence on discordant practices, researchers often present an ahistorical portrait of communities and actually contribute to the invention of cultures.[15] Although I agree with this view, I would add that the literature on poverty in the United States is filled with examples of researchers presenting individual narratives that reproduce stereotypes within their own culture despite good intentions to the contrary. It also has been my experience that sympathetic retellings of people's stories do not necessarily encourage sympathetic readings if they are dismissed as being unrepresentative, particularly by policymakers.

Although the major drawback of presenting multiple voices is that it prevents the reader from getting a fuller sense of the lives of individual men and women, this approach allows me to examine shared narrative conventions. This type of analysis focuses more on the existence of narratives outside individual experiences that help constitute men's and women's selves and subjectivity. Furthermore, by showing links between interviewees' statements and larger discursive repertoires made available to them, I hope to avoid exoticizing the accounts of men and women living in poor communities.

I spent a considerable amount of time in Trenton and nearby communities attending religious services with parents; going to birthday parties, cookouts, and church picnics; hanging out in people's apartments and homes; shopping at grocery stores; eating in neighborhood restaurants; driving around; sitting in on appointments at welfare offices; and visiting family court. Although my focus is on the language that parents used during interviews (which is documented in the transcripts), I draw on these experiences to interpret what people told me in interviews and to verify what cultural repertoires are available to them. Although I do not explicitly examine the use of language in social settings outside of the interview, the other conversations I heard about fatherhood, child support, and parenting informed my understanding of these issues.

Even though a systematic analysis of the language used in other social situations to discuss fatherhood would complement my approach in this study, I do not consider what parents told me in interviews to be less authentic simply because it did not occur in a natural setting. I view the interview, like discussions in people's homes and on the street, as performance. And because all linguistic accounts vary with the audience, the context, and time, they are always being modified and revised. Rather than trying to reveal the truth in what parents told me or to uncover what they *really* thought or felt, I focus on the cultural categories and resources that parents used to think about issues. I consider the statements made in the interview to be somewhere between public and private. They were made in the context of a private, one-on-one conversation, but they were addressed to someone whom they did not know well. Also, although the confidential nature of the interview may have encouraged more openness, the interviewees knew the content was intended for a larger audience (Scott 1990). Therefore, I argue that one test of the validity of my analysis would be to compare my findings with those of other researchers who have documented statements made in interviews and in participant observation with low-income parents. I engage these texts throughout this account. Although I look at new questions and present new research findings, our accounts of similar issues are largely consistent.

APPENDIX B

TABLE 1. Selected Characteristics of Mothers

Characteristics	African American Mothers	White Mothers	All Mothers
Average age	24	26	25
Average number of children	2	2	2
Average age of focal child[a]	2	3	2
Education and employment (%)			
Less than high school	45	38	42
High school diploma or GED	5	12	8
More than high school	50	50	50
Currently employed	5	31	17
Welfare status			
Child received AFDC	100	94	97
Child received Medicaid only	0	6	3
n	20	16	36

[a]The focal child refers to the parent's youngest child who has received welfare.

TABLE 2. Selected Characteristics of Fathers

Characteristics	African American Fathers	White Fathers	All Fathers
Average age	26	30	27
Average number of children	2	2	2
Average age of focal child[a]	3	6	4
Education and employment (%)			
Less than high school	35	22	31
High school diploma or GED	25	44	31
More than high school	40	33	38
Currently employed	65	56	62
Welfare status			
Child received AFDC	100	78[b]	93
Child received Medicaid only	0	22	7
n	20	9	29

[a]The focal child refers to the parent's youngest child who has received welfare.
[b]This figure includes one father who was uncertain about whether his child had received AFDC.

NOTES

1. For example, these sentiments are expressed by several of the contributors to Horn, Blankenhorn, and Pearlstein's (1999) edited volume. See also Blankenhorn 1995 and Popenoe 1996.

2. The Clinton-Gore administration introduced the goal of strengthening fatherhood as a top priority, and President Clinton issued this directive to federal agencies in 1995 (White House 1995). President George W. Bush's appointment of the former president of the National Fatherhood Initiative, Wade Horn, to be assistant secretary of health and human services, and his support of responsible fatherhood programs, also signals the Bush administration's interest in fathers.

3. This image was popularized in Bill Moyers's television special titled "The Vanishing Family: Crisis in Black America" that aired on CBS on January 25, 1986. Moyers's widely watched documentary gave viewers a glimpse of poor, urban communities in which young men fathered numerous children outside of marriage as an expression of their masculinity and then nonchalantly abandoned these children to the welfare system. Viewers witnessed young, unmarried men who not only lacked a sense of responsibility to their children but also actually bragged about having children whom they did not support. One young man who made a prominent appearance on the show had six children by four different women and justified his failure to support his children by saying, "The majority of the mothers are on welfare. And welfare gives them the stipend for the month. So what I'm not doing, the Government does" (Griswold 1993, 237).

4. Of those never-married mothers who had a child support award or agreement, approximately 48 percent received some payment in 1997 (U.S. Census Bureau 2000, 7). Although most never-married mothers do not receive child support, the creation of the In-Hospital Paternity Acknowledgment Program has led to substantial increases in the numbers of paternities established in recent years (Committee on Ways and Means 2000, 475).

5. The Fragile Families and Child Wellbeing Study is a new, nationally representative

study of unmarried parents and their children that was designed to fill this gap. For information about the study see http://crcw.princeton.edu/fragilefamilies/. Other national surveys have also added questions about fatherhood in response to the growing interest in this field. Some of these surveys include unmarried fathers in their samples (see Marsiglio et al. 2000; U.S. Department of Health and Human Services 2001).

6. See Appendix A for more discussion of the interview format.

7. See note 5. Interviews with unmarried parents in the FFCW study are initially conducted at the time of their child's birth; follow-up interviews are conducted when the child is twelve, thirty, and forty-eight months old. The total sample includes approximately 4,890 families (i.e., 3,704 births to unmarried parents and 1,186 births to married parents). These data are representative of nonmarital births in each of the twenty cities studied and are representative of all nonmarital births in U.S. cities with populations greater than 200,000. See Reichman et al. 2001 for more information about the FFCW study's research design. Sara McLanahan and Irwin Garfinkel are the principal investigators of the Fragile Families and Child Wellbeing Study. I am part of a network of scholars that helped design and pilot the study.

8. The current analysis focuses on language as a way to understand the cultural categories through which unmarried parents perceive their experiences and through which their experiences attain meaning (Gusfield 1989). Sociologists have approached language—and the meaning systems that it entails—as a social construction that has a constraining effect on people. This view is summarized in Berger and Luckman's well-known statement: "Society is a human product. Society is an objective reality. Man is a social product" (1967, 61). Recent investigations of culture have also placed language and communication at the center of their analytical frameworks (Wuthnow 1987). In this work, language is often approached as a "meaning constituting system: that is, any system—strictly verbal or other—through which meaning is constructed and cultural practices organized and by which, accordingly, people represent and understand their world, including who they are and how they relate to others" (Scott 1988, 34).

9. See Mills 1940 for an earlier discussion of strategies of action and Hannerz 1969 for a discussion of cultural repertoires.

10. In this study, I use the term "responsibility" in its general sense and analyze how parents' ideas about this subject emerge in interviews. However, in the literature on fatherhood, the term "responsibility" has sometimes been used in a normative way. For example, Doherty, Kouneski, and Erickson (1998) offer a "value advocacy" approach to defining this term. Drawing on Levine and Pitt 1995, they define responsible fathering in regard to establishing legal paternity and sharing with the mother the emotional and physical care as well as continuing financial support of the child. The authors suggest that marriage is optimal for promoting responsible fatherhood. The term "responsibility" has also been used in a body of empirical studies in a specific but non-normative way (i.e. Lamb et al., 1987).

11. Other qualitative studies of low-income fathers include Achatz and MacAllum 1994; Furstenberg 1995; Allen and Doherty 1996; Hamer 1998, 2001; Johnson, Levine, and Doolittle 1999; and Roy 1999. I was unable to include a discussion of Hamer's (2001) work because my own work was already in press at the time of its release. However, Hamer's findings, like those of other qualitative work in this field, are largely consistent with those presented in this book.

12. Research on fatherhood has grown substantially over the last decade, as academic interest in fathers, as well as funding from the federal government and foundations, has increased. See Marsiglio et al. 2000 for an excellent overview of developments in this field. A relatively small proportion of this research focuses on low-income, unmarried fathers. See the previous note for exceptions.

1. Studying Unmarried Parents

1. Interviewees' names used in this book are pseudonyms that were chosen either by the interviewee or by the author.

2. In 1995, the percentage of births in which the mother received no prenatal care was more than twice as high in Trenton than in the state as a whole, the percentage of children born at low birth weights was about 37 percent higher, and the infant mortality rate was about 45 percent higher (Millhill Child and Family Development Corporation and the Association for Children of New Jersey 2001).

3. Cumbler (1989, 187–188) suggests that Trenton's economic decline began in the 1920s but did not accelerate until the 1950s and 1960s. According to Cumbler, Trenton was at the forefront of a national economic pattern characterized by decreases in manufacturing jobs and increases in public- and service-sector employment.

4. In 1992, Hill Refrigeration was one of the six major employers in Trenton. The five other top employers included the state of New Jersey, St. Francis Medical Center, Helene Fuld Medical Center, Mercer Medical Center, and the Hibbert Group (Mercer County Planning Board 1992).

5. The third largest racial/ethnic group was Hispanic, comprising 14 percent of the population in Trenton, 6 percent in Mercer County, and 9 percent in Middlesex County (U.S. Census Bureau 1990).

6. The Hispanic population in Trenton increased to approximately 22 percent (U.S. Census Bureau 2001).

7. In 1996, Trenton had twenty "Brownfield sites," that is, former industrialized sites that have been abandoned or have been seriously underutilized (Millhill Child and Family Development Corporation and the Association for Children of New Jersey 2001).

8. In 1995, the average single mother with two children in the United States participating in the AFDC or food stamp program received $377 per month in cash benefits and $214 in food stamps. The combined value of AFDC and food stamps left women 44 percent below the poverty line (Committee on Ways and Means 1996).

9. I interviewed 85 parents, 20 of whom were not included in the final sample. These 20 parents served as "informants" for this study and provided important points of comparison. For example, many of these parents had not received state assistance and were not subject to mandatory paternity establishment and child support regulations. Therefore, their relationships with the child support system were often quite different from those of parents whose cooperation was required.

10. I chose not to interview Hispanic parents because they comprised a small segment of the Trenton population relative to whites and African Americans. See n. 5.

11. Census data indicated that white, single-parent households with incomes below the poverty line were more likely to be distributed throughout Mercer and Middlesex Counties than to be concentrated in Trenton. New Jersey vital statistics also suggested that nonmarital births to white women were distributed across these counties. Therefore I sampled more white parents in areas adjacent to Trenton than in the central city.

12. In 1996, about 83 percent of children living with unmarried parents resided only with their mother (U.S. Census Bureau 2001b).

13. About 71 percent of nonmarital births occur to women age twenty and older, and the majority of teenagers who have a child outside of marriage are legal adults (that is, they are at least eighteen or nineteen years old). Birth rates for teenagers have also declined since 1994, particularly among blacks (Ventura and Bachrach 2000; Ventura et al. 1995).

14. In the sample of African American parents, one mother and her child had left AFDC within the past year but still received Medicaid, and five fathers had children who

had left AFDC within the last few years. Among white mothers and their children, five had stopped receiving AFDC in the past two years, and one had stopped receiving it five years prior to the study. All of these women and their children still received assistance from the Women, Infants, and Children (WIC) program and therefore had incomes below 125 percent of the poverty line. Three white fathers had children who had stopped receiving AFDC in the past three years. Finally, I decided to include one white father who had never seen his child and was unsure about whether or not the child received AFDC. Because his child's mother worked before the pregnancy as a go-go dancer, had stopped working during the pregnancy, and had received no financial assistance from him or from her family, he thought she could have received some form of public assistance, particularly at the time of the birth. By including this father, I was also able to examine an extreme case of a father who had never seen his child.

15. In 1996 and 1997, the public high school graduation rate in Trenton was about 30 percent for students who, four years earlier, had been enrolled in ninth grade (Millhill Child and Family Development Corporation and the Association for Children of New Jersey 2001).

16. In 1995, African American males eighteen years old and over had twice the unemployment rate of white males (8.8 versus 4.3 percent) (U.S. Bureau of Labor and Statistics 2001). These data do not include the number of men who are "jobless" and not currently seeking employment. See Wilson 1996 for an analysis of the prevalence and effects of joblessness among black fathers in poor communities.

17. The FFCW data are representative of nonmarital births in cities with populations over two hundred thousand.

18. Of non-Hispanic, black, and white parents in the FFCW sample, the mean age of black mothers was 24 and of white mothers was 23, while the mean age of black fathers was 27 and of white fathers was 26. About 37 percent of black mothers and 31 percent of white mothers did not have a high school diploma, about 33 percent of black mothers and 42 percent of white mothers had a high school diploma or GED, and about 31 percent of black mothers and 28 percent of white mothers had education or training beyond high school. In comparison, about 28 percent of black fathers and 33 percent of white fathers did not have a high school diploma, about 44 percent of black fathers and 34 percent of white fathers had a high school diploma or GED, and about 28 percent of black fathers and 33 percent of white fathers had some education or training beyond high school.

19. The age of the focal child (i.e., the youngest child who received public assistance) ranged from one month to fourteen years.

20. Approximately 81 percent non-Hispanic black parents in the FFCW sample were involved in romantic relationships at the time of their child's birth: 37 percent of these parents were cohabiting and another 44 percent were involved in romantic relationships but were not cohabiting. Similarly, 83 percent of non-Hispanic white parents were romantically involved at the time of the birth. However, 66 percent of white parents were living together, and only 17 percent were involved in relationships but were not living together.

21. WIC is a federally funded program that provides nutritional supplements such as milk, cheese, and formula to infants, children under five, and pregnant or breastfeeding women. I sampled from WIC because its clients closely matched the total population of women on welfare.

22. Seven African American mothers and 12 white mothers were contacted through WIC, 11 African American mothers and 3 white mothers were contacted through personal referrals, 1 African American mother and 1 white mother were contacted through flyers at a day care center, and 1 African American mother was contacted on the street.

23. What I said to parents varied, but I would usually tell them I was in school and

writing a report or book on the experiences and opinions of unmarried parents. I added that I was interested in learning about how families were changing and about the involvement of fathers in their children's lives in these new circumstances. Sometimes I talked about my interest in the child support system. I always noted that they would receive $20 for participating.

24. Three mothers called immediately before the interview to cancel, and I was unable to reschedule.

25. In some cases, I conducted more than one interview with parents.

26. I offered interviewees $5 for each referral in addition to the payment for the interview. Although parents were certainly motivated by the economic compensation, I do not believe this tainted the interviews. Respondents had to be willing to spend a significant amount of time with me talking about their personal life. Thankfully, most parents were enthusiastic about being interviewed; however, I did not want to interview people who were interested for strictly altruistic or ideological reasons. I also thought it was appropriate to compensate people for the time and effort they gave me. Although some parents said it was not necessary for me to pay them for the interview, I always did. When they expressed concern about taking money from me or when it threatened to violate our established rapport, I reminded parents that the money did not come out of my pocket.

27. The more informal conversations I had with women as a group or individually revolved around our status as unmarried women. However, at times our differences within this shared identity were emphasized. For example, because I was not a mother, I was alternatively advised to finish school before having children or to have children before I got much older. I was also told that I could be a good mother. My whiteness was also sometimes a point of conversation with African American mothers and usually was handled with friendly humor and questions about my experiences.

28. I asked for feedback on why a few men did not provide their names or follow through on interviews. One father told me that his friend was "in trouble with child support" and did not want to take any chances. Another father felt hurt that he could not see his new baby and said he would have difficulty talking about it. A third father who was interviewed told me that his brother would not participate because he felt guilty about his relationship with his daughter. These responses suggest that I interviewed more highly involved fathers. Furthermore, some fathers probably misunderstood what I was doing. This became apparent when one father showed up for the interview in dress clothes because he thought he would be speaking to a group or possibly be on a television talk show. As with women, I was able to give fathers more information about the interview when we spoke on the telephone after our first introduction.

29. Although some men who did not show up at our first scheduled meeting were interviewed at a later time, I had four no-shows with black fathers and one with a white father with whom I could not reschedule, in part, it seems, because of these logistical difficulties.

30. For example, I would occasionally get collect calls from one father asking me to come to a gas station immediately to interview one of his friends who stopped by.

31. Ten African American fathers were sampled from the street, seven were sampled from personal referrals, and three responded to fliers for the study.

32. Seven white fathers were sampled through referrals, and two were sampled from a program for noncustodial fathers.

33. Daniel Patrick Moynihan's 1965 report, *The Negro Family: The Case for National Action,* opened the contemporary policy debate about the role of public policy in promoting two-parent families. Although its focus was on black families, the report drew public attention to the changing structure of families and called for a national response to this issue. At the time this report was released, however, less than 8 percent of all births in

the United States occurred to unmarried women (Ventura and Bachrach 2000). The Moynihan report also focused on the fact that approximately 25 percent of black children were born to unmarried parents. This is about same proportion (22 percent) of children who are now born to unmarried white parents. In light of these trends, Charles Murray (1993) has expressed concern over the emergence of a white "underclass."

34. Births to unmarried white women make up the largest percentage of births outside of marriage in the United States (40 percent), followed by births to black (32 percent) and Hispanic (25 percent) women. However, the proportion of births outside of marriage is higher among black and Hispanic parents than white parents. Approximately 69 percent of births to black women and 42 percent of births to Hispanic women are nonmarital, compared with about 22 percent of births to white women (Ventura and Bachrach 2000).

2. Separation of Reproduction and Marriage

1. The analytical framework in this chapter draws on Burke's (1989) view of how individuals select, define, and understand events through language and Mills's (1940) discussion of vocabularies of motive. Mills suggests that these vocabularies are developed in response to specific situations and expressed in ways that are appropriate to an intended audience. Because the accounts I examine were solicited in interviews, I recognize them as explanations also constructed for the imagined reader and me. I do not examine parents' discursive strategies in other situations outside of the interview.

2. See Luker 1996 on the separation of reproduction and marriage.

3. Preliminary evidence from the Fragile Families and Child Wellbeing (FFCW) study shows that almost 7 out of 10 unmarried mothers and more than 5 out of 10 unmarried fathers had incomes at or below 200 percent of the poverty line (McLanahan et al. 2001). Between 1983 and 1988, only 21 percent of women who had experienced a nonmarital birth had been educated beyond high school (Ventura et al. 1995, 21). In recent years, nonmarital birth rates have declined among African Americans and teenagers while they have increased among whites (Ventura and Bachrach 2000). See chap. 1, n. 34, for differences in nonmarital childbearing by race and ethnicity, and chap. 1, n. 13, for distributions by age.

4. The percentage of nonmarital births has risen because births to unmarried women increased while births to married women declined. Data from the early 1990s show that this pattern is the result of increasing birth rates among unmarried women as well as increasing numbers of unmarried women at childbearing ages. As more women postponed marriage, a decrease in birth rates among married women also occurred (Ventura and Bachrach 2000, 3–4).

5. Between 1965 and 1998, the percentage of unmarried women aged 20 to 24 increased from 33 to 73 percent and the percentage of unmarried women aged 25 to 29 increased from 13 to 45 percent. The percentage of unmarried women also increased among females aged 18 and 19 and aged 30 to 44 (Ventura and Bachrach 2000).

6. Most of the increase in the number of cohabitors occurred among non-Hispanic white women (Ventura and Bachrach 2000, 8).

7. Hypotheses about the effects of women's economic independence on declining marriage rates have not been supported consistently by the empirical research (Lichter 1995; Moore 1995). See Bane and Ellwood 1994 (109–117) on the effects of welfare and Oppenheimer 1997 on the effects of women's employment.

8. Economists tend to attribute increases in earnings inequality to the higher premium placed on skilled labor. Some of the causes for the rising value of skilled labor include increases in automation, globalization, and immigration as well as institutional

changes such as declines in the minimum wage and unionization (Danziger and Reed 1999).

9. Scholars also point to the unequal sex ratio between low-income African American men and women (partly the result of a high rate of male incarceration and mortality rates) to explain declines in marriage (Tucker and Mitchell-Kernan 1995).

10. Studies have explored cultural and psychological motives underlying the decision to have a child outside of marriage among young low-income parents. Examples of these discussions include Dash 1989; Anderson 1989; Sullivan 1989; Burton 1990, 1995; Furstenberg 1991; and Musick 1993.

11. Although McLanahan and Sandefur (1994, 3) find that low income is the most important factor explaining negative outcomes for children who grow up in single-parent families, inadequate parental guidance and attention and lack of ties to community resources also contribute significantly to these outcomes.

12. The "feminization of poverty" in families headed by single women has been attributed to women earning less than men, to the failure of nonresident fathers to support their children at the same level as resident fathers do, and to low levels of government assistance for single-parent families in the United States (Garfinkel and McLanahan 1986).

13. These findings are consistent with Frank Furstenberg's (1991, 134) discussion of the fertility decisions of teenage parents. Furstenberg notes that "most attempt contraception but practice it irregularly. As a result, many drift into parenthood as an unintended result of having sex." He also suggests that individuals may "misjudge or distort their chances of becoming pregnant in contrast to the chances of everyone else."

14. According to the National Survey of Family Growth, approximately 78 percent of never-married women and 63 percent of formerly married women characterized their pregnancies as unintended. Approximately 31 percent of married mothers also indicated that they had had unintentional pregnancies (Ventura and Bachrach 2000, 9, 11).

15. This figure includes more than 50 percent of African American parents and approximately 40 percent of white parents in the study.

16. Although abortion rates among unmarried white and black women are similar, some survey results indicate that African Americans are less accepting of abortion than are whites (see Thornton 1995).

17. Before 1973, approximately 19 percent of nonmarital births to white women and 1.5 percent to black women resulted in formal adoption, but these percentages dropped to 1.7 percent and less than 1 percent, respectively, between 1989 and 1995 (Ventura and Bachrach 2000, 12).

18. It is also important to note that seven white parents in the study had been married previously. Two of these fathers had had brief marriages to "legitimate" an earlier unplanned pregnancy, and one mother forged her own mother's signature in an attempt to marry before she was legally permitted to do so. These parents may have revised earlier explanations about marital decisions.

19. Wilson (1996, 104) observes that "inner-city black males and females believe that since most marriages will eventually break up and since marriages no longer represent meaningful relationships, it is better to avoid the entanglements of wedlock altogether. For many single mothers in the inner city, nonmarriage makes more sense as a family formation strategy than does marriage. Single mothers who perceive the fathers of their children as unreliable or as having limited financial means will often—rationally—choose single parenthood."

20. Approximately 76 percent of black mothers and 60 percent of black fathers reported that the wife having a steady job was very important, compared with 54 percent of white mothers and 25 percent of white fathers.

21. Wilson (1996, 101) writes that the attitude of many young single African American

fathers is, "'I'll get married in the future when I am no longer having fun and when I get a job or a better job.'"

22. In fact, Gerinomous (1991) and Luker (1996) argue that having children as teenagers may be beneficial to some mothers. Luker (1996, 170) also suggests that middle-class women may not envision a "good time" to have a baby: "in the new global economy (and in the face of a declining middle class) the absence of a social structure that supports both work and motherhood has created a situation in which there is never a 'good' time to have a baby. Thus, the birth patterns of poor and affluent women in the United States have begun to bifurcate, as each group tries to come to terms with the difficulties of having children in a country that provides so little support. Poor women continue the traditional American pattern of early childbearing, because in this way they can become mothers before they enter the paid labor force and while they can make moral claims on kinfolk who will help with the childrearing. Affluent women, on the other hand, tend to wait until they are well established in the labor force before having a child."

23. Other mothers I interviewed adopted a different strategy; they decided to have their children when they were young adults and to enter the labor force when their children began school (see previous note).

24. See Brooks-Gunn and Duncan 1997 for a review of the effects of poverty on children.

25. See Luker 1996 (151–154) for a discussion of the concepts of "wantedness" and "unintendedness" in regard to childbearing.

26. Fathers' expectations about marriage are higher than mothers' largely because the fathers who participated in the study were more likely to be in committed relationships than were those who did not participate (Waller 2001). Approximately 51 percent of black mothers and 65 percent of black fathers thought there was a good or almost certain chance of marrying their child's other parent, compared with 71 percent of white mothers and 86 percent of white fathers.

27. Parents' accounts also seem to draw from conflicting vocabularies about love and marriage that represent relationships as highly particularistic choices and as binding commitments (Hopper 1993; Swidler 2001).

28. This theme appears in what the *New York Times Magazine* dubbed the love song of the summer in 1995, "I'll Be There for You/You're All I Need to Get By," by popular hip-hop artists Method Man and Mary J. Blige (see Tatley 1995).

3. Models of Fatherhood

1. Different models of fatherhood also coexisted in previous historical periods, rather than displacing each other or changing in a unilinear way (Mintz 1998). The discussion of these models is informed by the available historical research on fathers, which primarily documents the experiences of white middle-class men (see Griswold 1993).

2. See Swidler 1986 and 2001 for a discussion of cultural "tool kits."

3. Many scholars note that without the right to own property, slave fathers had no legal control over their children and could not exercise patriarchal control (Griswold 1993, 20), but see Mann 1988 for a critique of this view. Many historians are also reluctant to characterize slave families as matriarchal. Herbert Gutman (1976, 190–191) contends that naming practices among slave families dramatized the importance of black fathers. In contrast to the slave owners' practice of recognizing descent through the mother, many slave children were named after their fathers, particularly first-born sons. After emancipation, Jones (1985, 68) suggests that black sharecropping families developed patterns of family and work life that resembled "premodern" patterns. In the rural South, the "nu-

clear" family was situated within and closely tied to larger networks of family and community. Some writers argue that these family patterns were influenced by "African survivals" that centered on children and that recognized "blood ties" rather than marital bonds (Sudarkasa 1988; Miller 1993).

4. According to Jones (1985, 99–100), "Black working women in the South had a more equal relationship with their husbands in the sense that the two partners were not separated by extremes of economic power or political rights; black men and women lacked both. Oppression shaped these unions in another way. The overlapping of economic and domestic functions combined with the pressures imposed by a surrounding, hostile white society meant that black working women were not so dramatically dependent upon their husbands as were middle-class white wives. Within black families and communities, then, public-private, male-female distinctions were less tightly drawn than among middle-class whites. Together, black women and men participated in a rural folk culture based upon group cooperation rather than male competition and the accumulation of goods."

5. Earlier in the century, psychological theories of child development proposed that fathers participate in children's socialization and act as their "pals" (Griswold 1993).

6. During the Depression, the breadwinning model also remained in place, despite steep declines in men's employment. However, scholars argue that failure to provide undermined men's sense of masculine identity (Griswold 1993, 146–151).

7. Functionalist sociology also supported a clear separation between maternal and paternal responsibility.

8. See Griswold 1993 (219–269). As we saw in the previous chapter, Ehrenreich (1984) argues that a "flight from commitment" also emerged at this time, when fathers found it more difficult to provide for their families.

9. See LaRossa 1997 and Griswold 1993 for historical discussions of "new fatherhood" in the 1920s and 1930s.

10. See Pleck 1997 for an extensive review of the literature on paternal involvement. This review points to some important increases in involvement among fathers in two-parent families over the last three decades.

11. The emerging popular awareness of deadbeat dads appears in cover stories of *Newsweek* (Waldman 1992) and *People* (Schneider, Sugden, and Duffy 1995).

12. See Tucker 1997 for a social and cultural critique of the song "Mybabydaddy."

13. Tupac Shakur, the popular rap artist murdered in 1996, illustrates some of these contradictions. Although his lyrics and style drew on images of urban violence and machismo and he served time for sexual assault, he also wrote songs expressing sensitivity, respect, and gratitude toward single mothers raising children alone. These songs include "Keep Your Head Up," "Brenda's Got a Baby," and "Dear Mama," which was nominated for a Grammy in 1995. Tupac was unsure of the identity of his own biological father (Marriott 1996).

14. Other African American groups contested this view, however. For example, African American Agenda 2000, a group that includes prominent black women activists and leaders such as Angela Davis, released a statement critical of the Million Man March. An excerpt from this statement, explaining why the group did not support the march, reads, "No march, movement, or agenda that defines manhood in the narrowest terms and seeks to make women lesser partners in this quest for equality can be considered a positive step" (Wiggins 1995).

15. Although Lewis argues that this culture arises as a functional adaptation to conditions of deprivation, he suggests that when conditions improve, individuals who have absorbed the culture of poverty as children are not "psychologically geared to take full advantage of changing conditions or increased opportunities which may occur in their lifetime" (Lewis 1975, 169).

16. Unlike Swidler (2001, 25), I do not focus on how individuals shift from one part of their repertoire to another during the course of an interview.

17. Gadsden's (1999) family culture concept is similar to Stack and Burton's (1993) description of "kinscripts." Both studies use these concepts to examine members of black extended families.

18. Bourdieu (1984) uses the concept of *habitus* to describe the set of cultivated dispositions shared by people in similar social locations.

19. Membership in various groups may also allow parents to select cultural resources more easily. As Berger (1991, 13) suggests, "magnitudes of felt freedom and unfreedom are determined outcomes of the interaction between the 'pull' of personal and group interests generated by social location, and the 'push' of accessible ideologies (cognitive, moral, and aesthetic)." He argues that some "freedom" to choose among cultural resources arises from membership in diverse and multiple groups.

20. See Lamont 2000 on the availability of cultural resources. In a discussion of how diverse audiences read fiction, Radway (1991, 468) observes that readers actively engage texts and construct signifiers "as meaningful signs on the basis of previously learned interpretive procedures and cultural codes." Drawing on Stanley Fish, she suggests that people read differently because they belong to "different interpretive communities" and have different purposes for reading.

4. Interpreting Paternal Responsibility

1. See Daly 1995 for a discussion of how married fathers of young children draw from diverse models of fatherhood.

2. In particular, I look at how parents use symbolic boundaries to differentiate themselves from other groups, situations, or ideas to define their own identities and to uphold conscious or unconscious perceptions of worthiness or purity (Douglas 1966; Lamont 1992, 2001).

3. These five parents include three white fathers, one African American father, and one white mother.

4. Nancy Fraser (1989) identifies "needs" and "interests" as two of the primary languages for making political claims in contemporary American culture. A "rights" discourse represents the third language for making claims.

5. Approximately 95 percent of unmarried mothers interviewed at the time of their child's birth said they wanted the father to be involved in raising the child. Of the fathers who were interviewed, almost 100 percent said they wanted to be involved in raising the child. These parents might have had particularly high hopes for involvement given the timing of the interviews. Consistent with reports of mothers in this study, white mothers in the FFCW survey were slightly less likely to want the father to be involved than were black mothers.

6. In the FFCW survey, approximately 67 percent of unmarried mothers and 50 percent of unmarried fathers considered showing love and affection to the child to be the most important activity. Approximately 5 percent of unmarried mothers and 12 percent of unmarried fathers reported that providing direct care to children was the most important activity in which fathers could participate. Other choices included teaching children about life, providing protection, and serving as an authority figure. Approximately 82 percent of white mothers and 60 percent of white fathers ranked love and affection first compared with 62 percent of black mothers and 42 percent of black fathers.

7. Allen and Doherty (1996) also find that African American teenage fathers say that "being there" is an important aspect of being a good father.

8. Lamb et al. (1987) identify three types of involvement by fathers: engagement, ac-

cessibility, and responsibility. Engagement involves direct interactions with children, accessibility refers to supervision or the potential for interaction, and responsibility refers to taking ultimate responsibility for children's welfare, including managing children's activities (see Lamb 2000; Marsiglio, Day, and Lamb 2000). The parents I interviewed defined involvement more in terms of engagement and accessibility than responsibility. Because most fathers in this study lived apart from their children, accessibility often implied the potential for interaction rather than direct supervision (Marsiglio, Day, and Lamb 2000). See chapter 5 for more on these concepts.

9. An example of these ideas about role models appears in Kunjufu 1985. See Kelley 1996 for a different perspective on male role models in the black community.

10. In the FFCW survey, 8 percent of unmarried mothers and 19 percent of unmarried fathers ranked "Teaching child about life" first. When this item is combined with another item of paternal guidance (serving as an authority figure), 14 percent of mothers and 22 percent of fathers ranked these as the most important activities. Approximately 4 percent of white mothers and 10 percent of white fathers ranked teaching first compared with 9 percent of black mothers and 23 percent of black fathers. Only 2 percent of the white mothers interviewed and 3 percent of the white fathers ranked authority first compared with 6 percent of black mothers and 4 percent of black fathers.

11. Some parents suggested that mothers "have an advantage" disciplining daughters.

12. Fraser (1989, 165) uses the term "internally dialogized" to identify how political claims are made in reference to competing arguments.

13. These numbers represent responses to a question about how parents would describe a good father (either abstractly or specifically). Although I analyzed the entire interview transcript to interpret parents' accounts, their responses to this item provide a sense of how frequently parents invoked various models of fatherhood.

14. Approximately 6 percent of white mothers and 14 percent of white fathers ranked financial support as the most important paternal activity, whereas 29 percent of white mothers and 14 percent of white fathers ranked this as least important. In comparison, approximately 16 percent of black mothers and fathers ranked financial support as most important, whereas 20 percent of black mothers and 16 percent of black fathers considered it least important. In a study of divorced and never-married African American fathers, Hamer (1997) finds that these men rank the most important fathering activities in ways that are generally similar to the rankings by parents in this study and in the FFCW study. In another study of never-married African American couples, Hamer (1998) finds that mothers emphasized economic provision more than fathers, but that mothers were willing to forgo economic support for emotional and social support of children. Hamer reports that these fathers stress their non-economic roles and think of their economic role as supporting the mother's efforts to take care of their children. Conversely, Furstenberg (1992) suggests that low-income single mothers value emotional support more than fathers do, whereas fathers value economic provision more than mothers do. Unlike those parents interviewed in the Furstenberg and Hamer studies, the unmarried mothers and fathers I spoke with typically expressed congruent beliefs about the relative importance of emotional and economic support.

15. Edin and Lein (1997, 158–167) report that one-third of "welfare-reliant" women in their study received monetary support from nonresident fathers and another third reported receiving in-kind assistance.

16. However, Bitler (1998) finds that more aggressive child support enforcement at the state level reduces fathers' contact with their children and suggests that time and money are substitutes for fathers affected by these mechanisms.

17. Joblessness and low income have been found to have a negative effect on the psychological well-being of unmarried African American fathers, and these effects are exac-

erbated by subjective feelings of discouragement at fulfilling the provider role (Bowman and Sanders 1998).

18. Analyzing data from General Social Surveys conducted between 1972 and 1989, Wilkie (1993) finds a decline in men's endorsement of the provider role, which is related to cohort succession.

19. In the FFCW survey, both married and unmarried parents ranked "love and affection" as the most important paternal activity. As noted earlier, about 67 percent of unmarried mothers and 50 percent of unmarried fathers considered showing love and affection to the child to be the most important activity, compared with 74 percent of married mothers and 60 percent of married fathers. About 14 percent of unmarried mothers and 22 percent of unmarried fathers considered teaching children about life and serving as an authority figure to be the most important activities, compared with 14 percent of married mothers and 21 percent of married fathers. Finally, about 12 percent of unmarried mothers and fathers considered economic support to be the most important activity, compared with 5 percent of married mothers and fathers. These results show that married parents ranked economic support lower than did unmarried parents, perhaps because support is less a concern for parents with greater financial resources. As indicated earlier, unmarried white parents also ranked the importance of financial support lower than did black parents on both measures. Like married parents, white unmarried parents may also perceive themselves and their partners to have better employment and earnings prospects than do their black counterparts.

5. Departures from Paternal Responsibility

1. However, Pleck (1997, 69) finds that several studies show high agreement among individual reports by mother-father pairs. See Pleck 1997 for a description of methodological challenges involved in measuring paternal involvement.

2. Parents seemed to react to my gender when talking about their own, or their partner's, lack of involvement more than when talking about any other issue. Mothers often appealed to our shared identity as women, whereas fathers often defended themselves against possible criticisms of their behavior by women.

3. Furstenberg (1995, 135) reports a similar finding based on his discussions with low-income mothers.

4. See chapter 6 for more discussion of father–child contact.

5. Arendell (1995, 157–158) finds that many divorced fathers also talk about their involvement in relation to that of absent fathers, making their own effort appear greater in comparison.

6. Men's public discourse was also much "harder" on the street than in the interview. One father I interviewed mentioned the differences between men's public and private talk, suggesting that street talk was a more defensive, exaggerated, and tough language.

7. See Lamb 2000 and Marsiglio, Day, and Lamb 2000 for further explanation of these terms.

8. In a review of studies of fathers in two-parent families, Pleck (1997) finds an increase in fathers' engagement with and accessibility to their children over the last three decades. At the same time, he suggests that there is still a large difference between the levels of a mother's versus a father's involvement with their children.

9. Mothers play with their children more than fathers do, but play constitutes a smaller proportion of their interaction with children compared with that of fathers (see Lamb 2000).

10. Hochschild (1989) observes that the married mothers she interviewed felt more re-

sponsible for children and experienced more strain in taking care of them than the fathers did.

11. Researchers have also identified stories that men and women commonly tell to help them manage their identities after a divorce and negotiate the transition to being single (Reissman 1990; Vaughan 1990 [1986]; Hopper 1993). Vaughan (1990 [1986], 141), for example, pointed out that these patterned explanations help both partners understand the divorce and describe it in socially acceptable ways. To do so, a partner may neutralize or discredit the other's story. In the process of separating from a spouse, partners may also distance themselves from their children, who represent and remind them of the relationship (Vaughan 1990 [1986], 54).

12. According to Arendell (1995), fathers use emotion management strategies, such as absence, resistance, and noncooperation, to reestablish their identities and regain a sense of power after divorce. Arendell suggests that men with traditional ideas about gender (that is, that men and women are essentially different and have different roles) used a more traditional discourse and strategies of paternal participation. A minority of less traditional men had cooperative relationships with the mother and adopted more innovative responses to parenting after divorce. Although gender ideology influences the responses of fathers I interviewed, I did not observe a direct correspondence between a father's ideology and his level of paternal involvement.

13. At a more general level, factors such as the father's motivation, skills, and self-confidence; support, including support from the mother, for the father's involvement; and institutional practices may influence paternal involvement (Lamb et al. 1987; Lamb 2000). Doherty et al. (1998) suggest that fathers' engagement with their children may vary, depending on social, economic, and institutional contexts, factors specific to the father, factors related to co-parental relationships, factors related to the child, and factors related to the child's mother. See Pleck 1997, and Davis and Perkins 1996 for reviews of factors influencing paternal involvement in two-parent families. Pleck's review indicates, for example, that fathers tend to be more involved with boys than girls. Studies examining differences in involvement by a father's race or ethnicity and social class show mixed results.

14. These accounts describe different levels of disengagement, including fathers who had no contact with their child, fathers who saw their child a few times a year, and fathers who reduced their involvement because of specific problems.

15. Although none of these mothers had doubts about the identity of their child's father, three fathers were uncertain about their paternity at the time of the interview. See chapter 6 for more discussion of this issue.

16. Previous research shows that mothers often mediate a father's involvement with their children (see Arendell 1996) and may act as gatekeepers in situations in which they are living together as well as when they have separated (Marsiglio et al. 2000).

6. Recognizing Biological and Social Paternity

1. The history of paternity is discussed in chapter 7. At the time of this study, paternity was established for about half of children in New Jersey and nationwide who were in the federal child support, or IV-D, system (either because their parents received welfare or had requested public child support services). In 1998, paternity was established for approximately 64 percent of children in the IV-D program nationwide, after the development of in-hospital paternity establishment programs (Office of Child Support Enforcement 2000).

2. This study sampled men who said they were unmarried fathers, and therefore it

missed men who did not believe they had any children. At the same time, 3 of the fathers I interviewed expressed uncertainty about their paternity at the time of the interview. Another father had requested a paternity test, and 3 mothers reported that the father of their children had requested a paternity test to resolve this issue. An additional 10 parents (5 fathers and 5 mothers) said that either the father or the mother had raised some question about paternity, which was later resolved informally. Proportionally more white parents than black parents reported that paternity had been contested.

3. However, four white parents who had been in committed relationships before the pregnancy said they or their child's father had denied paternity when they had found out about the pregnancy. About two-thirds of African American parents and three-quarters of white parents report having been in committed relationships at the time of the pregnancy.

4. Other studies also document the role of physical resemblance in informal paternity establishment (e.g., Liebow 1967; Anderson 1989; Furstenberg 1995).

5. The trial judge could determine whether the child was old enough to have "settled features" to allow a fair "viewing" by the jury. In a famous paternity case, *Berry v. Chaplin,* a California jury asked Charlie Chaplin, the mother, and the child to stand next to each other to determine physical resemblance. Chaplin was found to be the father of the child even though blood testing excluded him as the biological father (Melli 1992, 38–40). Although this practice has become obsolete, physical resemblance can still be admitted as evidence in cases of disputed paternity (Melli 1992; Committee on Ways and Means 2000, 478).

6. In situations in which a child is receiving welfare, the state will pay the cost of the paternity test if a man is found not to be the child's father.

7. See Johnson 2001 for an analysis of unmarried fathers' early support of and involvement with their children. Based on early data from the FFCW study, Johnson finds that the kind of relationship unmarried parents had at the time of the birth, particularly whether or not they were living together, was the strongest predictor of support and involvement.

8. Judges could in fact consider the birth certificate as evidence in a paternity hearing (U.S. Department of Health and Human Services 1990, 28).

9. Liebow (1967) and Furstenberg and Talvitie (1980) also discuss paternal surnames as indicators of paternal commitment. Furstenberg and Talvitie find that children who received their father's surname were more likely to have contact with and receive support from their father during the first five years of their lives.

10. As we saw earlier with the birth certificate, most parents in the FFCW study had not yet given the child the father's last name at the time of the interview.

11. Only a few parents talked about the last name as an important symbol of legitimacy and respectability. White parents were more likely to do so than were African American parents, perhaps because nonmarital childbearing continues to be more stigmatized in white families. Most parents, in fact, suggested that many name options were acceptable, including hyphenation and changing the child's name when he or she got older.

12. See chapter 7 for more discussion of how paternity establishment fits into the child support process.

13. Legal paternity also gives children rights to inheritance, although this is less relevant for the children of poor fathers.

14. Some New Jersey hospitals had recently begun to implement programs that allowed parents to establish paternity in the hospital at the time of birth. As a result of the 1996 welfare reform legislation, establishing paternity in the hospital is now common practice.

15. Other researchers have pointed to the important role played by the families of young parents in recognizing paternity (e.g., Rainwater 1967; Anderson 1989). Perhaps because I interviewed adults rather than adolescents, the parents' families seemed to play a less important role in this process.

16. Lamb et al. (1987) and Hawkins and Palkovitz (1999) describe a variety of ways that a father's involvement can be measured beyond paternal contact and support. For example, Palkovitz and Hawkins (1999) identify multiple types of paternal involvement to include its cognitive, affective, economic, spiritual, and ethical dimensions. As we saw in chapter 4, parents refer to some of these types of involvement in their discussions of paternal obligation.

17. Although a review of recent studies of paternal involvement does not show consistent differences by race or ethnicity (Pleck 1997), Lerman (1993, 46) finds that unmarried African American fathers are more likely to live close to their children and visit them than are Hispanic or white fathers. Stier and Tienda (1993) report that black nonresident fathers living in low-income areas in Chicago who participated in the Urban Poverty and Family Life Survey visit their children more often than do fathers of other racial and ethnic groups in low-income neighborhoods.

18. These NLSY figures report contact for men in the 30–34 age bracket and for women in the 28–32 age bracket. Because these numbers represent maximum involvement with any child born outside of marriage, they may be upwardly biased. At the same time, older fathers such as these generally had less contact with their children than did younger fathers (Lerman and Sorensen 2000, 144–146).

7. Reconciling Formal and Informal Systems of Paternal Support

1. See Mincy and Pouncy 1999 for more on unmarried parents and the formation of public policy.

2. Previous versions of this chapter appeared in Waller and Plotnick 1999, 2001.

3. The earliest U.S. laws pertaining to paternity had their roots in the sixteenth-century English Poor Laws, which considered children born outside of marriage *filius nullius*, that is, child and heir of no one as well as "an offense against God's law and man's law." Because children born to unmarried parents had no legally recognized relationship to them and because parents had no rights or obligations to their "illegitimate" children, support for these children usually fell to the local community (Teichman 1982; Grossberg 1985; Melli 1992).

4. See Waller and Plotnick 1999 for a longer discussion of recent child support policy and how the contemporary child support system works. A summary of federal child support legislation and of current national policy and administrative procedures is in Committee on Ways and Means 2000, section 8. Other information on child support policy and administration is available from the federal Office of Child Support Enforcement at http://www.acf.dhhs.gov/programs/cse.

5. PRWORA includes several measures to improve paternity establishment. States must also set up a central registry of all IV-D support orders and any support order issued or changed after October 1998; a centralized, automated unit for collection and disbursement of payments; and a directory to which employers must report information on new employees. Information in these files is used to create a Federal Case Registry and National Directory of New Hires to track parents across state lines. Other new enforcement tools are also included. These reforms were enacted the year after I completed my interviews with New Jersey parents.

6. PRWORA (U.S. Congress 1996) begins by stating,

The Congress makes the following findings: (1) Marriage is the foundation of a successful society. (2) Marriage is an essential institution of a successful society which promotes the interests of children. (3) Promotion of responsible fatherhood and motherhood is integral to successful child rearing and the well-being of children. (4) In 1992, only 54 percent of single-parent families with children had a child support order established and, of that 54 percent, only about one-half received the full amount due. Of the cases enforced through the public child support enforcement system, only 18 percent of the caseload has a collection. (5) The number of individuals receiving aid to families with dependent children (in this section referred to as "AFDC") has more than tripled since 1965. More than two-thirds of these recipients are children. Eighty-nine percent of children receiving AFDC benefits now live in homes in which no father is present.... (6) The increase of out-of-wedlock pregnancies and births is well documented as follows.... (7) An effective strategy to combat teenage pregnancy must address the issue of male responsibility, including statutory rape culpability and prevention. The increase of teenage pregnancies among the youngest girls is particularly severe and is linked to predatory sexual practices by men who are significantly older.... (8) The negative consequences of an out-of-wedlock birth on the mother, the child, the family, and society are well documented as follows.... (9) Currently 35 percent of children in single-parent homes were born out-of-wedlock.... (10) Therefore, in light of this demonstration of the crisis in our Nation, it is the sense of the Congress that prevention of out-of-wedlock pregnancy and reduction in out-of-wedlock birth are very important Government interests and the policy contained in part A of title IV of the Social Security Act (as amended by section 103(a) of this Act) is intended to address the crisis.

7. At the time this study was conducted, cooperation involved providing the father's name and any additional available information, such as address, place of employment, and Social Security number. Since passage of the 1996 welfare legislation, mothers must also appear at child support interviews and hearings or face sanctions.

8. In cases of noncooperation, states also have the option of reducing mothers' food stamp benefits and denying food stamps to noncustodial fathers.

9. Between 1984 and 1996, federal law set the monthly pass-through at $50 for all welfare families. The 1996 reforms allowed states to modify this rule and most have done so (Gallagher et al. 1998). New Jersey has retained the $50 pass-through. Only Wisconsin allows the full amount of child support to be passed through to the family and disregards this payment when calculating welfare benefits.

10. Because the custodial parent is female in the overwhelming majority of cases nationwide (85 percent in 1998) (U.S. Census Bureau 2000, 1) and all of the custodial parents in the study are female, I use gender-specific language throughout the remainder of this discussion.

11. When establishing the amount of each order, states use formal guidelines to ensure that they comply with federal laws aimed at rationalizing procedures for setting awards and reducing judicial discretion. There are three types of approaches states use to set orders: income shares, percentage of income, and the Melson-Delaware guidelines. New Jersey uses income shares guidelines (along with thirty other states) that base the order on the combined income of both parents (Committee on Ways and Means 1996, 543). Fifteen states use the percentage-of-income guidelines, in which the percentage of the noncustodial parent's income that is to be paid is based on the number of children he or she has. The Melson-Delaware guidelines include a self-support reserve for parents (Committee on Ways and Means 1996, 543).

12. This description of the child support process in New Jersey is based on the procedure that child support staff said they used at the time of this study.

13. The Current Population Survey asks custodial parents without a legal child support order or with an informal agreement why no legal agreement had been established. In 1997, the most common response was that they did not feel the need to make it legal. Overall, approximately 13 percent said the child lived with the other parent part of the time, 13 percent said they could not locate the parent, 16 percent said they did not want to have contact with the other parent, 18 percent did not legally establish paternity, 19 percent did not want the other parent to pay, 22 percent said the other parent provides what they can, 25 percent said the other parent could not afford to pay, and 32 percent did not feel the need to make child support legal. Another 15 percent cited other reasons. These percentages do not add to 100 because parents could cite more than one reason (U.S. Census Bureau 2000, 3).

14. Achatz and MacAllum (1994) also suggest that fathers in the program were put off by the idea that parents who paid formal child support were more responsible than those who contributed informally.

15. Other studies of low-income parents' perceptions of the child support system report that parents object to the state keeping most of the child support payment (e.g., Furstenberg 1992; Sherwood 1992; Sullivan 1992; Achatz and MacAllum 1994; Edin 1995; Johnson and Doolittle 1998; Johnson, Levine, and Doolitte, 1999; Roy 1999). The endnotes report findings from other studies to document the similarity of low-income parents' responses to child support regulations in diverse locations (some of these findings were not emphasized in the original studies). See Waller and Plotnick 2001 for a review of this research. The framework for this review was developed from the current study.

16. The actual value of what the mother received was about $35 after her food stamps were reduced.

17. Achatz and MacAllum (1994, 81) find that most fathers in the program they evaluated reported spending more than $50 each month on their child. Edin and Lein (1997, 44) indicate that mothers on welfare reported receiving, on average, $39 a month in cash from fathers in addition to in-kind support.

18. Recent implementation of hospital-based paternity establishment and heightened enforcement of penalties for noncooperation and nonpayment under PRWORA will probably give parents less opportunity to evade paternity establishment regulations.

19. Whereas Edin (1995) considered the act of giving incomplete information to be "covert noncompliance," some of the practices described to me by parents I interviewed seemed to constitute more passive avoidance rather than active resistance. The differences in findings could reflect variations between the sites at which the research was conducted, including diverse enforcement practices and labor market conditions. See Sorensen and Turner 1996 for a review of research on administrative and other factors associated with differences in paternity establishment rates.

20. The U.S. Department of Health and Human Service's paternity establishment manual (1990, 26), distributed to welfare and child support workers who handle IV-D cases, advises:

> The mother's duty to cooperate requires more than simply appearing for an interview and providing "yes" or "no" responses to questions. She must assist in providing and gathering the information which will help locate and contact the alleged father. She must supply any documents helpful to her case, such as the child's birth certificate, hospital bill, baptismal record, or statements written by the alleged father referencing or acknowledging the child. If the mother refuses to answer questions, fails to provide requested information, or gives vague and evasive responses, explain the consequences of non-cooperation. Caution her that non-cooperation may jeopardize her public assistance grant. Document the circumstances and immediately notify the IV-A [welfare] agency of the situation.

21. Similarly, Achatz and MacAllum (1994, 84) note that to keep mothers happy and deter them from seeking formal child support orders, fathers attempt to maintain friendly relationships and make voluntary financial contributions.

22. In three other cases in which mothers talked specifically about domestic violence in relation to child support, mothers wanted formal support but did not want the father to have rights to the children.

23. In fact, one mother reported that the father became more abusive after a child support order was established.

24. Zelizer (1994, 77–78) observes that many social scientists have contrasted "reciprocal, affective, socially bound" gifts with the impersonal, instrumental character of money. However, Zelizer argues that money can also be "gifted." One of the things that characterizes gifts is that they "do not call for immediate reciprocation except in the form of appreciation, and they assume the long-term duration of a relationship." The personalization of gifts is also extremely important. According to Zelizer, "The good gift bears the mark of its donor and is clearly intended for a specific recipient."

25. Achatz and MacAllum (1994, 76) also suggest that men believe child support deprives them of an important part of fathering their children. They argue that most fathers prefer to purchase items for their children because "(1) they are visible symbols of responsible fatherhood in the community, (2) they are tangible and gratifying, and (3) they give the fathers control over how the money is spent." Similarly, Roy (1999, 439–444, 447–448) notes the importance of in-kind and voluntary support.

26. Sullivan (1992, 16) and Achatz and MacAllum (1994, 75) also observe that low-income fathers resent the state "forcing" them to pay child support; Sullivan notes that this statement reflects a general belief that the courts should not interfere in their families.

27. Achatz and MacAllum (1994, 76–79) also find that some fathers object to the child support system because it places unconditional trust in women when it assigns them support payments rather than allowing fathers to purchase needed items themselves.

28. Furstenberg (1992, 52–53) observes that women commonly object to the inefficiency of the child support system, including the difficulty of filing a claim, the inability of the system to collect payments from men, the inability or unwillingness to pursue men who evade the system, and the impersonal nature of the child support agency. Mothers are frustrated that they cannot talk or write to anyone in the child support agency about these concerns, and they have little confidence that their concerns will be addressed.

29. The minimum award set for noncustodial parents ranges from $21 to $179 per month (U.S. Department of Health and Human Services 2000; Roberts 2001).

30. New Jersey charges from the date that a request for support is filed; some states, however, charge retroactive support, sometimes from the time of the child's birth (U.S. Department of Health and Human Services 2000; Roberts 2001).

31. Presumably, the mother of O'Shen's children did not report this informal support to the welfare agency.

32. See also Achatz and MacAllum 1994 and Johnson, Levine, and Doolittle 1999.

33. Another important issue that fathers mention frequently, but that is not part of the enforcement process, is concern over visitation rights.

34. Sherwood (1992), Johnson and Doolittle (1998), and Johnson, Levine, and Doolittle (1999) also document concerns about using imprisonment as an enforcement tactic. Although low-income fathers believe that incarceration for nonsupport is likely (Johnson, Levine, and Doolittle 1999), Johnson and Doolittle (1998, 280) observe that "The perceived importance and likelihood of jail often is greater than would be statistically justified."

35. See Johnson, Levine, and Doolittle 1999 (100–103) for another discussion of low-income African American fathers' perceptions of the legal system and child support authorities in particular.

36. Johnson and Doolittle (1998, 279–280) report that many men were told the court

considered these to be gifts rather than support payments, and therefore they would not be counted. Johnson and Doolittle also note that in several sites at which they conducted research, men who had made informal contributions could be "locked down" until a sufficient payment was made. Achatz and MacAllum (1995, 85) observe that because almost all of the men they interviewed had contributed something to their children at some point, "nearly all expected to get some leniency or credit for having provided informal support." Achatz and MacAllum (1994, 86) also note that a few men they spoke with came to their hearings "with a shoebox of receipts in tow."

Conclusion

1. Most of these child support policy options were developed in collaboration with Robert Plotnick. For a longer discussion of these options, including an explanation of possible drawbacks, see Waller and Plotnick 1999.

2. At the time of this writing, President Bush's budget for fiscal year 2003 included federal matching funds to share with the states (at their option) the cost of passing through up to $100 in child support payments to families receiving welfare. The matching funds would restore states' incentive to pass through at least some portion of the child support payment and might encourage more states to pass through an amount greater than $50.

3. See Primus and Castro 1999, and Primus and Daugirdas 2000 for more on this option.

4. See Roberts 2001 for a detailed discussion of state child support policies related to arrears and recommendations on how to develop state programs to forgive arrears.

5. A review of some studies shows that levels of current physical abuse among welfare recipients ranged from 15 to 32 percent and levels of abuse during adulthood ranged from 34 to 65 percent (Raphael and Tolman 1997).

6. The federal earned income tax credit is intended to boost the incomes of low-wage workers with children. Because the credit is refundable, workers who do not earn enough to pay taxes can still receive this benefit, which can have as much value as a $2 per hour wage increase (Primus 2001).

7. Increases in employment and declines in welfare use have followed a period of strong economic growth, an expansion of the earned income tax credit, and the implementation of work requirements under TANF (Primus 2001).

8. As such, states might also consider creating publicly funded jobs for parents who cannot find employment. Federal regulations imposing a five-year time limit on welfare should also be reconsidered, and states should be given more flexibility to relax the proportion of the caseload exempted from these time limits.

9. See Waller 2001 on policy efforts to promote marriage among unmarried parents. See also Primus and Daugirdas 2000 and Primus 2001 for proposals to assist nonresident fathers and strengthen fragile families.

Appendix A

1. As the sampling proceeded, I changed an earlier version of the flyer that said I was interviewing single mothers to read "unmarried mothers" in response to some women who said they did not fit the criteria because they were involved in relationships with their child's father or another partner. Mothers and fathers read "single" to mean not only an "unattached" parent but also a custodial parent. The fact that parents in committed relationships and parents without sole custody of their children did not consider themselves single parents points to the diversity of mothers' and fathers' relationships and parenting arrangements.

2. I was a graduate student at Princeton at the time I collected these data.

3. Because I wanted to give something back to the extremely busy social service providers who offered their assistance to me, I helped the WIC program raise money for children's play centers at the sites. I also went door to door in Trenton for their children's vaccination drive.

4. Many of these questions were simply used as prompts, when parents did not introduce topics spontaneously.

5. I also conducted some follow-up interviews and spoke to several parents on the phone at least one time after their interviews.

6. One of the reasons I paraphrased this information was that some of the men and women I interviewed had difficulty reading.

7. Frankenberg (1993, 31–32) explains this by writing that "evasive or vague responses mark one as something specific by interviewees, be it 'closed-mouthed,' 'scientific,' 'rude,' 'mainstream,' 'moderate,' or perhaps 'strange'—and many of those are negative characterizations in some or all of the communities in which I was interviewing. My ability to conduct interviews successfully involved a complex set of adjustments in self-presentation, but never a presentation of myself as neutral." She also notes some of the unavoidable ways in which her respondents may have perceived her, regardless of her self-presentation.

8. In their discussions of African American knowledge-validation processes and linguistic styles, Patricia Hill Collins (1989) and Thomas Kochman (1981) point to the importance of speakers revealing their interests, motivations, and personal views to gain the acceptance and trust of their listeners. Collins notes that some of the values at the core of the African American epistemological standpoints that derive from family, religious, and other cultural traditions resemble those at the center of what writers have identified as a woman's standpoint. Collins suggests, for example, that speakers who cite personal experience, demonstrate emotion and empathy, and make use of dialogue are found to be more credible than are others. Knowledge claims are also evaluated in reference to the speaker's character and integrity.

9. Some parents requested much more information from me than others did. I found that some men and women seemed to prefer attentive listening to interjection, while others preferred to have a discussion with me either during or after the interview. In one case, a father interviewed me about my interests and experiences for about an hour and a half after his interview.

10. Although in most cases the information parents requested pertained to nonsensitive subjects (such as applying for Pell Grants for community college), a serious situation occurred when one of the fathers I interviewed indicated he was suicidal. I gave him the number of a suicide hotline, and following their advice and the advice of a psychologist, I called and met with him again. He called later to thank me and let me know he was doing better. I participated with parents after the interviews in other ways as well. For example, upon request, I accompanied some women on meetings with their welfare caseworker and to family court. I gave electric fans to a few mothers during the hot summer months. After becoming friends with a few parents, I offered them rides, loaned them money, and acted as a reference for them. Finally, one woman who acted as a key informant on this project asked me to be the godmother of her youngest child, and I provided her with financial assistance.

11. I conducted these interviews when I was aged twenty-seven and twenty-eight.

12. A few parents with post–high school education and the working-class parents I interviewed (as informants) took more note of the fact that I attended Princeton than other interviewees did. In a few cases, it seemed to affect their self-presentation during the interviews, for example, in their choice of words and how they described their employment status.

13. I also knew that one of the parents who sought me out had a crack addiction.

14. In one interview, the father of a woman I interviewed was drunk and particularly disruptive. She seemed to be inhibited and embarrassed by his behavior. Although most of his comments to me were benign, at one point he said, "You're not going to fuck with her [mind], are you?" and repeatedly made appeals to me as "a good Irish girl" to drink with him.

15. To counter these tendencies, Abu-Lughod (1993) adopts a writing strategy that she calls "tactical humanism," that is, focusing on a limited number of speakers to allow readers access to the complexity of individuals' lives while attempting to avoid the conventions of life story approaches that can invent an individual's "life."

BIBLIOGRAPHY

Abu-Lughod, Lila. 1993. *Writing Women's Worlds: Bedouin Stories.* Berkeley: University of California Press.

Achatz, Mary, and Crystal A. MacAllum. 1994. *Young Unwed Fathers: Report from the Field.* Philadelphia: Public/Private Ventures.

Allard, Mary Ann, Randy Albeda, Mary Ellen Colten, and Carol Cosenza. 1997. *In Harm's Way? Domestic Violence, AFDC Receipt, and Welfare Reform in Massachusetts.* Boston: University of Massachusetts, McCormack Institute and the Center for Survey Research

Allen, William D., and William J. Doherty. 1996. "The Responsibilities of Fatherhood as Perceived by African American Teenage Fathers." *Families in Society* 77(3): 142–155.

Anderson, Elijah. 1989. "Sex Codes and Family Life among Poor Inner-City Youths." *Annals of the American Academy of Political and Social Science* 501: 59–78.

Arendell, Terry. 1986. *Mothers and Divorce: Legal, Economic, and Social Dilemmas.* Berkeley: University of California Press.

———. 1995. *Fathers and Divorce.* Thousand Oaks, Calif.: Sage.

———. 1996. "Co-Parenting: A Review of the Literature." Philadelphia: National Center on Fathers and Families, University of Pennsylvania. Available at <http://www.ncoff .gse.upenn.edu>.

Bane, Mary Jo, and David T. Ellwood. 1994. *Welfare Realities: From Rhetoric to Reform.* Cambridge: Harvard University Press.

Bellah, Robert N., Richard Madsen, William M. Sullivan, Ann Swidler, and Steven M. Tipton. 1985. *Habits of the Heart: Individualism and Commitment in American Life.* Berkeley: University of California Press.

Berger, Bennett M. 1991. "Structure and Choice in the Sociology of Culture." *Theory and Society* 20 (1): 1–19.

Berger, Peter L., and Thomas Luckmann. 1967. *The Social Construction of Reality: A Treatise in the Sociology of Knowledge.* Garden City, New York: Anchor Books.

Bernard, Jessie. 1981. "The Good Provider Role: Its Rise and Fall." *American Psychologist* 36(1): 1–12.

Bitler, Marianne P. 1998. "Fathers' Time versus Fathers' Money: Effects of the Child Support Enforcement System." Ph.D. dissertation. Massachusetts Institute of Technology.

Blankenhorn, David. 1995. *Fatherless America: Confronting Our Most Urgent Social Problem.* New York: Basic Books.

Bourdieu, Pierre. 1984. *Distinction: A Social Critique of the Judgement of Taste.* Cambridge: Harvard University Press.

Bowman, Phillip J., and Reliford Sanders. 1998. "Unmarried African American Fathers: A Comparative Life Span Analysis." *Journal of Comparative Family Studies* 29(1): 39–56.

Brooks-Gunn, Jeanne, and Greg J. Duncan. 1997. "The Effects of Poverty on Children." *Future of Children* 7(2): 55–71.

Bumpass, Larry, and Hsien-Hen Lu. 2000. "Trends in Cohabitation and Implications for Children's Family Contexts in the United States." *Population Studies* 54 (1): 29–41.

Burawoy, Michael, ed. 1991. *Ethnography Unbound: Power and Resistance in the Modern Metropolis.* Berkeley: University of California Press.

Burke, Kenneth. 1989. *On Symbols and Society.* Edited and with an introduction by Joseph R. Gusfield. Chicago: University of Chicago Press.

Burton, Linda. 1990. "Teenage Childbearing as an Alternative Life-Course Strategy in Multigenerational Black Families." *Human Nature* 2: 123–143.

——. 1995. "Family Structure and Nonmarital Fertility: Perspectives from Ethnographic Research." In *Report to Congress on Out-of-Wedlock Childbearing* (PHS 95–1257), 147–165. U.S. Department of Health and Human Services. Washington, D.C.: U.S. Government Printing Office.

Clark, Kenneth B. 1965. *Dark Ghetto: Dilemmas of Social Power.* New York: Harper & Row.

Clifford, James, and George E. Marcus, eds. 1986. *Writing Culture: The Poetics and Politics of Ethnography.* Berkeley: University of California Press.

Collins, Patricia Hill. 1989. "The Social Construction of Black Feminist Thought." *Signs* 14(4): 745–773.

Committee on Ways and Means. U.S. House of Representatives. 1996. *Green Book: Background Material and Data on Programs within the Jurisdiction of the Committee on Ways and Means.* Washington, D.C.: U.S. Government Printing Office.

——. 2000. *Green Book: Background Material and Data on Programs within the Jurisdiction of the Committee on Ways and Means.* Washington, D.C.: U.S. Government Printing Office.

Cumbler, John T. 1989. *A Social History of Economic Decline: Business, Politics, and Work in Trenton.* New Brunswick: Rutgers University Press.

Daly, Kerry J. 1995. "Reshaping Fatherhood: Finding the Models." In *Fatherhood: Contemporary Theory, Research, and Social Policy,* ed. William Marsiglio, 21–40. Thousand Oaks, Calif.: Sage.

Danziger, Sheldon. 2000. Preface to *Coping with Poverty: The Social Contexts of Neighborhood, Work, and Family in the African-American Community,* ed. Sheldon Danziger and Ann Chih Lin, ix–xvi. Ann Arbor: University of Michigan Press.

Danziger, Sheldon, and Deborah Reed. 1999. "Winners and Losers: The Era of Inequality Continues." *Brookings Review* 17(4): 14–17.

Dash, Leon. 1989. *When Children Want Children: The Urban Crisis of Teenage Childbearing.* New York: William Morrow.

Davis, James Earl, and William Eric Perkins. 1996. "Fathers Care: A Review of the Literature." Philadelphia: National Center for Fathers and Families, University of Pennsylvania. Available at <http://www.ncoff.gse.upenn.edu>.

Demos, John. 1986. *Past, Present, and Personal: The Family and the Life Course in American History.* New York: Oxford University Press.

Doherty, William J., Edward F. Kouneski, and Martha F. Erikson. 1998. "Responsible Fathering: An Overview and Conceptual Framework." *Journal of Marriage and the Family* 60: 277–292.

Doolittle, Fred, Virginia Knox, Cynthia Miller, and Sharon Rowser. 1998. *Building Opportunities, Enforcing Obligations: Implementation and Interim Impacts of Parents' Fair Share.* New York: Manpower Demonstration Research Corporation.

Doolittle, Fred, and Suzanne Lynn. 1998. *Working with Low-Income Cases: Lessons for the Child Support Enforcement System from Parents' Fair Share.* New York: Manpower Demonstration Research Corporation.

Douglas, Mary. 1966. *Purity and Danger: An Analysis of the Concepts of Pollution and Taboo.* London: Routledge and Kegan Paul.

Driscoll, Anne K., Gesine K. Hearn, V. Jeffrey Evans, Kristin A. Moore, Barbara W. Sugland, and Vaughn Call. 1999. "Nonmarital Childbearing among Adult Women." *Journal of Marriage and Family* 61: 178–187.

Edin, Kathryn. 1995. "Single Mothers and Child Support: The Possibilities and Limits of Child Support Policy." *Children and Youth Services Review* 17 (1/2): 203–230.

Edin, Kathryn, and Laura Lein. 1997. *Making Ends Meet: How Single Mothers Survive Welfare and Low-Wage Work.* New York: Russell Sage Foundation.

Ehrenreich, Barbara. 1984. *The Hearts of Men: American Dreams and the Flight from Commitment.* Garden City, N.Y.: Anchor Press.

Ellwood, David T. 2000. "Anti-Poverty Policy for Families in the Next Century: From Welfare to Work—and Worries." *Journal of Economic Perspectives* 14: 187–198.

Frankenberg, Ruth. 1993. *White Women, Race Matters: The Social Construction of Whiteness.* Minneapolis: University of Minnesota Press.

Fraser, Nancy. 1989. *Unruly Practices: Power, Discourse and Gender in Contemporary Social Theory.* Minneapolis: University of Minnesota Press.

Frazier, E. Franklin. 1939. *The Negro Family in the United States.* Chicago: University of Chicago Press.

Furstenberg, Frank F., Jr. 1988. "Good Dads—Bad Dads: Two Faces of Fatherhood." In *The Changing American Family and Public Policy,* ed. Andrew Cherlin, 193–218. Washington, D.C.: Urban Institute Press.

——. 1991. "As the Pendulum Swings: Teenage Childbearing and Social Concern." *Family Relations* 40: 127–138.

——. 1992. "Daddies and Fathers: Men Who Do for Their Children and Men Who Don't." In *Caring and Paying: What Mothers and Fathers Say about Child Support,* ed. Frank Furstenberg, Jr., Kay Sherwood, and Mercer Sullivan, 34–56. New York: Manpower Demonstration Research Corporation.

——. 1995. "Fathering in the Inner City: Paternal Participation and Public Policy." In *Fatherhood: Contemporary Theory, Research, and Social Policy,* ed. William Marsiglio, 119–147. Thousand Oaks, Calif.: Sage.

——. 2001. "The Fading Dream: Prospects for Marriage in the Inner City." In *Problem of the Century: Racial Stratification in the United States,* ed. Elijah Anderson and Doug S. Massey, 224–246. New York: Russell Sage.

Furstenberg, Frank F., Jr., and Andrew J. Cherlin. 1991. *Divided Families: What Happens to Children When Parents Part.* Cambridge: Harvard University Press.

Furstenberg, Frank F., Jr., and Kathy Gordon Talvitie. 1980. "Children's Names and Paternal Claims: Bonds between Unmarried Fathers and Their Children." *Journal of Family Issues* 1(1): 31–57.

Gadsden, Vivian. L. 1999. "Black Families in Intergenerational and Cultural Per spective." In *Parenting and Child Development in "Nontraditional" Families,* ed. Michael E. Lamb, 221–246. Mahwah, N.J.: Lawrence Erlbaum Associates.

Gallagher, L. Jerome, Megan Gallagher, Kevin Perese, Susan Schreiber, and Keith Watson. 1998. *One Year after Federal Welfare Reform: A Description of State Temporary Assistance for Needy Families (TANF) Decisions as of October 1997.* Washington D.C.: Urban Institute. Available at <http://newfederalism.urban.org/>.

Garfinkel, Irwin. 1992. *Assuring Child Support: An Extension of the Social Security System.* New York: Russell Sage Foundation.

Garfinkel, Irwin, and Sara S. McLanahan. 1986. *Single Mothers and Their Children: A New American Dilemma.* Washington, D.C.: Urban Institute Press.

Garfinkel, Irwin, Sara S. McLanahan, and Thomas L. Hanson. 1998. "A Patchwork Portrait of Nonresident Fathers." In *Fathers under Fire: The Revolution in Child Support Enforcement,* ed. Irwin Garfinkel, Sara S. McLanahan, Daniel R. Meyer, and Judith A. Seltzer, 31–60. New York: Russell Sage Foundation.

Geronimous, Arline T. 1991. "Teenage Childbearing and Social and Reproductive Disadvantage: The Evolution of Complex Questions and the Demise of Simple Answers." *Family Relations* 40: 463–471.

Gerson, Kathleen. 1993. *No Man's Land: Men's Changing Commitments to Family and Work.* New York: Basic Books.

Glaser, Barney G., and Alselm L. Strauss. 1967. *The Discovery of Grounded Theory.* Chicago: Aldine.

Goffman, Erving. 1959. *The Presentation of Self in Everyday Life.* New York: Doubleday.

Goodnough, Abby. 1995. "The Day the Jobs Got Up and Moved Away: For One County, a Stunning Loss Seems Beyond Control." *New York Times,* 3 July, sec. 13NJ, 1.

Griswold, Robert L. 1993. *Fatherhood in America: A History.* New York: Basic Books.

Grossberg, Michael. 1985. *Governing the Hearth: Law and the Family in Nineteenth Century America.* Chapel Hill: University of North Carolina Press.

Gusfield, Joseph R. 1989. Introduction to *On Symbols and Society.* Chicago: University of Chicago Press.

Gutman, Herbert G. 1976. *The Black Family in Slavery and Freedom, 1750–1925.* New York: Pantheon Books.

Hamer, Jennifer F. 1997. "The Fathers of 'Fatherless' Black Children." *Families in Society* 78(6): 564–578.

———. 1998. "The Definition of Fatherhood: In the Words of Never-Married African American Custodial Mothers and the Non-Custodial Fathers of Their Children." *Journal of Sociology and Social Welfare* 25(4): 81–104.

———. 2001. *What It Means to Be Daddy: Fatherhood for Black Men Living Away from Their Children.* New York: Columbia University Press.

Hamilton, William L., Nancy R. Burstein, August J. Baker, Alison Earle, Stefanie Gluckman, Laura Peck, and Alan White. 1996. *The New York State Child Assistance Program: Five-Year Impacts, Costs, and Benefits.* Cambridge, Mass.: Abt Associates Inc.

Hannerz, Ulf. 1969. *Soulside: Inquiries into Ghetto Culture and Community.* New York: Columbia University Press.

Haskins, Ron, and Wendell Primus. 2001. "Welfare Reform and Poverty." Welfare Reform Brief No. 4. Washington, D.C.: Brookings Institution. Available at <http://www.brook.edu>.

Hawkins, Alan J., and Rob Palkovitz. 1999. "Beyond Ticks and Clicks: The Need for More Diverse and Broader Conceptualizations and Measures of Father Involvement." *Journal of Men's Studies* 8(1): 11–32.

Hochschild, Arlie, with Anne Machung. 1989. *The Second Shift.* New York: Avon Books.

Hopper, Joseph. 1993. "The Rhetoric of Motives in Divorce." *Journal of Marriage and the Family* 55: 801–813.

Horn, Wade F., David Blankenhorn, and Mitchell B. Pearlstein, eds. 1999. *The Fatherhood Movement: A Call to Action.* Lanham, Md.: Lexington Books.

Illouz, Eva. 1997. *Consuming the Romantic Utopia: Love and the Cultural Contradictions of Capitalism.* Berkeley: University of California Press.

Jarrett, Robin L. 1997. "African American Family and Parenting Strategies in Impoverished Neighborhoods." *Qualitative Sociology* 20 (2): 275–288.

Johnson, Earl S., and Fred Doolittle. 1998. "Low-Income Parents and the Parents' Fair Share Program: An Early Qualitative Look at Improving the Ability and Desire of Low-Income Noncustodial Parents to Pay Child Support." In *Fathers under Fire: The Revolution in Child Support Enforcement,* ed. Irwin Garfinkel, Sara S. McLanahan, Daniel R. Meyer, and Judith A. Seltzer, 253–301. New York: Russell Sage Foundation.

Johnson, Earl S., Ann Levine, and Fred C. Doolittle. 1999. *Fathers' Fair Share: Helping Poor Men Manage Child Support and Fatherhood.* New York: Russell Sage Foundation.

Johnson, Waldo E., Jr. 2000. "Work Preparation and Labor Market Experiences among Urban, Poor, Nonresident Fathers." In *Coping with Poverty: The Social Contexts of Neighborhood, Work, and Family in the African-American Community,* ed. Sheldon Danziger and Ann Chih Lin, 224–261. Ann Arbor: University of Michigan Press.

———. 2001. "Paternal Involvement among Unwed Fathers." *Children and Youth Services Review* 23 (6/7): 513–536.

Jones, Jacqueline. 1985. *Labor of Love, Labor of Sorrow: Black Women, Work, and the Family from Slavery to the Present.* New York: Vintage.

Kaufman, Jerry, and Martin Bailkey. 2001. "Farming Inside Cities." *Land Lines* 13(1): 1–3.

Kelley, Robin D. G. 1996. "Countering the Conspiracy to Ignore Black Girls." In *Faith of Our Fathers: African-American Men Reflect on Fatherhood,* ed. Andre C. Willis, 157–171. New York: Dutton.

Kochman, Thomas. 1981. *Black and White Styles in Conflict.* Chicago: University of Chicago Press.

Kunjufu, Jawanza. 1985. *Countering the Conspiracy to Destroy Black Boys.* Vols. 1–3. Chicago: African-American Images.

Ladner, Joyce. 1995. *Tomorrow's Tomorrow: The Black Woman.* 1971. Reprint, Lincoln: University of Nebraska Press.

Lamb, Michael E. 1987. *The Father's Role: Cross-Cultural Perspectives.* Hillsdale, N.J.: Lawrence Erlbaum Associates.

———. 2000. "The History of Research on Father Involvement: An Overview." *Marriage and Family Review* 29(2/3): 23–42.

Lamb, Michael E., Joseph H. Pleck, Eric L. Charnov, and James A. Levine. 1987. "A Biosocial Perspective on Paternal Behavior and Involvement." In *Parenting across the Lifespan: Biosocial Dimensions,* ed. Jane B. Lancaster, Jeanne Altmann, Alice S. Rossi, and Lonnie R. Sherrod, 111–142. New York: Aldine de Gruyter.

Lamont, Michèle. 1992. *Money, Morals and Manners: The Culture of the French and the American Upper-Middle Class.* Chicago: University of Chicago Press.

———. 2000. *The Dignity of Working Men: Morality and the Boundaries of Race, Class, and Immigration.* New York: Russell Sage Foundation; Cambridge: Harvard University Press.

LaRossa, Ralph. 1997. *The Modernization of Fatherhood: A Social and Political History.* Chicago: University of Chicago Press.

Lazere, Ed, Shawn Fremstad, and Heidi Goldberg. 2000. "States and Counties Are Taking Steps to Help Low-Income Working Families Make Ends Meet and Move up the Economic Ladder." Washington, D.C.: Center on Budget and Policy Priorities. Available at <http://www.cbpp.org>.

Lerman, Robert. 1993. "A National Profile of Young Unwed Fathers." In *Young Unwed Fathers: Changing Roles and Emerging Policies,* ed. Robert I. Lerman and Theodora J. Ooms, 27–51. Philadelphia: Temple University Press.

Lerman, Robert, and Elaine Sorensen. 2000. "Father Involvement with Their Nonmarital Children: Patterns, Determinants, and Effects on Their Earnings." *Marriage and Family Review* 29: 137–158.

Levine, James A., and Edward W. Pitt. 1995. *New Expectations: Community Strategies for Responsible Fatherhood.* New York: Families and Work Institute.

Lewis, Oscar. 1959. *Five Families: Mexican Case Studies in the Culture of Poverty.* New York: Basic Books.

——. 1975. "The Culture of Poverty." In *Life Styles: Diversity in American Society* 2d ed., ed. Saul Feldman and Gerald W. Thielbar, 167–176. Boston: Little, Brown.

Lichter, Daniel T. 1995. "The Retreat from Marriage and the Decline in Nonmarital Fertility." In *Report to Congress on Out-of Wedlock Childbearing* (PHS 95–1257), 137–146. U.S. Department of Health and Human Services. Washington, D.C.: U.S. Government Printing Office.

Liebow, Elliot. 1967. *Tally's Corner: A Study of Negro Streetcorner Men.* Boston: Little, Brown.

Lincoln, C. Eric, and Lawrence H. Mamiya. 1990. *The Black Church in the African American Experience.* Durham, N.C.: Duke University Press.

Luker, Kristin. 1996. *Dubious Conceptions: The Politics of Teenage Pregnancy.* Cambridge: Harvard University Press.

Mann, Susan A. 1988. "Slavery, Sharecropping, and Sexual Inequality." In *Black Women in America: Social Science Perspectives,* ed. Micheline R. Malson, Elisabeth Mudimbe-Boyi, Jean F. O'Barr, and Mary Wyer, 133–157. Chicago: University of Chicago Press.

Mare, Robert D., and Christopher Winship. 1991. "Socioeconomic Change and the Decline of Marriage for Blacks and Whites." In *The Urban Underclass,* ed. Christopher Jencks and Paul E. Peterson, 175–202. Washington, D.C.: Brookings Institution.

Marriott, Michel. 1996. "Shots Silence Angry Voice Sharpened by the Streets." *New York Times,* 16 September, A1.

Marsiglio, William, Paul Amato, Randal D. Day, and Michael E. Lamb. 2000. "Scholarship on Fatherhood in the 1990s and Beyond." *Journal of Marriage and the Family* 62: 1173–1191.

Marsiglio, William, Randal D. Day, and Michael E. Lamb. 2000. "Exploring Fatherhood Diversity: Implications for Conceptualizing Father Involvement." *Marriage and Family Review* 29(4): 269–293.

McAdoo, Harriette Pipes, ed. 1988. *Black Families.* 2d ed. Newbury Park, Calif.: Sage.

McAdoo, John Lewis. 1988. "Changing Perspectives on the Role of the Black Father." In *Fatherhood Today: Men's Changing Role in the Family,* ed. Phyllis Bronstein and Carolyn Pape Cowan, 79–92. New York: John Wiley.

McLanahan, Sara, Irwin Garfinkel, and Ron Mincy. 2001. "Fragile Families, Welfare Reform, and Marriage." Welfare Reform Brief No. 10. Washington, D.C.: Brookings Institution. Available at <http://www.brook.edu>.

McLanahan, Sara, Irwin Garfinkel, Nancy E. Reichman, Julien Teitler, Marcia Carlson, and Christina Norland Audigier. 2001. "The Fragile Families and Child Wellbeing

Study Baseline Report." Princeton: Center for Research on Child Wellbeing, Princeton University.

McLanahan, Sara, and Gary Sandefur. 1994. *Growing up with a Single Parent: What Hurts, What Helps.* Cambridge: Harvard University Press.

Melli, Marygold S. 1992. "A Brief History of the Legal Structure for Paternity Establishment in the United States." In *IRP Special Report 56A,* 31–42. Madison: Institute for Research on Poverty, University of Wisconsin.

Mercer County Planning Board. 1992. *Mercer County at a Glance.* Trenton, N.J.

Meyer, Daniel R., and Maria Cancian. 2001. *W-2 Child Support Demonstration Evaluation Phase 1: Final Report.* Vols. 1 and 2. Madison: Institute for Research on Poverty, University of Wisconsin.

Miller, Andrew T. 1993. "Social Science, Social Policy, and the Heritage of African-American Families." In *The "Underclass" Debate: Views from History,* ed. Michael B. Katz, 254–289. Princeton: Princeton University Press.

Millhill Child and Family Development Corporation and the Association for Children of New Jersey. 2001. *Trenton and Mercer County Kids Count 2001: A City and County Profile of Child and Family Well-Being.* Trenton and Newark, N.J.

Mills, C. Wright. 1940. "Situated Actions and Vocabularies of Motive." *American Sociological Review* 5(6): 904–913.

Mincy, Ronald B., and Hillard Pouncy. 1999. "There Must Be 50 Ways to Start a Family." In *The Fatherhood Movement: A Call to Action,* ed. Wade F. Horn, David Blankenhorn, and Mitchell B. Pearlstein, 83–104. Lanham, Md.: Lexington Books.

Mincy, Ronald B., and Elaine J. Sorensen. 1998. "Deadbeats and Turnips in Child Support Reform." *Journal of Policy Analysis and Management* 17(1): 44–51.

Mintz, Steven. 1998. "From Patriarchy to Androgyny and Other Myths: Placing Men's Family Roles in Historical Perspective." In *Men in Families: When Do They Get Involved? What Difference Does It Make?* ed. Alan Booth and Ann C. Crouter, 3–30. Mahwah, N.J.: Lawrence Erlbaum Associates.

Mishel, Lawrence, Jared Bernstein, and John Schmitt. 1999. *The State of Working America: 1998–1999.* Ithaca, N.Y.: Cornell University Press.

Moore, Kristin. 1995. "Executive Summary: Nonmarital Childbearing in the United States." In *Report to Congress on Out-of-Wedlock Childbearing* (PHS 95–1257), v–xxii. U.S. Department of Health and Human Services. Washington, D.C.: U.S. Government Printing Office.

Moynihan, Daniel P. 1965. *The Negro Family: The Case for National Action.* Office of Policy Planning and Research, U.S. Department of Labor. Washington, D.C.: U.S. Government Printing Office.

Murray, Charles. 1993. "The Coming White Underclass." *Wall Street Journal,* 29 October, A12(W), A14(E), col. 4.

Musick, Judith S. 1993. *Young, Poor, and Pregnant: The Psychology of Teenage Motherhood.* New Haven: Yale University Press.

National Center for Children in Poverty. 1999. *Map and Track: State Initiatives to Encourage Responsible Fatherhood.* Available at <http://cpmcnet.columbia.edu/dept/nccp/>.

National Women's Law Center and the Center on Fathers, Families, and Public Policy. 2000. *Family Ties: Improving Paternity Establishment Practices and Procedures for Low-Income Mothers, Fathers, and Children.* Washington, D.C.: National Women's Law Center; Madison, Wisc.: Center for Fathers, Families and Public Policy.

Newman, Katherine. 1992. "Culture and Structure in the Truly Disadvantaged." *City and Society* 6: 3–25.

Oakley, Ann. 1981. "Interviewing Women: A Contradiction in Terms." In *Doing Feminist Research,* ed. Helen Roberts, 30–61. London: Routledge and Kegan Paul.

Office of Child Support Enforcement. 2000. *Twenty-third Annual Report to Congress.* Available at <http://www.acf.dhhs.gov/programs/cse/rpt/annrpt23/index.html>.

Oppenheimer, Valerie Kincade. 1997. "Women's Employment and the Gain to Marriage: The Specialization and Trading Model." *Annual Review of Sociology* 23: 431–453.

Pleck, Joseph H. 1987. "American Fathering in Historical Perspective." In *Changing Men: New Directions in Research on Men and Masculinity,* ed. Michael Kimmel, 83–97. Newbury Park, Calif.: Sage.

———. 1997. "Paternal Involvement: Levels, Sources, and Consequences." In *The Role of the Father in Child Development,* 3d ed., ed. Michael E. Lamb, 66–103. New York: John Wiley & Sons.

Popenoe, David. 1996. *Life without Father.* New York: Martin Kessler Books.

Primus, Wendell. 2001. "What Next for Welfare Reform? A Vision for Assisting Families." *Brookings Review* 19, no. 3 (summer): 17–19.

Primus, Wendell, and Charita Castro. 1999. "A State Strategy for Increasing Child Support Payments from Low-Income Fathers and Improving the Well-Being of Their Children through Economic Incentives." Washington, D.C.: Center on Budget and Policy Priorities. Available at <http://www.cbpp.org>.

Primus, Wendell, and Kristina Daugirdas. 2000. *Improving Child Well-Being by Focusing on Low-Income Noncustodial Parents in Maryland.* Baltimore: Abell Foundation.

Probation Child Support Enforcement Services. 1990. *The New Jersey Expedited Process for Child Support: Its History and Operation.* Trenton, N.J.

Radway, Janice. 1991. "Interpretive Communities and Variable Literacies: The Functions of Romance Reading." In *Rethinking Popular Culture: Contemporary Perspectives in Cultural Studies,* ed. Chandra Mukerji and Michael Schudson, 465–486. Berkeley: University of California Press.

Rainwater, Lee. 1970. *Behind Ghetto Walls: Black Families in a Federal Slum.* Chicago: Aldine.

Rainwater, Lee, and William L. Yancey, eds. 1967. *The Moynihan Report and the Politics of Controversy.* Cambridge, Mass.: MIT Press.

Raphael, Jody, and Richard M. Tolman. 1997. *Trapped by Poverty, Trapped by Abuse: New Evidence Documenting the Relationship between Domestic Violence and Welfare.* Chicago: Taylor Institute and Ann Arbor: University of Michigan Research Development Center on Poverty, Risk, and Mental Health.

Reichman, Nancy, Julien Teitler, Irwin Garfinkel, and Sara McLanahan. 2001. "Fragile Families: Sample and Design." *Children and Youth Services Review* 23 (4/5): 303–326.

Riessman, Catherine Kohler. 1990. *Divorce Talk: Women and Men Make Sense of Personal Relationships.* New Brunswick, N.J.: Rutgers University Press.

Roberts, Paula. 1999. "Setting Support When the Noncustodial Parent Is Low Income." Washington, D.C.: Center for Law and Social Policy. Available at <http://www.clasp.org/pubs/>.

———. 2001. *An Ounce of Prevention and a Pound of Cure: Developing State Policy on the Payment of Child Support Arrears by Low Income Parents.* Washington, D.C.: Center for Law and Social Policy. Available at <http://www.clasp.org/pubs/>.

Rodman, Hyman. 1963. "The Lower-Class Value Stretch." *Social Forces* 42(2): 205–215.

Roy, Kevin. 1999. "Low-Income Single Fathers in an African American Community and the Requirements of Welfare Reform." *Journal of Family Issues* 20(4): 432–457.

Schneider, Karen, Jane Sugden, and Tom Duffy. 1995. "Daddy Meanest." *People,* 4 September, 40–45.

Schudson, Michael. 1989. "How Culture Works: Perspectives from Media Studies on the Efficacy of Symbols." *Theory and Society* 18 (2): 153–180.

Schwartz, Pepper. 1994. *Peer Marriage: How Love between Equals Really Works.* New York: Free Press.

Scott, James C. 1990. *Domination and the Arts of Resistance: Hidden Transcripts.* New Haven: Yale University Press.

Scott, Joan W. 1988. "Deconstructing Equality versus Difference: Or, the Uses of Poststructuralist Theory for Feminism." *Feminist Studies* 14 (1): 33–50.

Seltzer, Judith A., and Yvonne Brandreth. 1994. "What Fathers Say about Involvement with Children after Separation." *Journal of Family Issues* 15(1): 49–77.

Seltzer, Judith A., Nora Cate Schaeffer, and Hong-Wen Charng. 1989. "Family Ties after Divorce: The Relationship between Visiting and Paying Support." *Journal of Marriage and the Family* 51: 1013–1032.

Sewell, William H., Jr. 1992. "A Theory of Structure: Duality, Agency, and Transformation." *American Journal of Sociology* 98(1): 1–29.

Sherwood, Kay E. 1992. "Child Support Obligations: What Fathers Say about Paying." In *Caring and Paying: What Mothers and Fathers Say about Child Support,* ed. Frank F. Furstenberg, Jr., Kay Sherwood, and Mercer Sullivan, 57–76. New York: Manpower Demonstration Research Corporation.

Sorensen, Elaine, and Robert Lerman. 1998. "Welfare Reform and Low-Income Noncustodial Fathers." *Challenge* 41(4): 101–116.

Sorensen, Elaine, Ronald Mincy, and Ariel Halpern. 2000. "Redirecting Welfare Policy toward Building Strong Families (No. 3)." Washington, D.C.: Urban Institute. Available at <http://www.urban.org>.

Sorensen, Elaine, and Mark Turner. 1996. "Barriers in Child Support Policy: A Review of the Literature." Philadelphia: National Center on Fathers and Children, University of Philadelphia. Available at <http://fatherfamilylink.gse.upenn.edu/org/ncoff>.

Sorensen, Elaine, and Chava Zibman. 2000a. "To What Extent Do Children Benefit from Child Support?" Discussion paper 99–11. Washington, D.C.: Urban Institute. Available at <http://newfederalism.urban.org>.

——. 2000b. "A Look at Poor Dads Who Don't Pay Child Support." Discussion paper 00–07. Washington, D.C.: Urban Institute. Available at <http://newfederalism .urban.org>.

——. 2001. "Poor Dads Who Don't Pay Child Support: Deadbeats or Disadvantaged?" Series B, No. B-30. Washington, D.C.: Urban Institute. Available at <http://new federalism.urban.org>.

Stacey, Judith. 1991. "Backward toward the Postmodern Family: Reflections on Gender, Kinship, and Class in the Silicon Valley." In *America at Century's End,* ed. Alan Wolfe, 17–34. Berkeley: University of California Press.

Stack, Carol B. 1974. *All Our Kin: Strategies for Survival in a Black Community.* New York: Harper and Row.

Stack, Carol B., and Linda M. Burton. 1993. "Kinscripts." *Journal of Comparative Family Studies* 24 (2): 157–170.

Stier, Haya, and Marta Tienda. 1993. "Are Men Marginal to the Family? Insights from Chicago's Inner City." In *Men, Work, and Family,* ed. Jane C. Hood, 23–44. Newbury Park, Calif.: Sage.

Sudarkasa, Niara. 1988. "Interpreting the African Heritage in Afro-American Family Organization." In *Black Families* 2d ed., ed. Harriette Pipes McAdoo, 27–43. Newbury Park, Calif.: Sage.

Sullivan, Joseph. 1995. "Whitman Apologizes for Remark on Blacks." *New York Times,* 14 April, B6.

Sullivan, Mercer L. 1989. "Absent Fathers in the Inner City." *Annals of the American Academy of Political and Social Science* 501: 48–58.

——. 1992. "Noncustodial Fathers' Attitudes and Behaviors." In *Caring and Paying: What Mothers and Fathers Say about Child Support,* ed. Frank F. Furstenberg, Jr., Kay Sherwood, and Mercer Sullivan, 6–33. New York: Manpower Demonstration Research Corporation.

Super, David A., Sharon Parrott, Susan Steinmetz, and Cindy Mann. 1996. "The New Welfare Law." Washington, D.C.: Center on Budget and Policy Priorities. Available at <http://www.cbpp.org>.

Swidler, Ann. 1986. "Culture in Action: Symbols and Strategies." *American Sociological Review* 51: 273–286.

——. 2001. *Talk of Love: How Culture Matters.* Chicago: University of Chicago Press.

Tatley, Stephan. 1995. "The No. 1 Summer Song of Love." *New York Times Magazine,* 13 August, 32.

Teichman, Jenny. 1982. *Illegitimacy: An Examination of Bastardy.* Ithaca, N.Y.: Cornell University Press.

Thornton, Arland. 1995. "Attitudes, Values, and Norms Related to Nonmarital Fertility." In *Report to Congress on Out-of-Wedlock Childbearing* (PHS 95-1257), 201–215. U.S. Department of Health and Human Services. Washington, D.C.: U.S. Government Printing Office.

Thornton, Arland, and Deborah Freedman. 1982. "Changing Attitudes toward Marriage and Single Life." *Family Planning Perspectives* 14 (6): 297–303.

Tucker, Belinda M., and Claudia Mitchell-Kernan, eds. 1995. *The Decline in Marriage among African-Americans.* New York: Russell Sage Foundation.

Tucker, Cynthia. 1997. "Of Fuddy-Duddies and Babydaddies." *Times-Picayune,* 31 March, Metro B5.

U.S. Bureau of Labor Statistics. 2001. Local Area Unemployment Statistics. Available at <http://www.bls.gov>.

U.S. Census Bureau. 1990. U.S. Census Data. Available at <http://www.census.gov>.

——. 1995. "Child Support for Custodial Mothers and Fathers, 1991," by Lydia Scoon-Rogers and Gordon H. Lester. Current Population Reports, series P60-187. Available at <http://www.census.gov/prod/2/pop/p60/p60-187.pdf>.

——. 1999. "Child Support for Custodial Mothers and Fathers, 1995," by Lydia Scoon-Rogers. Current Population Reports, series P60-196. Available at <http://www.census.gov/prod/99pubs/p60-196.pdf>.

——. 2000. "Child Support for Custodial Mothers and Fathers, 1997," by Timothy Grall. Current Population Reports, series P60-212. Available at <http://www.census.gov/prod/2000pubs/p60-212.pdf>.

——. 2001a. American Factfinder. <http://factfinder.census.gov>.

——. 2001b. "Living Arrangements of Children: Fall 1996," by Jason Fields. Current Population Report P70-74. Washington, D.C.: U.S. Census Bureau. Available at <http://www.census.gov/prod/2001pubs/p70-74.pdf>.

U.S. Congress. 1996. *Personal Responsibility Work Opportunity Reconciliation Act, Public Law 104-193.* Washington, D.C.: U.S. Government Printing Office. Available at <http//www.access.gpo.gov/nara/publaw/104publ.html>.

U.S. Department of Health and Human Services. 1990. *Paternity Establishment.* 3d ed. Washington, D.C.: U.S. Government Printing Office.

——. 2000. "State Policies Used to Establish Child Support Orders for Low Income, Non-Custodial Parents." Office of Inspector General. Washington, D.C.: U.S. Government Printing Office. Available at <http://www.hhs.gov/oig/oei/reports/a479.pdf>.

——. 2001. "Promoting Responsible Fatherhood." Department of Health and Human Services fact sheet. Available at <http://www.hhs.gov/news/press/2001pres/01fsfatherhood.html>.

Valentine, Charles A. 1968. *Culture and Poverty: Critique and Counter-Proposals.* Chicago: University of Chicago Press.

Vaughan, Diane. 1990. *Uncoupling: Turning Points in Intimate Relationships.* 1986. Reprint, New York: Vintage Books.

Ventura, Stephanie J., and Christine A. Bachrach. 2000. *Nonmarital Childbearing in the United States, 1940–99.* National Vital Statistics Reports, vol. 48, no. 16. Hyattsville, Md.: National Center for Health Statistics.

Ventura, Stephanie J., Christine A. Bachrach, Laura Hill, Kelleen S. Kaye, Pamela A. Halcomb, and Elisa C. Koff. 1995. "The Demography of Out-of-Wedlock Childbearing." In *Report to Congress on Out-of-Wedlock Childbearing* (PHS 95-1257), 2–133. U.S. Department of Health and Human Services. Washington, D.C.: U.S. Government Printing Office.

Waldman, Steve. 1992. "Deadbeat Dads." *Newsweek,* 4 May, 46–51.

——. 1994. "Taking on Welfare Dads." *Newsweek,* 20 June, 34–38.

Wallace, Michelle. 1979. *Black Macho and the Myth of the Superwoman.* New York: Dial Press.

Waller, Maureen. 2001. *Unmarried Parents, Fragile Families: New Evidence from Oakland.* San Francisco: Public Policy Institute of California.

Waller, Maureen, and Robert Plotnick. 1999. *Child Support and Low-Income Parents: Perceptions, Practices, and Policy.* San Francisco: Public Policy Institute of California.

——. 2001. "Effective Child Support Policy for Low-Income Families: Evidence from Street Level Research." *Journal of Policy Analysis and Management* 20(1): 89–110.

White House. 1995. "Supporting the Role of Fathers in Families." Available at <http://fatherhood.hhs.gov/pclinton95.htm>.

Wiggins, Ovetta. 1995. "Letting Black Men Lead; Not All Sisters in Step but Support March Theme of Atonement." Bergen Record Corporation. *The Record,* 14 October, A01.

Wilkie, Jane Rilblett. 1993. "Changes in U.S. Men's Attitudes toward the Family Provider Role, 1972–1989." *Gender and Society* 7(2): 261–279.

Wilson, William Julius. 1987. *The Truly Disadvantaged: The Inner City, the Underclass, and Public Policy.* Chicago: University of Chicago Press.

——. 1996. *When Work Disappears: The World of the New Urban Poor.* New York: Alfred A. Knopf.

Wuthnow, Robert. 1987. *Meaning and Moral Order: Explorations in Cultural Analysis.* Berkeley: University of California Press.

Zelizer, Viviana A. 1994. *The Social Meaning of Money.* New York: Basic Books.

Index

Fraser, Nancy, 172*n*4, 173*n*12
Frazier, E. Franklin, 40
Freedman, Deborah, 23
Fremstad, Shawn, 145
Furstenberg, Frank, 23, 34, 35, 41, 45, 81, 92, 94, 110, 130, 132, 169*n*13, 173*n*14, 176*n*9, 180*n*28

Gadsden, Vivian, 46, 172*n*17
Garfinkel, Irwin, 3, 11, 113, 128, 142, 146, 147
Gender distrust, culture of, 35, 81, 126
Genetic paternity tests, 97, 113, 115, 176*n*6
Gerinomous, Arline T., 170*n*22
Gerson, Kathleen, 38, 39, 41, 42
Goffman, Erving, 98, 102
Goldberg, Heidi, 145
Goodnough, Abby, 8
Griswold, Robert L., 39, 40, 41, 55
Grossberg, Michael, 112
Guidance, 58–61, 107–8, 136, 173*n*10
Gutman, Herbert, 170*n*3

Halpern, Ariel, 3, 147
Hamer, Jennifer F., 173*n*14
Hamilton, William L., 142
Hannerz, Ulf, 35, 44, 45, 46, 81
Hanson, Thomas L., 128
Hawkins, Alan J., 177*n*16
Hochschild, Arlie, 174–75*n*10
Horn, Wade, 163*n*2
Housing arrangements
  methodological issues, 11, 165*n*12
  and paternal disengagement, 87–88, 175*n*16

Idealist model of marriage, 34–36, 170*nn*27, 28
Illouz, Eva, 34
Incarceration of fathers, 125–26, 128, 131. *See also* Criminal sanctions
Individualism, 23
Infant mortality, 165*n*2
Informal economic support
  and child support policy options, 144
  expectations of, 62–63
  extent of, 173*n*15, 179*n*17
  as indicator of social paternity, 108
  lack of formal credit for, 115, 129, 133, 181*n*36
  and parental child support preferences, 117–18, 179*n*14
  See also Formal child support system/informal economic support conflicts
Inheritance rights, 176*n*13
In-Hospital Paternity Acknowledgement Program, 163*n*4

In-kind assistance
  expectations of, 62–63
  extent of, 173*n*15
  fathers' preference for, 126, 180*n*25
  as indicator of social paternity, 108
  lack of formal credit for, 115
  and mother-father relationship, 125, 126, 180*n*27
  and negative impacts of child support system, 119–20, 125, 126, 127, 133, 181*n*36
Involved father model, 136, 172*n*7
  and economic support expectations, 66–67
  emergence of, 40, 55
  and guidance, 58
  and sex roles, 77

Jarrett, Robin, 33
Johnson, Earl S., 130, 132, 143, 146, 180*n*34, 181*n*36
Jones, Jacqueline, 170*n*3

Kaufman, Jerry, 10
Kouneski, Edward F., 164*n*10

Ladner, Joyce, 43
Lamb, Michael E., 38, 40, 55, 77, 172–73*n*8, 177*n*16
Lamont, Michèle, 4, 45
Language
  internally dialogized, 61, 173*n*12
  and political claims, 172*n*4
  and research approach, 4, 164*n*8
  vocabularies of motive, 168*n*1
Lazere, Ed, 145
Legal paternity establishment
  blood/genetic paternity tests, 97, 113, 115, 176*n*6
  extent of, 102, 175*n*1
  and formal child support system noncompliance, 120–21, 179*nn*18–20
  and inheritance rights, 176*n*13
  as method of paternity recognition, 102
  new emphasis on, 93, 175*n*1, 176*n*14, 177*n*5, 179*n*18
  vs. reciprocal recognition, 138
  and welfare, 10, 115
Lein, Laura, 13, 62, 173*n*15, 179*n*17
Lerman, Robert, 41, 106, 129, 177*n*17
Levine, Ann, 130, 132, 143, 146, 180*n*34
Levine, James A., 42
Lewis, Oscar, 42–43, 171*n*15
Lichter, Daniel T., 23
Liebow, Elliot, 5, 44, 66, 67, 94, 110, 176*n*9
Living arrangements. *See* Housing arrangements
Low birth weight, 165*n*2

Sex roles
and fatherhood models, 39–40, 136, 171nn5, 7
and paternal responsibility, 76–78, 140
Shakur, Tupac, 171n13
Sherwood, Kay E., 180n34
Slavery, 38, 170n3
Social paternity, 102–9
vs. biological paternity, 50–51, 94–95
indicators of, 105–9, 138
reciprocal nature of, 103–5
See also Paternal responsibility
Sorensen, Elaine, 3, 106, 113, 128, 129, 145, 146, 147
Stacey, Judith, 23
Stack, Carol B., 43
Stier, Haya, 177n17
"Street talk", 76, 174n6
Sullivan, Mercer L., 5, 10, 45, 94, 110, 132, 180n26
Surnames. *See* Naming
Survival strategies approach, 43
Swidler, Ann, 4, 44–45, 172n16

Tally's Corner (Liebow), 5
Talvitie, Kathy Gordon, 176n9
TANF. *See* Temporary Assistance for Needy Families
Temporary Assistance for Needy Families (TANF), 114–15
Therapeutic discourses, 40, 55
Thornton, Arland, 23
Tienda, Marta, 177n17
Tolman, Richard M., 145
Turner, Mark, 113, 128

Unemployment
and attitudes toward marriage, 22–23

community context, 8, 166n16
and economic support expectations, 173–74n17
extent of, 12
and negative impacts of child support system, 128–29, 130, 132
See also Economic constraints
Uniform Illegitimacy Act, 112–13
Uniform Parentage Act, 113

Valentine, Charles A., 44
Value stretch approach, 44, 45
"Vanishing Family, The: Crisis in Black America" (Moyers), 163n3
Vaughan, Diane, 175n11
Ventura, Stephanie J., 16, 22, 24, 26
Visitation rights, 72–73, 86, 180n33

Wallace, Michelle, 40
Welfare
and legal paternity establishment, 10, 115
mandatory cooperation requirements, 114–15, 118–24, 178nn7, 8, 179nn15–17, 19, 20
methodological issues, 10, 11, 165–66nn8, 14
and privatization, 3
PRWORA, 10, 114, 177–78nn5–7, 179n18
Whitman, Christine Todd, 10
WIC program. *See* Women, Infants, and Children (WIC) program
Wilson, William Julius, 8, 22–23, 35, 46, 169–70nn19, 21
Winship, Christopher, 23
Women, Infants, and Children (WIC) program, 13, 166n21

Zelizer, Viviana A., 180n24
Zibman, Chava, 3, 145, 146